THE GREAT FIRE OF LONDON

THE GREAT FIRE
OF LONDON

Stephen Porter

First published in 1996
This edition first published in 2009

The History Press
The Mill, Brimscombe Port
Stroud, Gloucestershire, GL5 2QG
www.thehistorypress.co.uk

British Library Cataloguing in Publication Data.
A catalogue record for this book is available from the British Library.

ISBN 978 0 7524 5025 4

Typesetting and origination by The History Press
Printed in Great Britain

CONTENTS

ACKNOWLEDGEMENTS

In preparing this book, I found myself reaping where many others had sown. I am especially grateful for the splendid work done by Walter Bell, Thomas Reddaway, Philip Jones, Robert Latham, William Matthews, Esmond de Beer and Henry Roseveare in making so many of the sources available in print, but I have also been able to draw upon the work of many historians of the period.

The Royal Commission on the Historical Monuments of England generously allowed me a period of study leave, and I have drawn extensively on the holdings of the National Monuments Record section of the Commission for the illustrations. My colleagues have been very helpful, and I would especially like to thank Ann Robey, Alan Cox, John Bold and Derek Kendall for much helpful advice. Michael Turner has shared his knowledge of town fires with me over many years. I would also like to thank Elizabeth McKellar for allowing me to consult her unpublished doctoral thesis, which proved to be very valuable.

For a number of reasons too tedious to relate, I managed to find myself writing this book while preparing another one for publication, and so my wife Carolyn needed to draw on extra reserves of forbearance to deal with my erratic behaviour and preoccupied state of mind. She managed this effortlessly, with her usual good humour, and also supplied large doses of help.

ONE

DANGERS AND PRECAUTIONS

There's no place ... better armed against the fury of the fire; for besides
the pitched Buckets that hang in Churches and Halls, there are divers
new Engines for that purpose.

James Howel, *Londinopolis*, 1658, p. 398

During Lemuel Gulliver's stay in Lilliput around 1700 a fire broke out
in the imperial palace when one of the empress's maids of honour
fell asleep while reading a romance and presumably knocked over
a candle. By the time Gulliver arrived at the scene the Lilliputians
had set up ladders against the walls of the empress's apartments; they
also had plenty of buckets for carrying water to the fire. But he soon
realised that because 'the flame was so violent' and the water had to
be carried 'some distance' their efforts were likely to be defeated and
the whole palace, not just the apartments, would be burnt down. In
this emergency he took drastic action and extinguished the blaze by
urinating violently and extensively over it.

Readers of Swift's brilliant satire would have recognised many of
the elements of this tale; how a minor domestic accident at night
could lead to widespread destruction, how a fire could overcome the
efforts of the fire-fighters even though they had plenty of equipment,
and the difficulties caused by the lack of a good supply of water close
by. Although Gulliver's timely action saved the palace, it was illegal
to make water within the precincts, and after some intrigues by his
enemies he faced impeachment. This, too, may have struck a chord
with contemporaries, for fire-fighters who took it upon themselves to
pull down buildings to create a fire-break and so check the progress of
the flames were liable to find themselves taken to court by the owners
of the property and compelled to pay the cost of rebuilding. Many
readers would also have been aware of the parallel between the fate
narrowly escaped by the imperial palace in Lilliput, which had 'cost so

many ages in erecting', and that of Whitehall Palace, part of which was gutted in a blaze in 1691 and the whole of the remainder, except for Inigo Jones's Banqueting House, by a fire in 1698. Gulliver's adventure must also have brought to mind the Great Fire of London of 1666, only sixty years before the publication of *Gulliver's Travels*, when Sir Thomas Bludworth, the lord mayor, called to the early stages of the fire, was said to have remarked that 'a woman might piss it out'.[1]

The conflagration that developed from the fire which Bludworth treated so dismissively was London's greatest single disaster and has come to be regarded as one of the major landmarks in English history, ranking in popular awareness with events of national importance such as the defeat of the Spanish Armada in 1588. It was all the more devastating because it came as the city was recovering from a severe outbreak of plague in the previous year, which, with high mortality levels from other diseases, had claimed almost 100,000 lives, nearly six times the normal death rate. There is something poignant in the fact that these two calamities came so closely together, and they have tended to be associated. Yet there were important distinctions between an epidemic and a conflagration. The most obvious one was that an epidemic brought death, and fire physical destruction, and so they affected the urban community in quite different ways. Their social impact also varied. Plague struck the poorer areas more heavily than the wealthier ones, not so much as a result of overcrowding and the conditions which it produced in the more impoverished districts, but rather because the better-off were able to leave the city for the duration of an outbreak, while the poor lacked that flexibility.[2] Fire, on the other hand, destroyed everything in its path; both the premises of wealthy merchants and the hovels of the poor were consumed by the flames. While the risk of a fire breaking out may have been greater in the overcrowded areas in which the poorer citizens lived, once it had taken hold it swept through rich and poor districts alike. The only avoiding action that a householder could take was to remove as many of the most valuable items as possible before the flames could reach them.

A further distinction was that in many years the danger from plague was much less immediate than that from fire. Although the plague had been endemic since the first onset of the Black Death in 1348, the outbreaks causing high mortality were intermittent. The worst death tolls from plague in seventeenth-century London came in 1603,

1625, 1636 and 1665, and during many of the intervening years there were so few deaths from the disease that many citizens may not have felt threatened by it. Only fifty-nine plague deaths were recorded in the *Bills of Mortality* during the five years before the outbreak of 1665.[3] But fire was an ever-present danger, perhaps slightly lessened during the damp winter months, but still there, as the conflagration at Nantwich, Cheshire, in December 1583 demonstrated.

It is indeed self-evident that fire is one of the principal threats to man's social and economic arrangements with its capacity to completely destroy both buildings and their contents in a relatively short time, leaving only scorched earth and charred remains. It is in cities and towns where the greatest damage can be done by fire, because of the concentration of buildings and the goods stored in and around them. That concentration makes it difficult to halt a fire once it has become established, with the blaze spreading from building to building, their fabric and contents providing ample fuel for the flames. But fire is also a menace to rural communities, for it can destroy houses, barns, stables and crops, both those harvested and in store and those standing in the fields, together with pasture, orchards and woodland.[4]

The city's population in the 1660s contained not only native Londoners, but also migrants from provincial towns and the countryside, all of whom would have been aware of the risk of fire. Yet an individual's vigilance did not bring complete security, for everyone depended on the care taken by their fellow-citizens as well as by themselves. A drunken or careless neighbour was to be feared and arson was regarded as one of the worst criminal offences.

However alert the citizens were, or tried to be, a degree of carelessness was inevitable and some accidents were unavoidable. Indeed, Londoners were periodically shaken out of their complacency by destructive blazes, both in the metropolis itself and elsewhere. Between 1600 and 1665 there were at least seventy substantial fires in English provincial towns. The most destructive of those which occurred in the years preceding the Great Fire destroyed 224 houses at Marlborough in 1653, 238 houses at Southwold in 1659 and 156 houses at Newport, Shropshire, in 1665.[5] Although the numbers of houses gutted in such fires were relatively small compared to the losses in the Great Fire, a high proportion of the buildings in each town was destroyed, and the disasters attracted much attention.

Of more immediate impact were the fires in London itself. A fire which began in an inn stable in Southwark in 1630 destroyed fifty houses before it could be controlled. This was followed by a potentially even more serious fire in February 1633, when a blaze among the buildings at the northern end of London Bridge spread out of control and not only wrecked about a third of the houses on the bridge itself, but also nearly eighty more in the parish of St Magnus the Martyr.[6] This fire was a frightening event on a prominent site and, as some of the houses at that end of the bridge were not rebuilt, the visible evidence of the destruction served as a reminder of the disaster. From time to time other fires did damage on a smaller scale, involving few houses, but no doubt causing much alarm in the neighbourhood. In May 1643 three houses in Aldermanbury were burned down, for instance, and in the April of the following year a fire in the parish of Christ Church destroyed houses and goods valued at £2,880.[7] Gunpowder stored both in buildings and on ships presented a particular danger. In January 1650 the detonation of seven barrels of powder on the premises of Robert Porter, a ship's chandler in Tower Street, began a fire which raged for two hours, wrecked fifteen houses and damaged twenty-six others so badly that they were uninhabitable. At least sixty-seven people were killed in this disaster, an unusually high death toll that was attributable to the explosion rather than the subsequent fire.[8] Smaller, but still serious, accidents occurred in July 1654, when two ships on the river blew up on successive days. The mid-1650s also saw fires in Threadneedle Street and Fleet Street, both of which were described as 'a great fire'.[9]

The news of fire disasters was transmitted by word of mouth and in correspondence, and also through the system by which funds were raised to help the victims of fire, flood, plague or other calamity. An application was made to the lord chancellor, who, if satisfied of the truth of the claim, authorised the issue of a brief describing the disaster, often in graphic terms, and asking for funds. The brief, a printed form, was then distributed over a specified area and collections were taken, usually as the congregation left church after a service, but in some cases by collectors going from house to house. The system was well developed by the 1660s, although not everyone reacted favourably to the number being presented, inviting their charity. After attending church on 30 June 1661 Samuel Pepys noted that 'the trade of briefes is come now up to so constant a course every Sunday, that we resolve to give no more to them'.[10] Whatever the response, the numbers issued during that period can only have served to increase the awareness of accidental fires. As well as briefs and pamphlets, the development of newspapers during the 1640s and 1650s provided a further means of publicising a fire and appealing for aid, both through news reports and notices placed by the victims. This process, still in its infancy in the 1660s, was to become one of the major methods for raising funds after a disaster, especially with the growth of provincial newspapers in the eighteenth century.[11]

Reaction to such disasters was to regard them as instruments of the vengeful hand of God. They were punishments inflicted on a sinful generation and warnings to repent and reform that should be heeded before it was too late. This was the interpretation thundered from the pulpits and recorded in the many sermons published in order to reach a wider public than the congregations who heard them. A fire at Banbury in 1628 destroyed over 100 houses, perhaps as much as one-third of the town. The rector, William Whateley, was a well-known Puritan with a reputation for long sermons delivered in a style which can be judged from his epithet 'the roaring boy of Banbury'. The fact that the fire had begun in a malt-house on a Sunday gave him ample scope to draw his parishioners' attentions to some moral lessons, which were stressed in his sermon on the disaster, pointedly entitled *Sinne no More, Banbury*.[12] The Puritan reformation at Banbury had already been under way for some time, for Whateley had been rector since 1610, whereas it was the particularly destructive conflagration at Dorchester in August 1613 which proved to be the stimulus for a similar movement there. Under the influence of its minister, John White, acting with the cooperation of civic leaders who were sympathetic to his aims, in the generation following the fire Dorchester was much 'improved'. The town was thought to have benefited from the disaster, not only morally, but also materially, 'knowledge causing piety, piety breeding industry, and industry procuring plenty unto it'.[13]

The pamphlet describing the fire at Dorchester was entitled *Fire from Heaven*, which succinctly expresses the contemporary view of the true nature of the disaster. Sinfulness, especially sabbath-breaking, was seen to have provoked the wrath of the Almighty, who 'out of just vengeance and judgement on the committers thereof hath often punished with fire'. There was ample testimony for this in the conflagration at Tiverton in 1612, which burnt 290 houses, and the 'sad and wonderfull fire' which swept through 'that seat of wickednesse the City of Oxford' in October 1644, destroying over 300 houses.[14] These were among the most destructive blazes in provincial towns in the seventeenth century and both occurred on Sundays. The Book of Jeremiah warns that the consequence of sabbath-breaking will be a fire that 'shall devour the palaces of Jerusalem, and it shall not be quenched'.[15]

Failure to observe the sabbath was not the only transgression likely to be punished by fire, however. The whole range of sins could provoke divine wrath. Yet it did not follow that the actual victims of fire were especially sinful. This was recognised by the wood-turner Nehemiah Wallington with respect to those whose homes were destroyed by the fire at London Bridge, who were not to be regarded as 'greater sinners than all the rest of the City of London because they suffered such things', any more than those who escaped such a catastrophe could be regarded as innocent of sin. The author of the pamphlet describing the conflagration which destroyed four-fifths of Northampton in 1675 wrote of the reasons for that disaster in much the same terms. The citizens of Northampton were not 'sinners above all Men', but their town had been turned into 'a burning Beacon' as a warning to other cities and towns of their fate 'except they receive and obey his Laws, and cease to provoke him, by their tolerated Disobedience'.[16] Similarly, the spate of fires in London in 1655 was interpreted by one preacher not in terms of specific shortcomings, but as the beginning of God's judgement on the world, which would be destroyed in the following year.[17]

Some allowance has to be made for an element of conventional piety in the accounts of fires, especially those which were intended primarily as appeals for relief. It was advisable for the sufferers to appear to be repentant and to strike the correct note in order to attract sympathy and assistance. But this should not disguise the underlying sincerity of the reports of disaster victims, for providentialism, derived from Calvinist theology, was not simply the orthodoxy of many of the clergy in seventeenth-century England. Divine intervention in human affairs was generally accepted, a part of the common psychology of the time that was expressed in private correspondence and personal diaries, as well as in publications.

Divine wrath could not only help to explain why fires had occurred, but also provide the basis for predictions of conflagrations to come. The late 1650s and early 1660s saw a number of gloomy prophesies specifically for London that were couched in these terms. Many Puritan preachers regarded it as the sinful city *par excellence* and characterised it as Babylon, or the bloody city. They anticipated a fiery end for London in the near future and graphically expounded their fears in their sermons. In 1657 Thomas Reeve, in his *God's Plea for Nineveh*, foresaw 'kindling sparks that will set all in a flame from one end of the city to the other' and two years later Daniel Baker's *Certaine Warning for a Naked Heart*, after condemning London's evil ways, predicted 'a consuming fire . . . which will scorch with burning heat all hypocrites, unstable, double-minded workers of iniquity'. The most detailed depiction of the city's fiery fate came in the Quaker Humphrey Smith's *Vision which he saw concerning London*, published in 1660. Smith wrote of a fire which none could quench and 'the burning thereof was exceeding great . . . All the tall buildings fell, and it consumed all the lofty things therein . . . And the fire continued, for, though all the lofty part was brought down, yet there was much old stuffe, and parts of broken-down desolate walls, which the fire continued burning against'. Smith did not live to judge how accurately his prophesy came true, for he died in Winchester gaol in 1663.[18]

Those who had been apprehensive for London's safety during the 1650s because of its wickedness must have been seriously alarmed after the Restoration. With the return of the court and its adherents, moral standards fell considerably and publicly. The character of Charles II's court was in marked contrast to that of his father, which had been chaste and aloof, and to that of Cromwell. Indeed, the king's own lechery was a byword.[19] Many of the returned Royalists who contributed to the general air of depravity were simply at a loose end. Sir William Coventry explained this in terms of their having been excluded from public business for the previous twenty years and so being unable to apply themselves to it. In his view the best of them were attending to their estates and family matters and the rest had given themselves over to debauchery.[20] Attention was focused especially on the theatres, which in many ways epitomised the new atmosphere in London. Closed since 1642, they were now reopened, with the novelty of actresses taking the female roles and apparently proving irresistible to 'severall young noblemen and gallants'. John Evelyn's opinion was that the Restoration theatre was 'fowle & undecent'.[21] Many evidently shared his view, but their collective indignation had no effect. Even protests by senior Anglican clergymen at the deplorable standards of behaviour were either ignored or ridiculed.

Faced with such moral backsliding, instead of the hoped-for reformation, the fears of those preachers who continued to warn of imminent doom for London could only be heightened. Their cause was not helped by the eclipse of their political allies. Indeed, the City was a target for snipers at both ends of the political and religious spectrum. While the Puritans deplored its sinfulness, Royalists blamed London for its crucial support for the Parliamentarian cause in the Civil War and the failure of its citizens to intervene to prevent the execution of the king. They therefore took practical steps to consolidate their power and weaken the influence of their opponents within London. The Restoration saw the removal from the corporation of prominent supporters of the Parliamentarian cause and Commonwealth regime, including Christopher Pack, John Barkstead, John Ireton, Robert Tichborn and Thomas Atkin, and the reinstatement of Royalists, such as Thomas Adams and Richard Browne, who had been expelled in 1649.[22] In addition, the Act of Uniformity of 1662 displaced those Puritan clergy who would not conform to the Anglican church, with approximately 130 ministers ejected from their livings in the diocese of London, 55 of them within the City.[23] In such a climate of moral and political disappointment, hopes for London's repentance receded further.

Forecasts of impending desolation could not be disregarded as the aberrations of eccentric preachers, for their predictions were apparently borne out by those fires which periodically threatened the city before they were checked. Indeed, their interpretation of fires as clear signs of divine displeasure and warnings of what might follow was shared by at least a section of the population. A generation earlier, Wallington was an eye-witness of the fire on London Bridge, close to his home in St Leonard Eastcheap. His response, confided in his journal, was that both mercies and disasters were attributable to God and that the calamity was a punishment for London's many sins.[24]

Mixed with Wallington's anxious chronicle of the sinfulness of the citizenry were observations of a more practical nature on how fortunate it was that there was no wind on the night of the fire, as there had been only a week before, and an awareness of the flammability of the contents of many of the buildings in Thames Street, close to the blaze. He concluded that much of the city could have been endangered if the conditions had not been so favourable.[25] Wallington's remarks highlight two elements which helped to determine the extent of damage caused by a fire. One was the weather at the time of the outbreak and over the previous few days, which was beyond human control, and the other was the storage of combustible goods, which was within the citizens' abilities to regulate. Indeed, providentialism did not lead to fatalism, and such dangers were tackled, as part of a range of fire precautions.

All urban communities took steps to minimise the risks of destructive blazes, through measures aimed at lessening the chance of fires beginning, limiting the means by which flames could spread and providing the means for fighting outbreaks. The inherent difficulties of preventing accidental blazes were enormous, for all householders required fire for lighting, heating and cooking, and tradesmen such as bakers, brewers, tallow-chandlers, distillers, dyers, maltsters, soap-boilers, potters and blacksmiths had to have ovens and furnaces on their premises. Some of the buildings in which they worked were made of combustible materials and many of their ovens and furnaces were inadequately constructed. These hazards were increased by the stocks of fuel kept in or close to their workshops. The cloth, metal and leather industries were all important elements in London's economy, scattered throughout the city but gradually tending to move outside the walls to the rapidly expanding suburbs. Despite this drift to the outer areas, on the eve of the Great Fire the textile and leather trades still accounted for more than a third of occupations in a district such as that around Cheapside.[26]

Inns were also a problem, for the hay and straw in their stables and outbuildings were potentially dangerous and the increasingly popular habit of smoking tobacco heightened the chance of an accidental fire in such surroundings, as elsewhere. London's riverside was probably its most dangerous district so far as fire was concerned, because its crowded yards, quays and storehouses were crammed with stocks of tar, pitch, hemp, sails and cordage. The vessels and their cargoes presented a similar risk and although they could be cast adrift into the river if a fire began on board, there was still the danger that they would drift ashore elsewhere or foul other ships and that burning debris could spread at random.

Despite the difficulties of controlling so many fire hazards, civic authorities attempted to enforce some restrictions, over the placing of hearths and furnaces, the storage of fuel, the dousing of fires and ovens overnight, and the building materials that were used. The regulations at London were imposed not only by the corporation and justices, but also by the government. This was understandable, for not only was it the principal city, but also the site of a royal palace to the west at Whitehall and the fortress of the Tower to the east. From a proclamation of 1580 to the Great Fire, successive governments issued a series of orders aimed at controlling the erection of new buildings, imposing minumum standards of construction and prohibiting the division of houses. The growth of London was an especial concern of the early Stuarts, with eight proclamations aimed at its regulation issued between 1602 and 1630.[27]

Of particular importance among fire controls was the prohibition of thatched roofs, for they caught fire easily and allowed flames to spread and rapidly engulf whole streets. Even where some buildings were tiled, burning fragments would blow from one thatched roof to another, making it difficult to check the flames. In a large blaze among houses of timber and thatch 'the flame and smoake therof is soe great, and violent that noe man is able to come neere those howses or to stand in the wynd to defend the fayer tyled howses'.[28] Only where practically all of the roofs were tiled or slated could this problem be overcome. Conflagrations in London in the eleventh and twelfth centuries amply demonstrated the need to prohibit thatching. This was attempted in the building regulations promulgated around 1200, although a concession allowed the retention of straw roofing if it was coated with plaster. Roof-tiles had come into use in a number of cities during the twelfth century and later orders in London dealt with their size and quality.[29] The difficulties of compelling householders to undergo the expense of re-roofing existing buildings must have made the replacement of thatch with tile or slate a slow process, but one which was virtually completed in London by the seventeenth century. John Stow attributed the absence of large-scale fires in the City to this policy.[30] It was indeed a notable success, for although similar regulations were attempted in other cities and towns, they were not universally observed, especially in those regions, such as East Anglia and the West Country, where thatching was so much easier and cheaper than tiling. Even in Norwich, the second largest city in Tudor

England, attempts made in 1509 and 1570 to enforce the use of tile seem to have made little impact, and thatched roofs were still reported there in the early nineteenth century.[31]

Some indication of the success achieved in London regarding roofing materials comes from the building regulations. For example, although a royal proclamation of 1620 mentioned that 'Hovels or other Sheds of Timber' should not be covered with thatch or boards, it was much more concerned with the use of timber and the congestion of buildings, suggesting that thatch had been largely eradicated. Like the other regulations of the period, this order specified that new buildings should be of brick or stone and that the upper storeys should not project outwards above the street. This practice, known as jettying, created a fire risk by narrowing the gap between buildings, making it easier for the flames to jump across. A building in St Margaret, Lothbury, had jetties which projected 4 feet at the first storey and 6 feet at the second, and one in Cousin Lane had a projection, described as a jetty, that was 39 feet long and was built out as far as 12 feet over the lane.[32] A policy that involved the replacement of existing buildings, as this did, was bound to take a long time to materialise, even if it could be adequately enforced. This also applied to building in stone or brick. The use of stone in the city during the Middle Ages had not been confined to churches and the larger monastic and public buildings. But it was a relatively expensive material and so was not likely to be adopted on a large scale for houses, especially during a period of rapid growth such as London experienced in the late sixteenth and early seventeenth centuries. Stow suggested that timber had replaced stone as the principal building material by the sixteenth century. Evidence from other towns also indicates that stone construction in vernacular buildings declined in the late Middle Ages. Henry VIII's topographer John Leland noted in the mid-sixteenth century that at Northampton 'Al the old building of the towne was of stone, the new is of tymbre'.[33]

Timber framing with lath and plaster infilling was by far the most common constructional method for both external and internal walling. Buildings erected in this way were often dismissively referred to as 'paper buildings', which stressed their flimsiness. In the years before the Great Fire there was anxiety not only about the extent of timber construction, but also that 'slight fir timber' was being used, 'fit for entertaining fire'.[34] Although the houses in the fashionable new areas to the west of the

City, such as the Earl of Bedford's development at Covent Garden, were of brick, attempts to compel rebuilding in that material in the City were slow to bear fruit. This was not because they were resisted, for landlords did observe the regulations, by requiring their tenants to use brick for new buildings. A lease of ground in Fetter Lane granted in 1632 stipulated that three houses of brick and timber should be built on the site, and the tenants evidently complied. Similarly, new brick houses were built in a court off Throgmorton Street in 1666 and some of them were 'scarcely finished' by the time of the fire.[35] But the rate of rebuilding was such that timber-framed buildings still predominated.

In 1658 James Howel expressed his disappointment that measures for the adoption of brick had not been more successful, because one effect would have been to make the City 'lesse subject to casual fyrings'. He was also aware of the aesthetic qualities of brick building, which would have 'conduced much to the beauty of her Streets and uniformity of Structure'. A petition from the Company of Tilers and Brickmakers a few years earlier had also pointed out that such building in brick was 'very graceful' to the City, as well as rehearsing the familiar arguments that brick-and-tile construction was a safeguard against fire and reduced the consumption of timber.[36]

The regulations issued between 1580 and 1666 reflect a widespread anxiety about the growth of the city and the deleterious effect which its expansion was thought to have on the economy and society of the remainder of the country, together with concern about the urban environment and the danger of fire. There seemed to be good cause for such concern, for the population of the metropolis grew from 120,000 in 1560 to 200,000 in 1600 and continued to rise, doubling to at least 400,000 by 1650. But the overall figures conceal changes in the pattern of growth. The influx was such that during the early seventeenth century the suburbs grew more rapidly and became more populous than the City. Indeed, from a peak of 135,000 inhabitants around 1640, the population of the City actually began to fall and by 1660 had dropped back to 105,000, a figure only slightly higher than that for 1600.[37] There was a further decline in the middle of the 1660s because of the plague. Most of those who had fled to escape the epidemic would have returned by the summer of 1666, anxious to secure their property and resume their businesses. Pepys moved his household to Woolwich early in July 1665, but brought them back to

London at the beginning of the following January, and Evelyn's wife and family, who left London for his house at Wotton in Surrey at the end of August, returned during the first week of February.[38] Indeed, those responsible for collecting the hearth tax reported that in London, unlike some provincial towns, the houses were 'presently filled' after the plague. Nevertheless, the population must have been reduced in the short term by the high mortality in the epidemic of 1665. This had affected the suburbs most severely, but the City itself had also suffered badly, with 15,200 deaths during the year in the parishes within the walls, almost two-thirds of them attributed to plague.[39]

At the time of the Great Fire, therefore, pressure on space within the City had eased considerably, although the consequences of the population boom remained. These included the shoddy buildings which had been rapidly constructed to cope with the demand. In 1647 a complaint was made that some empty houses in an alley off Finch Lane had been allowed to fall into ruin. Part of the structure had actually collapsed 'and by the fall thereof hath slaine three persons' and the remainder was supported on props. An almost equally dangerous house in Bucklesbury was 'very old and ruinous and propped up and was ready to fall' by the time of the fire. The subdivision of houses for occupation by several households and the interconnection of rooms between buildings increased the fire hazards. The Three Crowns in Christ Church parish, for example, had some rooms which were 'intermixed with other houses'.[40] Other problems included the conversion of structures such as stables, barns and haylofts into dwellings, and the erection of tenements in narrow alleys running back from the street front. By 1638 there were at least 857 dwellings within the City classified as tenements, almost a quarter of them in the riverside parish of St Michael Queenhithe. The situation was far worse in the suburbs, however, where 1,856 tenements were recorded in the two parishes of St Botolph without Aldgate and St Botolph without Bishopsgate.[41]

Enforcement of the various regulations aimed at preventing new building had evidently been unsuccessful. Some owners may have chosen to ignore the restrictions, hoping to get away with it, but others obtained licences granting them exemption. As a fee was payable for a licence, the process was regarded as a source of revenue, not just a means of controlling building. It was primarily to produce income that the process was revived in 1657, with an Act 'for preventing the multiplicity of Buildings in and about the Suburbs of London and within ten miles of the same'. Occupiers of houses erected since 1620, without four acres of adjoining land, were liable to a fine of a year's rent of the premises, although the City itself was exempt. This measure produced almost £41,000 in 1657–8.[42]

With or without a licence, much construction on new foundations evidently went ahead, as well as the subdivision of houses. The site of a stable and vacant ground in Little Old Bailey was used to erect forty dwellings, for example. Even where there were few infringements of the orders regarding new structures, the problems of pressure on existing accommodation remained. Although there seems to have been little new building within the City during the 1630s, there was still ample evidence of overcrowding and the division of property. St Margaret Moses, Friday Street, contained 'An Alderman's house' divided between four households, two households in another 'house divided' and 'an Inn divided into tenements', while Silver Street in St Alban's, Wood Street, contained a house with a separate family in each of its ten rooms, and in St Michael's, Cornhill, a property in Harp Alley contained six rooms 'let to 64 persons' and another in Harrow Alley had six rooms 'let to diverse'. Nor was the population a settled and stable one, a feature which attracted the attention of Abraham Hayne, rector of St Olave's, Hart Street, who complained of the 'sudden shifting and leaving of tenements and non-solvent people' in his parish.[43]

The alleys and courts behind the wealthier street-front properties contained about a third of the City's inhabitants, and it was in these dwellings that the worst overcrowding could be found, and hence the greatest risk of fire. Ralph Treswell's plans of various sites across London in the late sixteenth and early seventeenth centuries graphically convey the density of buildings and lack of open space, with small cottages of two and three storeys packed around the alleys and yards at the back of the larger buildings. The resultant social mixing of wealthy citizens in the more substantial shops and houses fronting the main streets and their poorer neighbours in the smaller and overcrowded properties to their rear seems to have been found throughout the City. Allhallows, Lombard Street, was one of the broad band of comparatively wealthy parishes that ran across the centre of the City from east to west, but nevertheless it contained more tenements than houses.[44]

Treswell's surveys also show that London dwellings contained a high proportion of heated rooms; a half of those in the average small- to medium-sized houses contained a fireplace.[45] Domestic fires were among the causes of fire described in the *Seasonable Advice for preventing the Mischief of Fire* issued by the lord mayor in 1643, with 'bad hearths, chimneys, ovens … clothes hanged against the fire … leaving great fires in chimneys' specifically mentioned. Other dangers that were itemised included the careless use of candles in hazardous surroundings, the disposal of hot cinders in baskets or wooden containers, lights placed where they could be knocked over, and the combustion of wet hay, straw or corn.[46]

The fire risks produced by overcrowding, inadequate, obstructed or clogged chimneys, the storage of fuel and dangerously placed workshops were not ignored. Indeed, in this respect as in others, the City was closely governed and regulated, not only by the corporation itself, but also by the officers of the twenty-four wards that lay north of the river. Fire hazards were reported and the offenders instructed to remove or correct the fault, with fines imposed on those who did not comply. Among other infringements of the byelaws, householders in Cornhill ward were reported for throwing out cinders, using a hot press, drying boards and storing wood chip in a room where fires were lit, and constructing dangerous chimneys. The assiduousness of the investigators is shown by the presentment of Humphrey Blake for having a stove which was a fire risk, although his house was not in a prominent position, for it stood at the rear of houses in Threadneedle Street.[47]

If the preventative measures failed and a fire did break out, a swift response was essential. *The Seasonable Advice* urged that smoke or the smell of burning should be investigated and not ignored. A fire that broke out at night was potentially more dangerous than one which began during daylight hours, not only because it took longer for fire-fighters to assemble, but also because a fire could be well established before it was detected. Fire protection was one of the night-watchmen's chief duties and during a hot dry spell the numbers of watchmen could be increased and householders instructed to leave pails of water outside their doors overnight, so that they were ready to hand in an emergency. Indeed, the Common Council required each householder in the City to keep a bucket of water by the street door during the summer months.[48]

The fire-fighting equipment that was available consisted chiefly of leather buckets, fire-hooks and ladders. The fire-hooks were used rather like grappling irons to unroof, or even to pull down, buildings in the path of the fire. Pickaxes, shovels, crowbars and chisels were also useful, for digging up water pipes and then cutting them open, and brooms and long-handled swabs were kept for beating out the flames. Hand-held water squirts were developed in the sixteenth century, but the major innovation during the period was the fire-engine, which was introduced in the second quarter of the seventeenth century and widely adopted in London and many provincial towns.

A ready supply of equipment was essential and was achieved by requiring the parishes and livery companies to keep a specified number of buckets, ladders and fire-hooks. In the early 1640s each of the larger companies was asked to hold three dozen buckets, two ladders, two 'great hooks with chains', pickaxes, spades and shovels, and one fire-engine. The companies and the wards also kept small brass squirts; Cornhill ward bought three of these in 1649, for example, for the modest sum of £11 10s, which also included twenty-seven buckets. Leather buckets dried out and split if not maintained and they were also likely to be taken away and used for purposes other than fire-fighting and either spoiled or mislaid. Because of this the numbers fluctuated considerably. The churchwardens of St Martin Outwich had custody of fifteen buckets in 1633, brought this up to thirty in 1640 with the purchase of another fifteen, but had only seven by 1652, before further purchases increased the stock to twenty-four, which became the standard number for the parish.[49]

Leather fire-buckets were obtained from the founders in Lothbury, who were also the principal manufacturers of fire-engines, which had been developed in Germany. John Jones, a merchant, was responsible for acquiring the first engines to be used in England. Acting with the help of his brother Roger and at the instance of the Court of Aldermen he brought two engines to London early in 1625, apparently from Nuremburg. In February that year he was granted a patent awarding him a fourteen-year monopoly for making and selling engines 'for the casting of water' and claimed that with a crew of ten a fire could be put out using an engine 'with more ease and speed' than 500 men equipped with buckets and ladders. Jones died during the severe outbreak of plague later in 1625, but the City invested in further acquisitions. In October Alderman Hammersley acquired two more engines, from

Hamburg, and by June 1626 he had brought over eleven other 'Engines or water spouts', which were distributed around the city.[50]

John Bate's *The Mysteries of Nature and Art*, published in 1634, included a description and sketch of an engine 'for spouting water', which he described as 'very useful for to quench fire amongst buildings'.[51] This rather understates the reaction to the effectiveness of these early engines, which created a favourable impression, not just in demonstrations, but actually in use at fires. In 1638, following a blaze at Arundel House in the Strand, the Privy Council wrote to the lord mayor and aldermen that it had been informed of 'the excellent use to bee made in Accidents of fier, of the new Engines for spowting of water'. The problem at Arundel House had been that the engines had arrived too late because none were kept in the nearby parishes, demonstrating that it was advisable that they should be 'neare & ready at hand' wherever a similar emergency might occur. The council therefore recommended that the City parishes should acquire their own fire-engines, the smaller ones joining together for the purpose and the larger ones providing their own, and it also instructed the Middlesex parishes to obtain engines.[52]

During the next few years further orders were made for the provision of engines in London. In 1642 the lord mayor instructed each of the twelve principal livery companies to obtain a fire-engine, as well as to ensure that their other fire-fighting equipment was in order.[53] Among those which did so were the Ironmongers' Company, the Goldsmiths' Company, which negotiated for an engine for £20 which would usually have cost £23, and the Drapers' Company, which bought 'an engine . . . for the better quenching of fire' from Mr Lambard, a Lothbury founder. Presumably this was the Leonard Lambert who, in 1638, had supplied the City with two engines for £44. Each of the wards was also directed to obtain an engine, which the lord mayor's precept described as 'this Instrument soe usefull & necessary to the securing of this Citty'.[54]

The Civil War and the fear of a blaze started by Royalist agents prompted the corporation to give close attention to all fire precautions, including the provision of equipment. The financial demands of the war and the disruption of internal trade and communications between London and many provincial towns interrupted the acquisition of fire-engines, however. The first towns to acquire an engine did so just before the Civil War, with Norwich, Worcester and Devizes all buying their first fire-engine in 1641.[55] After a hiatus during the war years the process resumed in the late 1640s, when such towns as Bristol, Gloucester and Marlborough bought their first engines.[56] Indeed, a sample of towns shows that almost a quarter of them, fifteen out of sixty-four, had acquired an engine by 1665. The same pattern was followed in London, with a resumption in the purchase of new engines after the Civil War. The Middle Temple, for example, bought an engine for £30 in 1650 and the Goldsmiths' Company replaced its engine with a new and larger one five years later.[57]

Fire-engines were, therefore, common items of equipment by the mid-1660s, especially in London. The principal supplier during the middle years of the century was William Burroughs, the City's founder, who was said to have made roughly sixty engines by about 1660,[58] but there were other makers in London, including John Shaw and Ahasuerus Fromanteel, a clock-maker. The particular advantages claimed for Fromanteel's engines were that they were so tough they would not break 'without extreme violence' and were small enough to be taken into a building. They could even be carried upstairs, an important consideration in the City, where the height of many buildings created problems in fighting fires on the upper floors.[59] In the vicinity of Cheapside, for example, many houses were of three storeys with attics and some in Cheapside itself were two storeys higher.[60] Unless the speedy carriage of water up several flights of stairs was feasible a dangerous delay was likely before a fire could be dealt with. In 1629 Wallington had a narrow escape when his servant and apprentice, sleeping in a garret where much flammable material was stored, awakened to find the bedding alight and, without water, had 'pissed out the fire as well as they could'.[61]

Fromanteel's claim for the durability of his fire-engines was designed to allay fears that such appliances were too easily damaged and put out of action. Complaints also show that it was not uncommon for engines to be useless when they were needed because of lack of maintenance. Another feature of the early seventeenth-century engines which restricted their capabilities was that they could throw only an intermittent jet of water. This was overcome by the invention of the air vessel by a Nuremburg maker in 1655, which permitted a continuous stream to be delivered on to the fire, although it may have been some time before this refinement was incorporated into the engines built in London.

Fire-engines represented a major advance in the technology of fire-fighting and they were adopted with considerable enthusiasm, but there were disappointments. Wallington claimed that the three engines deployed at the blaze on London Bridge in 1633 had been ineffective, for example. Yet some successes were recorded, including the 'great service' which the engines contributed to the dousing of the fire at Tower Street in 1650.[62] Whatever the quality or efficacy of the equipment, a good supply of water was essential, for the engines contained a tank of only limited capacity that had to be continually topped up by a bucket chain.

Water supplies came from the river and its tributaries, wells and aqueducts. The most notable improvement to the provision of water from the Thames came in the early 1580s, when the Dutchman Pieter Morice constructed 'an artificial forcier' which could deliver water from the river, at the northern end of London Bridge, as high as Leadenhall. He was granted a 500-year lease for the purpose in 1581 and a second, to extend the works, in the following year. A similar arrangement, with a substantial rectangular tower, was constructed at Broken Wharf by Bevis Bulmar in 1594–5 and a 'rare engine' designed by Sir Edward Ford in the 1650s could raise water from the river to a height of 93 feet. Supplies from the Thames reached even the smaller properties in the back streets. In 1640, for example, tenants of the Ironmongers' Company arranged for it to be brought into Hogshead Alley 'for prevention of the danger of fire'.[63]

Medieval supplies of water from the high ground to the north of the city included an aqueduct from Tyburn to a conduit in West Cheap, opened in 1236 and later extended, and one from Highbury to Cripplegate that was built in the 1420s. Clerkenwell and Smithfield could draw upon supplies of piped water laid on for St Bartholomew's, the Hospital of St John of Jerusalem, St Mary's nunnery and the Carthusian priory at the Charterhouse by the middle of the fifteenth century. Their aqueducts remained in use after the Dissolution and were considerably supplemented by an ambitious enterprise devised by Edmund Colthurst and undertaken by Hugh Myddelton in the early seventeenth century. This was the construction of a channel from Amwell and Chadwell in Hertfordshire to the New River Head in Clerkenwell, which was reached in 1613, from where water was distributed to other parts of the city in elm pipes.

By the 1660s London had a good supply of water from these various sources, but it was not completely reliable. In dry weather the levels in wells and the flow along the aqueducts could both be low, and it was more difficult to draw water from the river at low tide. Wallington anxiously noted the drought in 1654, when the conduit that supplied his and nearby parishes dried up during June and did not flow again until early October. The difficulties that would have resulted if a fire had broken out were obvious.[64]

The provision of fire-fighting equipment and an adequate supply of water were of little use unless they were deployed to good effect when a blaze began. Resolute action and good organisation were essential. Contemporaries were often critical of the way a fire was fought, contrasting the orderly response to such a crisis in continental towns with the confusion and lack of coordination in England. Writing a century before the Great Fire, John Fox complained of the lack of 'public or civil order in doing of things, neither any division of labour: but every man, running headlong together, catcheth whatsoever cometh to hand to quench the fire'. Things had not improved by the 1670s, if Andrew Yarranton's description of the typical reaction to a fire is to be believed: 'all the Rable runs crying Fire, Fire, to the great affrightment and amazement of most people near where the Fire is . . . Then one cries Pull down, and another cries, Blow up this House, another cries, Blow up that House. So grows a confusion not to be parallel'd'.[65]

Some authorities, including those in London, did issue instructions outlining the action to be taken when a fire broke out, but in fact common sense and experience were likely to be of more use than printed regulations. The important thing was to get as many people and as much equipment to the scene as quickly as possible and for the magistrates and parish officers to deploy them to best effect. A bucket chain was formed and as continuous a supply of water as could be achieved was thrown on to the flames and poured into the tanks of the engines. The *Seasonable Advice* recommended that there should be double rows of men on each side of the street, one rank passing full buckets and the other returning the empty ones. To avoid confusion, the area of the fire should be cordoned off so that the 'rude people' could be kept away. The same idea prompted those who prepared regulations at Oxford in 1671, when they ordered that students should be restrained from leaving their colleges when a blaze broke out 'excepting such who will be assistant in quenching the fire'.[66] Chaos was invariably counter-productive in dealing with fires and the magistrates were expected to take charge and provide the necessary direction, so that an outbreak could be extinguished before it became a major problem.

In terms of an awareness of the hazards of fire and attempts to reduce them, and the provision of fire-fighting equipment, by the mid-1660s London had achieved a great deal. The rapid growth of the early years of the century had caused problems with congestion and shoddy building, but in the City itself the population had fallen again and the greatest fire risk seemed to be in the less-well-regulated and overcrowded suburbs. Thatched roofing, the principal constructional risk, had been dealt with, although little could be done in the short term to reduce the extent of exposed timber and increase the use of brick. Nor could the lighting of fires and furnaces, or storage of flammable goods, within the built-up area be eradicated, but a check was kept and where the arrangements appeared hazardous those responsible were required to alter them. Indeed, an observer contemplating the risks and the evidence of fires, in London itself and the largest provincial cities, could reasonably have concluded that the measures followed were adequate to contain the occasional outbreak and prevent a conflagration. Bristol, Exeter and Newcastle all escaped major fires in the post-medieval period, and even Norwich, where the control of building materials proved more difficult, had not suffered a serious outbreak since 1507. Apart from Glasgow, where roughly one-quarter of the houses were destroyed in 1652, it was the smaller country market towns which had, in the recent past, suffered catastrophic fire damage. Needless to say, this did not mean that there was room for complacency, and a hot, dry and windy spell required the greater care of householders, extra vigilance from the watchmen and a readiness on everyone's part to turn out promptly in an emergency.

TWO

THE GREAT FIRE

... a fire, such as had not been known in Europe since the conflagration
of Rome under Nero, laid in ruins the whole city, from the Tower to
the Temple, and from the river to the purlieus of Smithfield.

Lord Macaulay, *History of England*, vol. 1, chap. 2

According to the thirteenth Book of Revelation, the number of
the Beast, one of whose attributes was the ability to bring fire from
heaven, was 666. For some time there had been increasing foreboding
that this indicated that 1666 would be a fateful year, and when it
actually arrived interest in the predictions naturally intensified. It was
widely assumed that the Year of the Beast would see the fall of Rome
and the overthrow of the Antichrist, generally equated with the Pope,
although other candidates were put forward, including Louis XIV.[1]
But there was also an apprehension that it would be destructive in
other ways.

Some almanac writers played down these long-standing prophesies
as 1666 approached, while others remained confident that it would be
a significant year. They later countered the charge that they had failed
to warn of the Great Fire with the accusation that Roger L'Estrange,
the king's surveyor of the press, had deleted their forecasts referring to
it, including one which had been so accurate that it had 'named the
month'. Richard Edlin, who took credit for successfully predicting
the plague of 1665, claimed that he had also forecast the fire, with his
prognostication that an astrological conjunction would bring 'great
Drought and Barrennesse, Conflagrations or great Destruction by Fire,
during the effects of that Conjunction, which will continue till the
latter end of the year 1666'.[2] This prediction apart, there was a lack
of clear guidance from the writers of the almanacs and apocalyptic
sermons as to what the year really had in store and many people
remained apprehensive. They included Pepys, who was curious enough

to buy a copy of Francis Potter's *An interpretation of the number 666*, published in 1642, and after perusing it he concluded that 'certainly this year of 1666 will be a year of great action, but what the consequence of it will be, God knows'. His erstwhile patron, the Earl of Sandwich, was also uneasy. Before he set out to take up his post as ambassador to Spain he confided to Pepys his fears that there would be 'some very great revolutions'.[3] When the fire came it was Mother Shipton, an early sixteenth-century fortune-teller, who was remembered as having prophesied that 'London in '66 should be burnt to ashes', although her forecasts as published in 1641 had contained nothing so specific.[4]

Plague and war must have been uppermost among the various anxieties at the beginning of 1666, together with some lingering concern that the more desperate of those hostile to the regime would attempt a coup. Perhaps the Fifth Monarchy men would see it as the appropriate year to establish the millennium, beginning with the overthrow of the earthly government of Charles II.[5] The early years of his reign were marked by a fear of anti-government plots, encouraged by Venner's Rising in the streets of London in 1661 and the Derwentdale Plot of 1663. The authorities did uncover one conspiracy, by several former Parliamentarian soldiers, although their ringleader, Robert Danvers, escaped. In April 1666 *The London Gazette* reported that the date set for their attempt was the rather obvious one of 3 September, the anniversary of the battles of Dunbar and Worcester and the death of Oliver Cromwell, and that the 'Hellish design' was to have included the firing of the city. The Danvers Plot was really no more than an obscure little intrigue and its potential danger was exaggerated by the government. Nevertheless, it did nothing to ease the worries of those who were fearful of an arson attack.[6]

Yet while the approach of 3 September may have caused some uneasiness that there might be an attempt to seize the City, such small-scale designs against an unpopular government were of much less concern to the majority of citizens in 1666 than the resurgence of the plague. Not surprisingly, it was expected that the disease would return with the warmer weather and the figures in the weekly *Bills of Mortality* were anxiously checked. Pepys noted 'a great fear' among the prostitutes around Drury Lane in the spring and was alarmed to be told that a hostelry in Chelsea for which he was headed had been shut up because of plague. In fact, London did not suffer a second year of epidemic and escaped relatively lightly, for fewer than 1,800 plague deaths were recorded in the Bills for the whole of the year.[7] It was in the provinces, not in the capital, that plague made the greatest impact in 1666. Over much of the country, it was as bad a year for plague as 1665 had been in London, although the disease varied considerably in its severity. The Essex towns of Colchester and Braintree, for example, suffered very high levels of mortality, with perhaps as many as half of their inhabitants falling victim, while other towns in the county emerged largely unscathed. In a reversal of the pattern of the previous year, Evelyn noted that the disease was widespread in and around Wotton, whereas London was almost free of it.[8]

Despite its relative freedom from plague in 1666, London could not escape the worsening economic conditions caused by the epidemic. The normal pattern of internal trade was interrupted by the precautions taken by many communities, especially attempts to cordon themselves off by restricting movement in and out, the understandable reluctance of merchants and carriers to visit infected places, and, not least, the general uncertainty that epidemic conditions engendered. London was the hub of the country's internal trade, as a consumer of manufactured goods, an industrial centre in its own right and a major market for agricultural produce, as well as being by far the largest port for exports and the distribution of imported goods.

Londoners also suffered from the interruption of the coastal trade by Dutch commerce raiders. The Second Dutch War had begun in February 1665 and the east-coast trade, which supplied the capital with coal and food, was especially vulnerable, with the danger that the Thames could be blockaded. Supplies of coal from the north-east of England and Fife were indeed badly disrupted, as they had been for a part of the first Civil War in the 1640s and during the First Dutch War of 1652–4. The tonnage of coal shipped from the Tyne in 1665 was only two-thirds of the annual average for 1660–4, and the figure for 1666 was even lower, at less than half of that average.[9] This caused rising prices, economic dislocation and popular discontent, exacerbated by the disruption of overseas trade.

Although a section of the merchant community had been in favour of the war as a means of taking commerce away from the Dutch, many found that in practice their own trade was reduced by the conflict. Those trading with the Baltic suffered a severe blow when the Dutch secured a diplomatic victory by persuading Denmark–Norway to close the Sound to British shipping. No British ships passed in or out of the Baltic during 1666, and only seven did so in 1667, although the average figure for 1660–4 had been over 100 vessels a year. Even more alarming was the vulnerability of merchantmen to Dutch privateers and warships, which led to the loss of perhaps as many as 500 vessels.[10] To add to these problems, France joined the war on the Dutch side in January 1666, thereby virtually isolating Britain diplomatically and considerably worsening her strategic position.

The war did bring some successes, such as conquest of the Dutch islands in the West Indies, the seizure of many merchant vessels and the capture of New Amsterdam, but these did not produce any immediate benefits to set against the difficulties caused by the conflict. Failure to achieve decisive success in any of the major fleet actions, despite a victory at the St James's Day Battle in July 1666, high levels of taxation, setbacks such as the loss of St Kitts in the West Indies to the French, the impressment of men to serve in the fleet, the depressing sight of the returning wounded sailors and the adverse effects of the war on London's trade produced a growing war-weariness in the city during the summer of 1666.[11] With the government's deteriorating financial position and the effect which that had on the maintenance of the fleet, there was little prospect of achieving any further tangible success from the war. Indeed, the last major stroke of the campaigning season was the burning of perhaps as many as 150 Dutch merchant vessels lying in the shelter of the islands of Vlie and Terschelling, together with Westterschelling and the town on Vlie. This was carried out by a squadron under Sir Robert Holmes in early August.[12] Both fleets put to sea again towards the end of that month, but the fierce easterly gale which sprang up not only prevented them coming into action, but actually drove the English fleet out of the North Sea and down the Channel to St Helen's Road off the Isle of Wight.

If the war produced a certain gloom, it did not generate the disaster anticipated by those who expected 1666 to be a year of catastrophe. It was the gale at the turn of the month, following the hot, dry summer experienced by much of Europe, that was the key to the imminent calamity. Although the temperature figures for south-east and midland England for the period do not provide a wholly reliable record, they are dependable enough to show that the mean figure for the summer months in 1666 was considerably higher than that for any year since 1659, when the record begins. Indeed it was 1.7°C above the mean for 1659–65 and both July and August were warmer than any of the corresponding months during those years.[13] Both 1665 and 1666 were also unusually dry years, confirmed by narrow growth rings on oak trees. The parched summer of 1665 was succeeded by a long period of drought in south-east England that began in November and continued until September 1666. Despite heavy storms in July, Anthony Wood at Oxford noted that water levels were low in the rivers and the rivulets were 'quite drye', and when John Evelyn reflected on the reasons for the scale of the Great Fire he recalled 'the long and extraordinary drought' of the preceding months.[14]

The fire that was to make 1666 so memorable began at the house of Thomas Farriner, a contractor supplying ship's biscuit to the Navy, in Pudding Lane early in the morning of Sunday, 2 September. He later claimed that the fire in the bakehouse oven had been put out by ten o'clock the previous night and that when he went to it at about midnight it did not have enough heat to light his candle. The house contained five other hearths and he went to one of them, where some embers remained, which he raked over before he went upstairs, to ensure that they were extinguished. He was also certain that the windows and doors were closed, so there was no draught through the house. Woken by smoke some time after one o'clock, the household discovered that a fire had broken out downstairs that was so well established that they could not use the stairs and instead were forced to escape through an upstairs window and along a gutter to a neighbour's house. Their maidservant, however, was so fearful of the dangerous climb that she remained behind and was killed. As he left, Farriner checked to see how far the fire had advanced and noticed that it had not yet touched the fuel in the yard, and also that it had not begun near the chimney or oven. When questioned by the committee established to determine the cause of the conflagration, he maintained that the fire did not start in or near the oven and that the faggots that were actually in it, placed there by his boy to dry, were recovered intact after the fire. Perhaps understandably reluctant to bear the awesome responsibility for the disaster that had ensued, Farriner insisted that a fire in his bakehouse was not the cause.[15]

A witness later claimed that the fire did not spread from Farriner's house to adjoining properties for an hour. Whether that was an exaggeration or not, it seems that a next-door neighbour was able to remove his goods before his house, too, caught fire. The flames gradually took hold of the nearby premises, however, and by three o'clock the fire was prominent enough for Pepys's servants in Seething Lane, over a quarter of a mile away, to be aware of it. Jane Birch, the maid, called her master, telling him that there was 'a great fire' in the City, but after watching for some time and judging where the fire was, and that it was 'far enough off', Pepys went back to bed.[16]

By this time the alarm had been raised; one account mentioned 'a great noise of drums'. The lord mayor was called to the scene from his house in Maiden Lane, Aldersgate, and made his unfortunate remark about how easy it would be to put out the blaze. It may have been at this point that he was advised to authorise the demolition of four houses and a shop close to the fire, which he did not do, reportedly asking, 'When the houses have been brought down, who shall pay the charge of rebuilding them?' Such fires were frequent, and he and his officers may not have thought this one unduly dangerous, although it should already have been apparent that the strong gale that had driven the fleet down the Channel would soon make it difficult to check the flames. A later judgement was that by the time fifteen or sixteen houses had caught fire, the chance of containing the blaze had already passed.[17]

Added to the problems caused by the high wind was the fact that this part of the City was a difficult one in which to deal with a major fire. Pudding Lane ran northwards from Thames Street to East Cheap in an area of narrow streets and alleys 'close built with wooden pitched houses'. Furthermore, many of the occupiers were tradesmen dealing in goods relating to shipping and seaborne commerce. The excavation of a brick-floored cellar in Pudding Lane has shown that barrels of wood pitch, a caulking agent, were stored there and that the building above was timber-framed with a tiled roof. The premises were entirely typical of the Thames Street area, which contained 'old paper buildings and the most combustible matter of Tarr, Pitch, Hemp, Rosen, and Flax', while the nearby wharves were stacked with timber and coal.[18]

With the failure to isolate the fire by demolishing the buildings around it, the flames, fanned by the high wind, did not lack plenty of combustible matter to allow them to spread. The account written by the clergyman Edward Waterhouse especially mentions the Star Inn, 'full of hay and other combustibles'. It stood on Fish Street Hill, which ran northwards from the bridge, backing on to premises in Pudding Lane only a few doors away from Farriner's. In such conditions, it soon became extremely difficult for the fire-fighters to operate, for the heat prevented them from getting close enough to the flames to take any effective action. Obviously, they could only throw the water from a bucket a short distance and, given the limited capacity and range of the engines, the fire 'in a short time became too big to be mastered by any Engines or working neer it'.[19]

The wind drove the blaze westwards through the flammable buildings along Thames Street to the west of Pudding Lane. The new houses erected after the fire of 1633 around the northern end of London Bridge were burnt down, even though some of them were 'of a stronger and more stately way of building' than those which they had replaced.[20] The water engine set up by Pieter Morice was also destroyed. It was one of the misfortunes of the early stages of the conflagration that this major supplier of the City's water was out of action at the time of the fire.[21] To make matters worse, water levels were so low that there was little flow at the conduits and as the fire spread the pipes were cut to provide a supply at a particular point, thereby preventing the passage of any more water to the fire-fighters further along. An account given by Bishop Lloyd and the Countess of Clarendon to Gilbert Burnet that the supply from the New River Head was cut off at the beginning of the fire, because the cocks there had been closed on the previous day by John Graunt, a Catholic, is almost certainly no more than one of the many anti-papist tales that were rife at the time. In fact, Graunt, best known as a political economist, did not become a member of the New River Company until later in the month and there is no evidence to support the allegation.[22]

Pepys was concerned enough to rise at about seven o'clock on the Sunday morning and check on the progress of the fire. He decided that it was further away than it had been when he watched it during the night and 'not so much as it was'. Only when Jane came to tell him that she had heard that more than 300 houses had been burnt down did he realise the seriousness of the situation. Although the figure could be no more than hearsay, it certainly indicated that the fire was an unusually large and threatening one. Pepys was not alone in reacting sluggishly to the early stages of the fire; a Dutch account mentioned that 'the fire took people by surprise'.[23] William Taswell, a schoolboy at Westminster, apparently knew nothing of the disaster until between ten and eleven o'clock on the Sunday morning, and he was alerted not by the sight or smell of smoke drifting downwind of the blaze, but by people 'running to and fro in a seeming disquietude and consternation' and then hearing the cause of their distress. The slowness of the response was attributed partly to the fact that it was a Sunday morning, when far fewer people needed to be up and about as early as on a weekday.[24]

Those near the fire necessarily reacted more quickly and threw what goods they could carry into boats and lighters on the river. Pepys noticed that many stayed in their houses until the last possible moment before fleeing.[25] The removal of their possessions was not helped by the limited access to the river. There was no quay along the north side of the Thames through the City, for many buildings stood on the water's edge, with some actually jettied out above the river on piles.

Other householders, whose premises were further away, remained comparatively relaxed. Queen Christina of Sweden's principal confidential secretary, Franciscus de Rapicani, who was on a visit to London, had a midday meal in Covent Garden with 'a fine company', including some people from the City, who were 'quite cheerful for so perilous and sorry a time'. His account adds, however, that some of his companions, on their return to the City, found that 'their houses had gone up in fire and smoke'. Pepys and his wife, too, had guests and 'we had an extraordinary good dinner, and [were] as merry as at this time we could be'.[26] Indeed, the speed of the fire and the way in which houses some distance from the front line of flames caught fire, as burning debris was spread by the wind, seem to have taken people by surprise. It was said that the blaze advanced so quickly that it destroyed about 100 houses an hour.[27]

By the end of Sunday the fire had burned along the riverfront for about half a mile, and had engulfed the area contained within an arc running from the river close to Queenhithe through the Bush Lane area to the top of St Michael's Lane and Fish Street Hill at Cannon Street, the northernmost point reached by this time. It had made little progress upwind, although it had burned as far as the south end of Love Lane. Inevitably, this modest eastward progress caused great concern for the safety of the Tower, although it was relatively secure while the wind continued to blow from the east or north-east. Among the more prominent buildings destroyed on Sunday were the halls of the Fishmongers', Dyers' and Watermen's Companies and the guildhall of the Hansa merchants at the Steelyard. A number of churches were gutted, including St Magnus the Martyr, St Margaret, New Fish Street, St George, Botolph Lane, and St Lawrence Pountney.

It was in Cannon Street that Pepys met with the, by now distraught, lord mayor, with orders from the king not to spare any property 'but to pull down before the fire every way'. Bludworth protested that he had indeed been supervising the demolition of houses, but that the fire had overtaken these efforts.[28] Pulling down buildings was the obvious, in fact by this stage the only, solution, but in such difficult conditions the opportunities to establish effective fire-breaks were few. Where the buildings were closely packed together an inordinate amount of labour and time was required to clear a space, with the added difficulty that it was not enough simply to destroy the buildings, but the materials and the other flammable goods already on the site had to be removed. With the strong wind behind them, the flames jumped across narrow gaps. Only the principal thoroughfares were broad enough to give this course of action a reasonable chance of success, if the buildings along them were cleared away to widen the space. Cornhill was a 'large and spacious street' and the houses on its south side were pulled down on Monday, as the fire approached, but the timber that had been left in the street caught alight and so the flames continued unchecked. Cheapside offered a similar opportunity to make a broad fire-break, although it was not taken, and John Rushworth alleged that when the fire reached it on Tuesday 'not tenn men stood by helping or calling for helpe'.[29]

Another criticism of the efforts to check the flames was that the fire-breaks were too close to the front of the fire. The creation of a break some distance ahead of the flames may have given the fire-fighters enough time to contrive an effective barrier. It had the further advantage that gunpowder could be used, destroying the buildings more quickly than could be achieved by demolition and so allowing a wider gap to be created in the time available. This could not be done close to the fire because of the all-too-obvious dangers of handling powder barrels in the face of a blaze which was emitting burning debris. The use of gunpowder was apparently suggested by sailors early on, but their advice was not followed. Evelyn claimed that it was opposed by 'some tenacious & avaritious Men, Aldermen &c.' because their houses would have been among the first to have been destroyed.[30] In any case, making a fire-break well away from the front of the fire created problems of its own. It implicitly sacrificed those buildings between the fire and the break, which would not only lose the fire-fighters the help of their occupants, but make their efforts even more difficult as the householders attempted to save their possessions, adding to the confusion.

From an early stage, many citizens faced the agonising choice between staying to help to douse the flames and concentrating on removing their own goods, and their dilemma increased as the fire grew in scale and the likelihood that it would be checked diminished. The impact on the fire-fighting effort of increasing numbers choosing to secure their possessions was not only to reduce the manpower available, but also to add to the chaos. Initially, those whose houses were threatened moved their goods relatively short distances, only to realise fairly quickly that they had to take them further away. Humphrey Stokes, a goldsmith in Lombard Street, took in a friend's belongings on Sunday, but his own house was burnt on the following day.

As the area threatened with destruction grew, so did the number of people whose premises were endangered. The Thames was the obvious escape route for those living in the area burnt on Sunday and Pepys described it as full of lighters and boats being loaded with their belongings, while other goods were floating in the water. This was still the picture on Monday, according to Evelyn, who saw the river 'coverd with goods floating, all the barges & boates laden with what some had time & courage to save'. Keyboard instruments seem to have been high on the list of valuables which householders tried to secure. Pepys reckoned that he saw a pair of virginals on two out of every three boats, although other evidence suggests that this exaggerated the proportion of households that possessed these instruments.[31]

As the flames spread away from the riverside, the same pattern was repeated in the streets. With the rising sense of urgency, verging on panic, came profiteering by those who were able to provide transport. Carts could only be obtained 'at most unhumane prices' that were later said to have been as high as £30 per load, although £4 or £5 seems to have been the common price, with porters charging 9s or 10s. Lady

Hobart claimed that it had cost her £20 'in porters and carts' to remove her goods and Pepys paid £8 for the two lighters that carried his goods downstream to Deptford.[32] Many could not afford such rates and so could save only what they could carry. Thomas Hayter, a clerk, carried away just 'some few of his goods' from his house in Fish Street Hill. Pepys was shocked to see the streets 'crowded with people, running and riding and getting of carts at any rate to fetch away thing[s]'. The congestion became so bad that on Monday an order was issued that no carts should be brought near the fire. This proved to be unenforceable and was withdrawn on the following day.[33]

Despite the crowded streets and the piles of debris that increasingly obstructed them, larger vehicles could get through. Lord Conway's servant was able to load some of the 'best chairs and fine goods' at his house in Queen Street into his coach and, by borrowing a team of horses, take them to Kensington. Those without their own transport found things more difficult, however. Families with servants discovered that their usefulness in arranging transport was limited, for if they went out they could be pressed into service to help fight the fire. Dr William Denton complained that two of his men had been detained in this way in a single morning, so that he 'dare not send a man out of doors'. Conveyances were, in any case, difficult to come by and on Tuesday afternoon there was not a boat, barge, cart or coach to be had at the Temple. Many householders had no choice but to rely on the help of strangers, sometimes with unhappy results. Taswell's family hired 'certain persons, assuming the character of porters, but in reality nothing else but downright plunderers', to help move their belongings, only to find that they had made off with goods worth £40. The opportunities for pilfering and looting from empty shops and houses were almost limitless.[34]

The prospect of a descent into chaos across the city was an alarming one for the government, which was anxious not only about the spread of the fire, but also a possible breakdown of law and order. The king had, of course, been told about the outbreak on Sunday morning and received a report from Pepys, who had checked on the fire's progress and talked to Sir John Robinson, the Lieutenant of the Tower, before hurrying to Whitehall. In the afternoon, both the king and the Duke of York went down the Thames by barge to watch the fire, landing at Queenhithe and giving orders for pulling down houses.[35] On Monday, as the fire continued to spread, Charles attempted to bring order to the efforts being made by establishing eight fire posts and putting the Duke of York in overall control. Strictly speaking, the lord mayor's authority in the City was paramount, but in such an emergency, and with his authority and that of the aldermen being 'little regarded', there could be no objections to the king's action. Without doubt the existing arrangements had been overwhelmed by the scale of the disaster and Bludworth's attempts at directing operations had been particularly ineffectual.[36]

The fire posts were placed around the conflagration and, at that stage, some distance from it. The western side of the City was covered by posts at Temple Bar, Clifford's Inn Gardens, Fetter Lane and Shoe Lane, while on its north side posts were placed at Cow Lane in Smithfield, Aldersgate and Cripplegate. The most easterly post was that at Coleman Street, for none was established in the broad arc around the edge of the fire between that point and the Tower. This may reflect an awareness of the vulnerability of the west of the City if the wind continued to blow from the east, and perhaps, too, a growing concern for the safety of Whitehall and even of Westminster. Control of each post was entrusted to a privy councillor or nobleman, who was assisted by three justices of the peace and the parish constables, with 100 men. In addition, thirty foot-soldiers, commanded by 'a careful officer', were assigned to each post. The City's trained bands had been called out on Sunday and some of them were assigned to guard the citizens' belongings that were being deposited in the available open spaces outside the walls. The militia from Hertfordshire, Middlesex, Surrey and Kent were now ordered to assemble near London, to be ready to relieve the City's trained bands if necessary.[37]

Worries about law and order were justified, for although nothing could be done to prevent minor offences, a more sinister development was the aggressive behaviour of citizens who vented their anger and frustration on suspected arsonists. Indeed, those manning the fire posts were kept busy taking into their charge people accused of deliberately starting fires, as much for their own protection as because there was any evidence against them. Lord Hollis and Lord Ashley had 'many brought to them in custody for crimes of this nature'. The war had put Frenchmen and Dutchmen high on the list of potential suspects, with the latter under particular suspicion because of fears of retaliation for Holmes's raid, and there were those who were 'ready to knock them all on the head wheresoever they meet them'.[38] This remark was based on more than rumour, for Taswell witnessed a Frenchman felled by a blow with an iron bar. But in an atmosphere where rumours of arson and plots were rife, any foreigner was likely to be set upon. A servant of the Portuguese ambassador was seized, having been seen putting a fireball into a house, although on investigation it proved to be no more than a piece of bread which he had picked up in the street. On another occasion, tennis balls in a Frenchman's chest were mistaken for incendiary devices and one man was thrown into prison because he had 'the appearance of a Frenchman'.[39] It was clearly advisable for anyone likely to be at risk to remain indoors. Some found this too restrictive. A member of the Swedish ambassador's retinue was 'so impatient at staying away from a lady-friend' that he went to visit her, but as he was trying to return he and his companion were stopped by a crowd, who were intent on hanging them from a house sign. They were saved only because a troop of the Duke of York's bodyguard happened to come by at that moment.[40]

Foreigners were not the only suspects. Because the fire had broken out so near 3 September, Nonconformist fanatics inevitably came to mind as the real villains and, as a papist plot could never be ruled out in such circumstances, some Catholics were arrested. After all, this disaster surely had the hallmarks of another 'Popish design' like the Gunpowder Plot, but one which had proved successful.[41] The logic of the conspiracy theory that the fire was started deliberately by enemies of the state demanded that there would be some follow-up, presumably a hostile force that would take advantage of the confusion and seize the city. This could be achieved by a force coming together within London, such as the 4,000 French and papists that Taswell heard were in arms, or by an invading army, hence the reports that 50,000 Dutch and French troops were on their way.[42]

The nature of the fire encouraged the notion that arsonists were at work. After the first few hours, when there was just one blaze around Pudding Lane, the fire had dispersed and become in effect several local fires, as the flames followed the path provided by the most combustible materials and the fire-fighters had some isolated successes in checking their advance. Moreover, fires began well ahead of the flames, apparently in buildings that should have been secure. When a man who had struggled to move his goods from his house in Bread Street to a friend's in Holborn then saw that house, and no others, catch fire, he became suspicious of the cause. Cases such as this, with fires 'breaking out in several places at so great distance from each other', did much to arouse fears that the fire was begun maliciously as part of a great conspiracy.[43] Of course, burning debris carried on the strong wind was bound to start fires in this way and many were aware of 'great flakes' blowing on to buildings ahead of the flames and setting them alight. The Duke of York, for example, saw the firebrand that started a fire at Dorset House and could confirm that it had not been ignited by a fireball. Yet even apparently straightforward incidents of this kind were open to differing interpretations. Pepys watched as the steeple of St Lawrence Pountney caught fire at the top 'and there burned till it fall down' and did not consider it suspicious, although Thomas Middleton, a surgeon, who also saw it, decided that here was evidence that the fire 'was maintained by design'. In such an atmosphere, arson was very much in the eye of the beholder.[44]

Despite the growing awareness that a major catastrophe was in the making, by dawn on Monday the fire had still destroyed only a comparatively small part of the area within the city walls. It made considerable progress during Monday, however, destroying perhaps five times as many churches as it had done on the previous day. Still driven by the easterly wind, it continued westwards along the riverside, where an attempt to make a fire-break at the market place at Queenhithe was wholly unsuccessful, towards Broken Wharf, Paul's Wharf and Baynard's Castle. The castle was a tall and substantial stone building fronting directly on the river, providing another possible point where the flames could be checked, but all hopes of that were to be disappointed and the structure was burned out. The fire also moved through the area north of Thames Street and the river, up to Old Fish Street and across Cannon Street. The post office in Cloak Lane, off Dowgate, was destroyed early on Monday morning and the company halls of the cutlers, vintners and salters were also gutted during the day. The churches in the area north of Thames Street that were destroyed included the 'fair parish church' of St Michael Paternoster Royal, where Richard Whittington was buried, together with the almshouses which he had founded, known as God's House.[45]

Eastwards, towards the wind, the flames made slower progress, not reaching Billingsgate until the early evening. As Monday drew to a close, St Mary-at-Hill had been destroyed, yet the fire-fighters around St Dunstan's-in-the-East, who included the scholars of Westminster

School under the direction of the dean, John Dolben, managed to isolate the building and prevent it from being entirely gutted, although it was badly damaged.[46] The fire in this sector was still roughly 300 yards away from the Tower. Nevertheless, steps were taken to bolster its resources, including a request for all fire-engines still at the naval yards at Woolwich and Deptford to be sent there, together with 'all persons, capable either by hand or judgement'.[47]

On Monday the fire began to destroy areas of a different character from those affected so far. The riverside consisted of some of the poorest parishes within the walls, but the flames now made inroads into the heart of the City, reaching some of its wealthiest districts. Lombard Street, with its 'divers fair Houses', Cornhill, Gracechurch Street and the western part of Fenchurch Street were all burnt out during Monday. The merchants and goldsmiths had anticipated the spread of the fire into their area and had already moved their valuables away. Because their wealth consisted principally of money, and bills and bonds, rather than bulky goods, it was easily removed. So easily, indeed, that some of them evidently felt that a modest tip was an adequate reward to those who helped them. This, at least, was a common opinion after the fire. Sir Richard Browne, the alderman of Langborne ward, was said to have had £10,000 in his chest and he rewarded those who had helped him save it with a payment of £4.[48] The goldsmiths and merchants first deposited their valuables in the Tower, from where they were later transferred to Whitehall, with Sir Robert Viner's removed to his brother's quarters in Windsor Castle.[49]

The Royal Exchange in Cornhill was one of the major casualties of this phase of the fire, both because of the value of the goods stored there and its significance as the London bourse. Built at the expense of Sir Thomas Gresham in 1566–7 and modelled on the Antwerp bourse of 1531, it was an imposing courtyard building with a tall clock tower, described by Thomas Vincent as 'the glory of the merchants'. The shops in its upper gallery were particularly favoured by those trading in silks and fine-quality cloths. As well as the goods in its many shops and stalls, its crypt housed the East India Company's stocks of pepper, which had not been removed. By the time the fire had burned through the building, all that remained, apart from the ruins, was Gresham's statue, which had toppled over but was intact, 'the Turrett where the Clock hanged . . . and halfe a pillar'.[50]

A little further east along Cornhill was the 'fair and beautiful' church of St Michael, with 'a proper cloister, and a fair churchyard' on its south side. The church was gutted, although its tower survived and was not demolished until 1721. St Peter's was also destroyed, but just east of this was Leadenhall, where the progress of the fire came to a halt. Leadenhall was a stone structure, strong enough to have served as the City's magazine for corn and arms, and a combination of its high walls and the timely encouragement which an alderman gave to the fire-fighters there, together with the fact that the flames were burning into the wind, proved to be enough to check the fire.[51]

At the west end of Lombard Street was the 'comely Parish Church' of St Mary Woolnoth, which was damaged, and beyond lay Poultry and Cheapside. These were now threatened by the fires spreading along the streets leading into them from the south, as well as those which had burnt Cornhill, Lombard Street and Threadneedle Street. The stone buildings of the former College of St Thomas of Acon, now the Mercers' Company chapel, temporarily checked the progress of the flames along Poultry, but early on Tuesday they spread into Cheapside. This became the most destructive day of the disaster. Perhaps because the front of the various fires was now so long, those fighting the flames were becoming exhausted, the wind continued to blow strongly and the water supply position had not improved, the blaze made more progress than on either of the previous days.

Those in charge of the fire-fighting had realised that they were unlikely to be able to check the fires before they had reached the city walls. During the night they had ordered the demolition of houses in Whitefriars, between Fleet Street and the river, several hundred yards ahead of the fire. The line of the River Fleet from Holborn Bridge to the Thames offered a possible fire-break, and the plan during Tuesday morning was to clear buildings along it to widen the gap. By that time the flames had reached the west end of Cheapside and were spreading northwards to engulf Guildhall.

Under the direction of the Duke of York, much effort had been put into halting the blaze at the Fleet. But the hope that it would be an effective fire-break proved to be a vain one. From St Paul's the fire 'rushed like a torrent down Ludgate Hill' and neither the city wall nor the Fleet proved to be effective barriers. By midday on Tuesday the flames had spread across the Fleet to Salisbury Court and the houses between it and the Bridewell. They 'raged so extreme in Fleet Street on both sides' that the fire-fighters had to withdraw and they considered that the next point where it might be checked was Somerset House. The fire reached the walls of the Temple by six o'clock and by dusk it could be seen 'from the very ditch the shore quite up to the Temple all in a flame, and a very great breadth'. Much of the Inner Temple was gutted, as were the buildings along Fleet Street, to within a few houses of St Dunstan's church on the north side and just opposite the church on the south.[52] There were now very real fears for Whitehall Palace and so buildings westwards of the Temple, from Somerset House as far as Charing Cross and Scotland Yard, were demolished or unroofed. The king and the courtiers had already begun to ship goods away by river. Clarendon later explained that his wife had been so fearful for the safety of Worcester House in the Strand, which they had occupied since 1660, that she 'caused all my goodes to be throwne into lighters for Twitnam [Twickenham], and into Cartes for my new house and other places'. A warrant was issued for the removal of the exchequer to Nonsuch House, near Epsom, and the money was actually loaded into vessels in preparation for the move.[53]

The city wall to the north of Ludgate also failed to prevent the spread of the fire, which ran along Butcher Row and Newgate Market to Newgate, and beyond the wall to Holborn Bridge. To the north of Newgate Street was Christ Church, one of the most impressive of the City's churches, 300 feet long and 64 feet high to the line of the roof, and the buildings of Christ's Hospital around the cloister of the former Grey Friars. The church was badly damaged and was later demolished and the destruction wreaked on the hospital buildings, with their contents, was estimated to be worth at least £8,000. Nevertheless, some parts of this group emerged from the fire relatively unscathed and the library built by Richard Whittington along the north side of the cloister in 1429 was in use until the early nineteenth century.[54] Eastwards, the fire also broke through the wall at Aldersgate, and its progress in this quarter was such that St Bartholomew's Hospital seemed to be threatened. In fact, the damage outside the gate was relatively limited, with only about thirty houses gutted. St Botolph's church survived and neither St Bartholomew's nor Smithfield were reached. There was also little destruction outside the line of the wall round to Cripplegate.[55]

St Paul's dominated the western part of the City that was destroyed on Tuesday. Because a programme of repair and restoration was about to begin, the building was under scaffolding by early September and Evelyn thought that the 'Scaffalds contributed exceedingly' to the spread of the flames when the building caught fire.[56] Another major factor was that goods had been carried into the building since the fire had begun. It was common for householders to take their possessions into churches for safety during major fires, acting on the understandable basis that they were the only reasonably fire-resistant structures open to the public. In many instances, the goods deposited in a church actually contributed to its destruction, acting as fuel and providing the means for the flames to spread through the building. This pattern was repeated at the London churches during the Great Fire,[57] and also at St Paul's, which because of confidence in 'the absolute security of that place' was filled with 'all sorts of goods' by Tuesday evening. So, too, was the church of St Faith beneath the cathedral. This served as the parish church for the stationers, whose premises were concentrated in the vicinity, and they now chose it as a secure place for their stocks, blocking up every aperture in an attempt to make it fireproof.[58]

Initially it was hoped that the cathedral, protected by the space around it, had escaped the general disaster, for when the flames reached the area on Tuesday the building did not catch fire. This was only a brief respite, however, for the roof ignited at about eight o'clock that evening as burning debris settled on it. Within an hour the blaze was so fierce that Taswell later claimed that he could read his pocket edition of Terence by the light of it, although he was in Westminster. The cathedral burned for several hours and eventually the roofs fell in, parts of the masonry disintegrated, and the vaulted roof of the choir collapsed, breaking through the floor and exposing to the flames the stationers' stocks in St Faith's underneath it. By the time the fire had burnt out, the cathedral was left as 'a smoking mass of lamentable ruins'.[59]

Along the northern edge of the conflagration, the early seventeenth-century buildings of Sion College, just within the walls, were all burnt. The fire post in Coleman Street had to be abandoned as the flames advanced, but the northern end of that street was saved. To the east, the flames destroyed the buildings along Throgmorton Street and the hall of the Drapers' Company, but its extensive garden acted as a fire-break. The fire made some progress along its eastern edge, in spite of the wind, during Tuesday, reaching, but not destroying, the Dutch church at Austin Friars and the church of St Martin Outwich at the junction of Threadneedle Street and Bishopsgate Street. Further south, towards the river, its progress along Tower Street and Thames Street, which had been closely watched since Sunday morning, now prompted decisive action to protect the Tower. Houses in Tower Street and Mark Lane were blown up and buildings that stood close to the Tower, in some places along its ditch, were demolished by cannon fire. Nevertheless, the fire 'came almost to the very Gates' of the Tower, having destroyed the whole area to the west. The Custom House, a tall and substantial Elizabethan building, was gutted, but Allhallows, Barking, to the north of Tower Street, narrowly escaped, despite its parsonage house and porch being burned.[60]

Pepys climbed the tower of Allhallows on Wednesday 'and there saw the saddest sight of desolation that I ever saw . . . the fire being spread as far as I could see it'.[61] The flames had reached the church during the night, but had made no further progress, and although Tuesday night had seemed 'more dreadful' than the previous one, conditions had begun to improve.[62] A change in the direction of the wind was detected late on Monday evening, which had encouraged the fire-fighters around Fleet Street and the Temple, but this was illusory and there was no respite until Wednesday, when the wind dropped completely. This proved to be crucial, despite the 'great fires' still burning all over the City, for they could be tackled in the changed conditions and the relative calm allowed further preparations to be made in case the fire picked up again. The flames at Fetter Lane and Shoe Lane were halted and then doused, and the lord mayor supervised the pulling down of a 'great store of houses' at Cripplegate. By midday on Wednesday the fire at Holborn Bridge was extinguished and by that evening all those to the west of the City, which had burnt so fiercely the day before, were out, except for that at Cripplegate. Resources could now be concentrated on this remaining blaze and it was eventually quenched, as was a further outbreak at the Temple, which was put out by about two o'clock on Thursday morning. In these hopeful circumstances, Wednesday night promised to be a comparatively restful one, only to be broken by the urgent news that the Frenchmen and Dutchmen were coming.[63]

Much work remained to be done on Thursday and 200 members of the militia from the nearby counties were ordered to relieve those who had been on duty in the City. They were also required to bring carts and tools so that the tasks of clearing the streets and property and damping down the ruins could be continued. On Friday the king visited the Tower and ordered the demolition of the remaining houses around the ditch and on Tower Wharf.[64]

The normal arrangements for supplying provisions had collapsed, with the destruction of the stocks within the City, together with the bakehouses and brewhouses. The markets, too, had been gutted. On Wednesday the king issued a proclamation directing suppliers to continue to bring in provisions every day. This was done to such good effect that when those camped in Moorfields were provided with biscuit from the Navy's stores they refused it, 'being unaccustomed to that kind of Bread'.[65]

With so much of the area within the walls destroyed, the inhabitants had been driven to find refuge elsewhere, initially in the suburbs and the open spaces around the City at Moorfields, Lincoln's Inn Fields, Gray's Inn Fields, Hatton Garden, St Giles's Fields and the piazza at Covent Garden. These quickly became crowded, however, with Moorfields said to be 'full of people', and so the refugees moved on, to Islington and Highgate. In a short time 'all the neighbour villages were filled with more people than they could contain, and more goods than they could find room for', so that many were forced to settle in the fields, which 'for many miles were strewed with moveables of all sorts, & Tents'.[66] To provide for those who had been displaced, temporary markets were set up, not only at Bishopsgate, Tower Hill and Smithfield, but further afield, at Clerkenwell, Islington, Finsbury Fields, Mile End Green and Ratcliff.[67]

The king's proclamations were hardly needed, so far as news of the fire itself was concerned. The ringing of the church bells in the early stages indicated to those within earshot that something was seriously amiss and places downwind soon had evidence of a major fire, with the pall of smoke drifting westwards. Gardens to the west of the City were covered by a layer of ash that included fragments of paper and linen, and also 'peices of Ceiling and playster work', and burning papers were blown as far as Cranbourne and Eton, in Berkshire.[68] The news was also spread by letters, hastily written, and word of mouth. Almost inevitably, some reports of the fire exaggerated the scale of the disaster. The Duke of Buckingham was told on Thursday that almost all the Strand had been burnt.[69] Such information may have emanated from those hearing the news at second or third hand, or who had seen the fire only from a distance and so could make no more than rough estimates of its extent.

So little was written from the City when the fire was still raging that it is chiefly letters and journal entries written after the conflagration had subsided that give an impression of conditions between Sunday and Wednesday. Pepys wrote up his entry for Sunday, but then sent his diary away with his other papers, and did not retrieve it until the following Saturday. Although several writers described the progress of the fire in terms of the individual days, it blazed continuously without respite, and in such conditions it was easy to become confused about the passage of time. Pepys thought that the four days of fire seemed like a week and he had almost forgotten what day it was.[70] Lack of rest and the unceasing noise of the fire and collapse of buildings contributed to this, as well as the lightness of the night sky, with 'the light of the fire supplying that of the sun'. During the days 'all the skie were of a fiery aspect, like the top of a burning Oven'. The air around the fire was 'so hot & inflam'd that at the last one was not able to approch it' and even on Thursday Taswell found the air still 'intensely warm'.[71] The extent of the fires was such that the whole city seemed to be on fire at once. This impression was increased when the flammable goods that had been pushed from the wharves into the Thames, because they were so bulky, caught alight as burning timbers fell into the water, which gave the impression that the river was on fire.[72] To the general horror of the flames and smoke was added the stench of burning buildings and those goods that were too unwieldy to be removed, ranging in pungency from pitch and turpentine to brandy and pepper.

Some accounts criticised the reactions of the citizens, chiefly for giving more attention to saving their goods than to tackling the fire. Windham Sandys described their response in simple terms based on social status: 'for the first rank, they minded only for their own preservation; the middle sort so distracted and amazed that they did not know what they did; the poorer, they minded nothing but pilfering'. He also implied that there was a certain resignation in the face of this disaster, while others, such as Evelyn, described an understandable state of alarm, with 'the shreeking of Women & children, the hurry of people'.[73] Indeed, the sheer danger of fire-fighting in those conditions was a factor in the citizens' behaviour, and at least six people met their death during the fire, beginning with Farriner's maid on the first night and including an elderly woman whose body Taswell saw near to St Paul's 'parched up as it were with the flames'.[74] Unless this was a gross underestimate, then the death toll was remarkably low. Despite the alarm and confusion, the elderly and infirm had been removed before the fire arrived, although some of them may have died later. The playwright James Shirley and his wife both died on the same day in October, perhaps as a result of being forced to abandon their home, which was destroyed, and adapt to makeshift accommodation. Soon after the fire it was predicted that the disaster would lead to physicians being in great demand.[75]

Despite the risks, there is evidence of individuals dealing with the crisis in a calm and practical manner by tackling fires in and around their own premises. The neighbours of John Vandermarsh, a merchant, later testified that he had been instrumental in saving houses adjacent to his in Lime Street, by his own efforts and by paying labourers to prevent the flames from spreading and to put them out. Having secured his goods, he paid £50 to have 'a great part' of one of the houses of which he was a tenant pulled down. Witnesses said that one side of the house caught fire and was beaten down, so that it 'lay open from top to bottom', and that water had damaged the ceilings and floors. Vandermarsh's efforts were particularly commendable as he was the son of a Dutchman, born in Haarlem and naturalised only two years earlier, and might have thought it prudent to lie low to avoid the anger directed at the Dutch, rather than draw attention to himself by demolishing property. John Gaze, a baker in Bishopsgate Street, also claimed to have saved nearby property by putting out the fire in his own house, part of which was destroyed.[76] Elsewhere, the presence of brick buildings, such as those in Fetter Lane, had helped to check the fire. The Earl of Clarendon noted that when the roof and other timbers burnt and fell into a brick building 'the walls stood and enclosed the fire' which then burned out without making further progress.[77] His observations were surely correct and confirmed the opinions of those who had argued for the widespread adoption of brick building within the City.

Yet even the presence of groups of brick buildings was not enough to stop the fire once it had become well established, nor were the efforts of the fire-fighters. The measures initiated by the king and Duke of York were sensible and practical ones, taking over direction from the City's officers, giving royal authority to the demolition of buildings, bringing organisation to the creation of fire-breaks and using patrols of the royal guards to keep order. In addition, they were both much in evidence providing supervision and encouragement, even helping to pass the buckets and work the fire-engines. Sandys, who was with the duke's entourage, praised his exertions and the risks that he ran while directing operations, and the king distributed guineas among the labourers.[78] None of their efforts before Wednesday so much as checked the advance of the fire, however, and the fire-breaks that had been prepared were overwhelmed.

With the dryness of the buildings and their contents after such a hot summer, there was little or no chance of getting the fire under control until the strength of the wind fell. A Dutch account commented that in those conditions the fire could not have been checked 'even with the help of half the world, had it been available'.[79] This was a rather melodramatic expression of an essential truth. The failure to contain the fire in Farriner's house or the premises immediately around it at the very outset had been crucial.

The ultimate responsibility rested with the lord mayor, who was described as 'a young man of little experience'.[80] A merchant trading to Turkey and a Committee of the East India Company, Bludworth was forty-six years old at the time of the fire and had entered City politics in 1658 as a common councilman. His rapid rise to lord mayor within seven years undoubtedly owed a great deal to his royalism. He was knighted at the Restoration and was elected to parliament for Southwark in 1660 and 1661. The commissioners implementing the Corporation Act appointed him as alderman of Portsoken ward in 1662 on the king's recommendation. While he had only a few years in public office behind him at the time of the Great Fire, he had already served the greatest part of his year's term as lord mayor.[81]

Bludworth's reputation has been tarnished by Pepys's judgement of him as 'a silly man' who was also 'very weak'. Pepys could be a harsh judge and may be a hostile witness in this case, having clashed with Bludworth earlier in the year over the pressing of men in the

City to serve in the Navy. On that occasion he concluded that the lord mayor was 'a mean man of understanding and despatch of any public business'.[82] But Pepys was by no means Bludworth's only critic. Indeed, he was criticised for 'delighting more in drinking and dancing than is necessary for such a magistrate' and 'much blamed' for the extent of the disaster by 'not pulling houses downe time enough'. He was clearly the target of a lampoon which observed that London had been burnt within five days 'All though a strong man and a stoute / Did say at first hee'd pisse it out'.[83] His reaction to the criticism was that it had been his misfortune 'to serve in the severest year that ever man did'.[84]

The case against Bludworth, as summarised by the Earl of Clarendon, was that although he arrived at the scene promptly, when he did so 'his consternation was equal to that of other men', and when pressed by those who were not as discouraged as he was to pull down the nearby houses, he would not act, thinking that it was 'not safe counsel'.[85] An inexperienced or uncertain person in a difficult situation, such as that which Bludworth faced on the night of 2 September, has to be prepared to take the advice of others and to follow the safest and most sensible course of action, regardless of possible legal or financial consequences. Whatever the portion of blame that can be fairly attributed to Bludworth, by Thursday morning a fire which had begun at a baker's in a side street four days earlier had destroyed much of the City.

THREE

TAKING STOCK

In three days the most flourishing city in the world is a ruinous heap,
the streets only to be known by the maimed remainder of the churches.

Letter to Philip Pedder, 13 September 1666,
Calendar of State Papers Domestic, 1666–7, p. 122

A disaster on the scale of the Great Fire created immediate and
massive problems. Some of them were practical matters similar to
those which followed any large-scale urban fire. Provision had to be
made for the homeless before the winter, for example, both in terms
of accommodation and cash assistance for those left destitute. Yet the
citizens who were best able to provide poor relief were themselves
among the victims. This was one reason that it was necessary to
establish the scale of the losses, by individuals taking stock of their
own position and by the City authorities assessing the overall extent of
the damage. But because of London's unique role there were further,
political, considerations, which did not apply after such catastrophes
elsewhere. It was advisable that the causes of the conflagration be
investigated, if only to ensure that the citizens' initial xenophobic
reaction would not lead them to prolong their search for scapegoats,
perhaps even turn their anger against the government itself. This was
not the only problem facing the government, however, for the fire
inevitably had some effect upon its own operations and the conduct of
the war against the United Provinces and France.

Even more immediate than these concerns was the possibility that
the fire could begin again if the wind sprang up. Both Pepys and
Taswell remarked how hot the ground was when they walked through
the ruined area on Wednesday and Thursday, and on Friday Evelyn
found himself climbing over 'mountaines of yet smoking rubbish',
with his hair almost singed and his feet made sore by the heat.[1] The

initial priority, therefore, was to make things safe by moving stocks of fuel out of the burnt area, clearing the streets and damping down the smouldering ruins. The task was eased by the rain that fell on the Sunday following the fire. A longer spell of rain, lasting for ten days, came in October, finally dousing the embers.

Those who ventured among the ruins soon after the fire had ended were struck by the completeness of the destruction. Most of the buildings had collapsed, so that it was almost possible to see from one side of the City to the other, and the river was visible from Cheapside.[2] The masonry of many of the churches and some of the company halls still stood, although a number of churches, such as St Mary-le-Bow, were completely ruined. Those which were recognisable were invaluable as landmarks in the confusion of wreckage and rubbish. Some of the buildings had fallen into the streets and Evelyn found that the lanes and narrower streets were 'quite fill'd up with rubbish'. The heat had been so intense that the church bells had melted, as had the chains along the streets and the hinges, bars and gates of the prisons. Scavengers searching through the ruins found lumps of metal 'mixed together and out of shape'. As Evelyn looked over the ruins of St Paul's he was shocked to see that not only had the bells melted, but so too had the large area of lead from the roof, the ironwork and the plate.[3]

Letters sent from London describing this calamity reached a readership anxious for accurate news. Word of the fire had spread rapidly. It had reached the neighbourhood of Hungerford by Tuesday and by Friday a rumour was circulating that 60,000 Presbyterians, with French and Dutch, had been up in arms during the fire and the king's forces had defeated them, killing 30,000 and taking many others prisoner. This nonsense was contradicted by a more reliable source of intelligence.[4] Yet many who heard of the fire assumed at once that it had been started deliberately, by 'implacable enemies' or 'Anabaptists and other disaffected persons'. At Newcastle it was observed that the meetings of Quakers and other sectaries had been well attended recently 'and little care is taken to hinder them'. In many places the militia were called out in case the fire was part of a wider plan, perhaps a 'hellish contrivance' of the French, Dutch and fanatics. This fear was so widespread that 'all townes stood upon their owne defence day and night'. The militia were still keeping a watch at Barnstaple on 11 September, because of a report that the plot was aimed not only at London, but at the destruction of the principal towns and cities in England. The governor of Hull set a strong guard and in Norwich the innkeepers were instructed not to lodge strangers until they had been questioned by the mayor, nor to allow them to leave the city without his order.

These anxieties were strengthened by rumours that began to circulate of fires elsewhere. Minor outbreaks now received considerable notice, such as a blaze in two houses in Bridgwater and one in a tanner's kiln in Chester, both of which were quenched with little damage. Fear of arsonists was rife, with suspects thrown into prison in Leicester and reports that suspicious persons seized near Lutterworth were carrying fire-balls as big as tennis balls. A rumour that a man had been seen handling a fire-ball near Warwick caused 'the whole town' to take to the streets, and the crowd had to be dispersed by the militia. Anthony Wood noted that two fires near Oxford on successive days soon after the Great Fire had been started deliberately.[5]

Such sharp reactions to the news of the fire were exacerbated by the lack of reliable information. The post office in Cloak Lane, off Dowgate Hill, was in the area burnt out on Monday morning and the consequent breakdown of the postal service with London raised suspicions that something was awry. Those who had received the 3 September issue of *The London Gazette* would have seen a short, but alarming, note to the effect that a major fire had broken out which had already blazed for two nights and a day and was continuing to burn 'with great violence'. This was enough to set its readers' imaginations racing, especially as no further issue appeared for a week. That number, for 3–10 September, began by explaining that publication had been interrupted 'by a Sad and Lamentable Accident of Fire lately hapned in the City of London'. In fact, the premises of its printer, Thomas Newcombe, were close to Baynard's Castle and had been destroyed.[6]

The *Gazette* was managed by Joseph Williamson, Lord Arlington's secretary, and the account of the fire printed in the issue of 10 September was effectively an official statement. Readers certainly seem to have regarded it as authoritative and welcomed it as providing hard news 'after such a diversity of reports'. It gave an account of the early stages of the fire and its subsequent progress, describing the efforts made to check the flames and stressing the role of the royal brothers. The measures that the king had taken for supplying the homeless with provisions were also noted, together with the extent of the citizens' gratitude for his efforts. While admitting the arrest of 'Divers Strangers' during the fire and announcing an enquiry into its causes, the report was at pains to stress that the fire was an accident. The way in which the flames had behaved in the strong wind led to the conclusion that the disaster was the result of 'an unhappy chance, or to speak better, the heavy hand of God upon us for our Sins, shewing us the terrour of his Judgment' not only in raising the fire, but also in stopping it 'when we were in the last despair'.

This point that the fire was a divine judgement was one which was widely accepted. Classical and biblical parallels with Troy and Jerusalem immediately sprang to mind, but so did the fate of Sodom and Gomorrah, and the need to repent was obvious.[7] Thomas Holden wrote to Williamson from Falmouth expressing the hope that the fire would be regarded by all as a judgement for sin, and Williamson also received a letter from Hugh Acland at Truro, who prayed that God would avert His judgements and 'give grace to all so to live as to divert the fierceness of His anger'. Another writer believed that everyone accepted that the fire was caused by the anger of the Lord for the sins of the people, pointing out that pestilence and fire had both come, and that unless the nation's conduct improved the Lord would 'empty his quiver of wrath'. Evelyn saw it as a punishment not only for sins, including those committed within the dissolute court, but also ingratitude for the deliverance from the 'late intestine calamities' and the restoration of the church and monarchy.[8]

Pepys's description of two services which he attended on the Sunday after the fire provides an indication of the mood in London in the aftermath of the disaster. The church was 'mighty full' in the morning and the 'melancholy but good' sermon was so moving that many in the congregation wept. Pepys was less impressed by the Dean of Rochester's preaching at the later service, however, and was particularly displeased by the description of the city as being 'reduced from a large Folio to a Decimo tertio'. Yet although some of the congregation at St Olave's, Hart Street, were deeply moved by the disaster, other citizens apparently showed no sign of contrition. On the previous day Sir Edward Atkyns had written to his brother giving an account of the fire, but concluding that 'you would wonder at the profaness of people, & how little some are concerned in this sad calamity'.[9]

A national fast day was observed on 10 October. This was an important occasion, with William Sancroft, Dean of St Paul's, preaching to the king and court, Seth Ward, Bishop of Exeter, to the Lords and Edward Stillingfleet, later Bishop of Worcester, delivering a sermon to the House of Commons, in St Margaret's, Westminster. The clergy generally presented the fire as a reprimand, a heavy judgement indeed, but also a mercy, for the destruction could have been much worse. A greater disaster could be visited on the country if repentance and reform did not follow this most explicit of warnings.[10] The message was evidently driven home with some fervour. Isaac Archer, the incumbent of Chippenham in Cambridgeshire, noted that the news of the fire 'struck mee with amazement'. His text on the fast day was from the book of Amos, chapter four, verse eleven, with its reference to Sodom and Gomorrah and 'a firebrand plucked out of the burning', and he endeavoured to develop his theme 'to worke my own soule, and the hearts of others to a submission to God, and a seeking his face, and imploring his helpe that we might, in this day of our distresse, prepare to meet our God by true repentance'.[11]

Pepys was in London and went to hear Stillingfleet, but could not stay for the sermon because the church was so full, as it was again later in the day when the preacher was Robert Frampton, later Bishop of Gloucester. While clergymen around the country were able to use the opportunity to drive home the moral lessons of the disaster, the services also provided the opportunity for a collection to help the victims. Frampton was a powerful preacher whose sermon a fortnight after the fire had reduced the king and courtiers to tears.[12] He and Stillingfleet moved the congregations at St Margaret's to such good effect that they donated £135 1s 3d, the fifth highest of the sums raised on 1,021 briefs read there between 1644 and 1793, exceeded only by collections for freeing English slaves in Algiers and Turkey and two appeals to help the French Protestants following the revocation of the Edict of Nantes. At Falmouth Francis Bedford preached 'a very learned and particular sermon' that was so effective that his congregation gave £7, although charitable collections there usually raised only 12s or 15s. The donations in Truro came to more than £20, which was thought to be a commendable sum, 'considering the meanness of the place'.[13]

Some communities had made donations even before the fast day and official collection. By 15 September, £100 had been collected in Lyme Regis. A thoughtful suggestion from Southwold, based on the town's own experience after the blaze there seven years before, was that the poor would be short of food in the aftermath of the fire and because cheese was then so cheap in Suffolk the local gentry could pay for a shipload to be sent to London. The Council of Ireland had a similar idea and investigated how 15,000 head of cattle might be sent to London, but because of current attempts to prohibit the import of livestock from Ireland, which came to fruition with an Act of Parliament early in 1667, this scheme had a political point to it, as well as a benevolent one. Indeed, emotions were running so high over the issue that the Irish charity for London was alleged in the Commons to be 'an abominable cheat, a piece of hypocrisy, a mischievous design to ruin the kingdom of England'.[14]

The fast day collections raised £12,794 and separate gifts added a further £1,077. This was a comparatively modest sum, considering the scale of the disaster, the immediate and widespread publicity it received and the prominence given to the collection, on a national fast day. A second collection was taken in 1668, but produced only £2,306. Indeed, all receipts for the fire victims came to only £16,201.[15] Funds raised to help the victims of the fire at Nantwich in December 1583 had reached £3,300 by March 1586, admittedly helped by particularly assiduous collectors. The response to the fire at Marlborough in 1653 had been even more generous, with £18,000 raised by 1658, and the appeal following the fire at Northampton in 1675 was to bring in £25,000.[16] Both Marlborough and Northampton, therefore, received more in financial aid than did London, for similar kinds of disasters that, while devastating those two communities, were on an infinitely smaller scale than the Great Fire.

A part of the explanation for the modest response may be that a considerable proportion of money given to charitable collections came from London. It was the principal contributor to the Nantwich collection, for example, with the City's donation of £600 contrasting sharply with the £54 sent by Bury St Edmunds, the £35 by Norwich and the £30 by York, and yet they were the largest sums received from other English towns.[17] After the fire at Marlborough the hope was expressed that 'the City will have a compassionate eye, and lend us

their help'. The single parish of St Stephen, Coleman Street, raised
£26 towards that collection and £48 4s 8d for Northampton, which
may be compared with donations towards the appeal after the Great
Fire of £32 in Derby and £23 in Lichfield.[18] It seems that the
wealthy metropolis was a major source of funds on such occasions and
when it was itself the victim the remainder of the country could not
make up the shortfall. Indeed, the immediate response from Norwich
to the Great Fire was that it would lose potential charitable gifts from
London for its own plague sufferers, rather than offering help to those
burnt out. A similar concern prompted the receiver of funds for 'the
poor visited people' at Cambridge to advertise his new address in The
London Gazette shortly after the fire. The town suffered from plague
in both 1665 and 1666, losing about a quarter of its population in the
outbreak.[19]

The anxiety in both places was understandable, given the severity of
the plague. Indeed, the fire coincided with the worst period of mortality
during the epidemic in Norwich, with 200 burials a week at the end of
August. Roughly 15 per cent of the city's population died in the year
to October 1666, with mortality levels in the poorest parishes running
at 25 per cent.[20] The presence of the plague in many places was an
important reason for the modest scale of the donations. It not only
inflicted a heavy death toll across much of the country, but also made
people reluctant to gather in a congregation for fear of infection, while
a door-to-door collection was no less hazardous. Many communities
must have felt that they were themselves in need of charity and could ill
spare money for London, although Colchester sent in a very creditable
£103, despite suffering heavily from plague. Furthermore, London had
benefited from a collection for its own plague victims in the previous
year, with £7,664 distributed by the lord mayor between July and
December 1665. This may have helped to take the edge off the response
to the appeal after the fire, which was the second plea for help for the
capital in little more than a year.[21]

Even in normal circumstances potential benefactors were cautious
about making donations too soon after receiving news of a fire, aware
that 'Rumour often exceeds Truth', and delayed until the scale of the
destruction was more certain.[22] This was hardly the case after the Great
Fire, however, for the magnitude of the disaster was never in doubt.
Some of the first reports of the conflagration included estimates of

the scale of the losses and those speculations were followed by an assessment of the area affected and the number of buildings destroyed.

On 10 September the king appointed Wenceslaus Hollar and Francis Sandford to take 'an exact plan and survey of the city, as it now stands after the calamity of the late fire'.[23] Hollar was a native of Prague who had come to London in the entourage of his patron the Earl of Arundel in 1636 and had remained in England thereafter, apart from a spell in Antwerp between 1644 and 1651. The foremost landscapist at work in Britain, his surveys of London, including those for a large-scale plan, together with his familiarity with the City, made him uniquely qualified to undertake such a project. Sandford was the author of the Genealogical History of the Kings of England, which appeared in 1677 and was illustrated by Hollar. Following the king's commission, Hollar worked quickly. His plan of the City showing both the area that had been burnt and its context within the metropolis was published before the end of the year. He also produced contrasting views of the City from the tower of St Mary Overy church in Southwark, showing it 'in its flourishing condition before the fire' and 'after the sad calamitie and destruction by fire'. The latter shows a ruined townscape sprinkled with the remains of the churches and some of the more substantial buildings, such as Baynard's Castle and the Custom House. Few of the houses still stood to any height, although many chimneys poked up from the ruins. The area shown by Hollar within which the buildings had been destroyed was measured at 436¾ acres. Only 75¾ acres inside the walls had escaped the fire.[24]

The number of houses destroyed was assessed in rough estimates made immediately after the fire. These included one which put the number of houses at between 14,000 and 16,000, and another one which reported the figure to be 12,000 houses. Excluding a particularly wild report that mentioned 55,000 houses, these evaluations were remarkably good. The detailed assessment by the corporation's surveyors, Jonas Moore and Ralph Greatrix, produced a figure of 13,200 houses destroyed.[25] Their efforts followed two attempts to obtain a comprehensive list of properties, ownership and tenure, preparatory to deciding on plans for rebuilding.

The first attempt, announced on 22 September, placed the onus on individual occupiers, who were required to submit this information and 'a perfect Survey of the Ground' within fourteen days of the order.[26] It seems unlikely, to say the least, that many occupiers responded to this directive. Fewer than 100 of the 1,100 householders in St Bride's and St Martin, Ludgate, submitted a return, for example.[27] For one thing, it was not an easy task, given the condition of the City in the immediate aftermath of the fire. The ruins of the collapsed buildings made it difficult to identify individual sites and clearance was slow because workmen, especially those in the building trades, were fully employed. Within a week of the fire it was observed that 'the late ruins of howses in the citty of London . . . gives so much imployment to carpenters, bricklayers and masons that they cannot be procured but by some speciall warrant'.[28] For another, many householders must still have been too busy arranging adequate accommodation and reviving their businesses before the onset of winter to be diverted to the less immediate, and potentially dangerous, task of clearing and surveying their house-site.

The failure of the attempt was tacitly admitted when, on 10 October, the task was entrusted to contractors, at a rate of 2s 6d per house. They were to be accompanied by the common councilmen, to ensure that owners were fairly treated, for it was understood that the survey was for 'the better stating thereafter every ones right and propriety'.[29] For their part, householders were given fourteen days to clear the debris from their ground and stack the bricks and stones, in order to help the surveyors. This, too, was an optimistic deadline and it is not clear that their survey was ever completed. Eventually, in November, the streets were cleared by contractors and arrangements made for the measuring and marking of the streets. The burnt area was divided into six districts for the purpose and the results of the survey were incorporated by John Leake into a single plan, engraved by Hollar.[30] The figure produced by Moore and Greatrix for the number of houses burnt presumably derived partly from such returns as were made, from individual cases and from the observations of the surveyors, as the work of clearing and staking out the streets proceeded. Sir William Petty accepted the figure of 13,000 and calculated that it represented a fifth of the total number of houses within the metropolis.[31]

The number of houses destroyed suggests that at least 65,000 people were made homeless by the fire. This may be too low, however. Applying the proportion of 85 per cent of the City's area that was gutted to a notional population of 90,000 (the figure of 105,000 for 1660 reduced by 15,000 to allow for the victims of the plague in 1665), produces an estimate of 76,500 citizens who had been burnt out. Neither of these figures is more than a rough approximation, but they do suggest that at least 65,000 and perhaps almost 80,000 Londoners lost their homes in the disaster, at a time when Norwich, the next largest English city, still contained fewer than 30,000 inhabitants.

Calculations based on the number of houses burnt purported to give the value of the property lost. Some keen statisticians produced figures for the losses even before the surveyors' estimate was available. In the middle of September Captain George Cocke, who was a Fellow of the Royal Society as well as a merchant and naval contractor, told Pepys that the rents of the houses destroyed were worth £600,000 per annum.[32] The figure derived from the surveyors' return of 13,200 houses destroyed was a much lower one of £330,000, based on an average annual rent of £25 per house. The further assumption that each house was worth twelve years' purchase, which was regarded as a 'low rate' compared with the norm at that period of sixteen years, produced an estimate of £3,960,000 for the value of the houses, equivalent to £300 per house.[33] This seems to have been rather high. In 1638 the average rental value within the City had been approximately £20 and pressure on space had eased since then as the population had fallen.[34] Indeed, Petty, writing in 1665, based his estimate of the value of houses within the City at £15 per annum and twelve years' purchase.[35] The comparable figure for the value of property destroyed in fires in four provincial towns during the period was £134 per house, but £170 10s at Warwick, which was probably the wealthiest of the four, although much less prosperous than London.[36] Comparison of these figures with the average for the Great Fire is difficult because the size, costs and rents of houses were so much greater in London than elsewhere. Nevertheless, they do suggest that the valuation is rather inflated, and substituting £25 with £20, for the rental value, produces a figure of £3,168,000 or £240 per house, rather closer to the average for the provincial towns.

The other sums included in the various assessments of the cost of the fire were more speculative. Indeed, Clarendon's opinion was that the value 'could never be computed in any degree'.[37] Household goods, money and 'wares' lost were put at roughly a half of the value of the houses. Other allowances included figures for merchandise, the cost of moving goods during and after the fire and the principal buildings destroyed. These included St Paul's Cathedral, eighty-seven parish churches (three more had been damaged), six consecrated chapels, fifty-two halls of the livery companies, Guildhall, the Royal Exchange, the Custom House, Blackwell Hall, the compters at Wood Street and Poultry, Newgate prison, Bridewell, the Sessions House, and the City gates at Ludgate, Newgate and Aldersgate. In 1667 the total figure was put at £7,370,000, but this was based on 12,000 houses and when adjusted for the higher number becomes £7,730,000. Those making the later calculations should have been better informed, but in fact compiled them on the same basis. In 1681 the total was put at £9,900,000 and a detailed estimate that appeared in 1720, which included allowances for such items as the building of the Monument, produced a figure of £10,788,500.[38]

The sums given in 1720 for the value of the houses, household goods, trade stock, books and paper total £7,610,000, equivalent to £576 10s per house. This is a higher average than in other contemporary fires for which there are comparable data; at Newport in 1665 (£148), at Northampton in 1675 (£145), in Southwark in 1676 (£135), at Wem in 1677 (£169) and at Warwick for the fire in 1694 (£232).[39] Nevertheless, it would be rash to attempt to revise the sums for the Great Fire in accordance with those for other towns, both because of London's relative wealth and the fact that its stocks of goods, which varied seasonally, were particularly high at the end of the summer, when the fire occurred. Indeed, while the values of the houses and contents lost in other fires are substantially lower than those in London in 1666, they do suggest that a figure of almost £8 million for those categories for the Great Fire is not wholly implausible, even though it was based on notional values for both buildings and goods.

Despite the scale of the losses, there was some relief that the wealthiest sections of the City's business community had escaped, if not unscathed, since their property had been destroyed, but at least with much of their wealth intact. The money, plate and papers taken into the Tower and then to Whitehall were estimated to be worth £1,200,000. This figure may be no more reliable than the gossip circulating in Paris that it was proving difficult for the owners to identify and reclaim their valuables. Because of the confusion over ownership, nothing could be removed, for 'every one claims and demands them and there is no judge or gentleman who can pronounce upon them because all show themselves to be interested'.[40] The merchants' problems in this respect reflected those of the victims who were left searching for the belongings which they had been unable to remove or keep with them.

The removal of goods from the fields to more secure storage had been facilitated by the king's proclamation of 5 September that all public buildings – churches, chapels, schools and 'other like Publick places' – should be available for that purpose. Nevertheless, some goods had gone astray and a further proclamation, issued on 19 September, designated the Honourable Artillery Company's armoury in Finsbury Fields as a clearing house, where valuables and goods could be taken for listing and, if all went well, restitution to their owners. It implied an amnesty, recognising that items had been taken from the ruins not only with the intention of returning them, or in ignorance of who they belonged to, but also 'wilfully'. Some stolen goods were recovered. Nathaniel Hubert had 'detained' items worth 3s 6d while helping to move them during the fire, but they were later restored to their owner and Hubert was gaoled, despite claiming that he had taken them only because he had not been paid for his efforts. Not all articles that were found to be missing after the fire had been burnt or stolen and some turned up many months after the disaster. The Weavers' Company archives had been dispersed and one volume was discovered as late as December 1667.[41]

Given such difficulties, there was a delay before many of those who had been burnt out could determine exactly what they had lost. Nevertheless, some victims were able to estimate their losses, especially their rental income, which could be calculated quickly and accurately. If a house stood within the area of the fire, then the rent which it produced would not be received until it was rebuilt and reoccupied. Among the largest losers of property was St Bartholomew's Hospital, with 190 of its houses destroyed, representing an annual loss of £2,104 in rents. The livery companies also suffered badly. Roughly a half of the 200 houses owned by the Drapers' Company were burnt down, with its yearly rental income falling from £1,257 13s 5d to £584 10s 2d as a result, and the rents from the Whittington Estate of the Mercers' Company fell to only one-sixth of the £400 per annum they had produced before the fire.[42]

Frances Aske was one of the individuals who knew only too well the effect of the fire. She was born and lived her whole life in St Dunstan's-in-the-West. In her late sixties at the time of the fire, she had been blind for some years and was increasingly infirm. Her sole income was a rent of £24 per annum from her house in Fetter Lane, and when it was burnt down she literally lost her only means of support and had to appeal for charitable help. This was a shattering blow and other owners, even though better off than Frances Aske, were badly affected by their loss. William Denton reported that his wife cried 'all day longe' because her property, which produced £86 per annum, had been gutted.[43]

In addition to those buildings completely destroyed, income was also lost from those over a wider area that had been damaged by being unroofed or even partly demolished to prevent the flames spreading. Most of them lay around the edge of the area destroyed in the fire, especially to the west, along the Strand. Houses near Strandbridge in the parish of St Mary Savoy had been 'demolished', for example, although they were over 400 yards from the point where the fire was halted. Even further away, houses erected by Sir John Denham in Scotland Yard during the early 1660s were 'uncovered and defaced' as a precaution, and the cost of repairs was more than £500.[44] Some allowance had to be made to the tenants of buildings that had been treated in this way, with rental income reduced or lost until they were restored.

Although most of the buildings that had been burnt were completely ruined, not all of the goods that had been left in them were destroyed. While curious observers such as Taswell wandered through the ruins, the burnt-out householders began to investigate whether any of their possessions had survived. The devastation on the surface was so extensive that there was scarcely a single piece of timber that had not been burnt, but some of the goods stored in cellars below ground remained intact. One report described how 'Vaults are daily open'd wherein are found immense quantitys of Pepper, Spices, and Wines, oyls and sugars, etc. safe and untoucht though the houses were fired'. Taswell noted that wood and other flammable goods in his father's cellar were undamaged.[45] Even so, fires continued burning among the 'coals, spirits, or other combustible matters' in some cellars long after they had been put out on the surface. Pepys saw a fire among logwood in a cellar in Tower Street as late as 1 December and smoke still drifting out of cellars the following March.[46]

Despite the appearance of almost total destruction, careful scavenging could discover something of value from among the surface debris. Coins with a value of £446 belonging to the Drapers' Company had melted and fused, but silver worth £115 0s 5d was recovered from the lumps that remained, and the Grocers' Company was able to retrieve 200 lb of silver from the melted deposits in the ruins of its hall. Even the base metals had some value, with iron retrieved from among the rubble fetching £20 per ton and holding out the prospect of a higher price when rebuilding began. With such rewards, scavenging could be a worthwhile occupation for both legitimate searchers and those prepared to search anywhere in the hope of a profitable discovery. The latter made the ruins unsafe to walk around, especially after dark.[47] Pepys got into the habit of travelling through the City at night with his sword drawn, even when in his coach.[48]

Those who had houses or lodgings in London but were away at the time of the fire could only await information of their losses. Many found themselves in this unenviable position. Indeed, it was said that the losses in the fire were so high because it had occurred when many people were out of London and there was no one to supervise the removal of their goods. Because the courts were not sitting, those houses around the inns of court and Fleet Street occupied by lawyers during term were empty.[49] Bulstrode Whitelocke, for example, was in Wiltshire. Based on information received by post on 10 September, he gloomily assessed his losses at nearly £1,000. His house in Fleet Street had been burnt, with only two loads of goods rescued from it, as well as another house, on which he had recently taken a lease, and the chamber in the Temple bought for one of his sons. He realised that he had lost 'some of the best things, & bookes and writings'. Thomas Bromley, too, was in the country at the time of the fire and lost books valued at £30, many of them Greek and Hebrew texts. His greatest sadness was for the loss of his copy of the Polyglot Bible, perhaps the six-volume edition *Biblia Polyglotta* of 1657, for which subscribers had paid £10.[50] John and Jane Turner lost all of their belongings in their house in Salisbury Court off Fleet Street, Pepys blaming John's brother for 'having not endeavoured . . . to save one penny'.[51] Even those who knew that some of their possessions had been removed before the fire reached them could not be certain that they would be able to recover those which had been saved, especially if it had not been possible to keep them together or arrange for someone to guard them. Henry Griffith, at Benthall in Shropshire, received a letter telling him that some of his goods had been rescued, but that a trunk of his taken out of a house in Lothbury and 'carried into the fields' had been stolen.[52]

Virtually all of the figures produced for the household and trade goods destroyed, lost and pilfered could only be estimates. None the less, some of the victims did produce valuations, albeit in round figures that are more indicative of the scale of the loss than the actual value of the goods. Among the biggest losers were the owners of heavy and bulky merchandise, which could not be moved. They included vintners such as Robert Davy, whose wines and other commodities in the Antwerp adjoining the Royal Exchange were valued at £1,500, and John and Mary Henthorne of the St John's Head tavern in Chancery Lane, pulled down to protect Lincoln's Inn, lost wines and goods worth £200 and building materials valued at £150. When the fire began Daniel Berry had stock with an estimated value of £500 at his dyehouse and wharf in Cousin Lane off Thames Street, which were burnt out, while the merchant John Jeffreys was said to have lost tobacco worth £20,000.[53]

The stationers attracted more attention than any other group, partly because the destruction of their stock in St Faith's was so spectacular. Other books and papers of theirs were cached at Stationers' Hall and Christ Church, and they, too, were burnt. The total value of their destroyed stock was put at £150,000, some said £200,000, with 'all the great booksellers almost undone'. Joseph Kirton found himself in debt by £2,000 or £3,000, although before the fire he had been worth £7,000 or £8,000, while the complete run of a nine-volume set entitled *Critici Sancti* was lost, at a cost to the bookseller Cornelius Bec and his partners of £13,000.[54] Some only narrowly avoided complete ruin. The destruction of the house and stock of the publisher and translator John Ogilby left him with barely £5, and when Samuel Thompson drew up his will two years after the fire he mentioned that his losses had been such that he regarded it as 'a special mercy' that he had anything left to bequeath to his children.[55]

Sympathy was expressed even for the unfortunate authors and editors whose works, having taken so much effort to produce, were destroyed before they could be distributed. William Dugdale's *Originales Juridiciales* had only recently come off the press and almost all of the copies were destroyed, as were 300 copies of his *History of St. Paul's Cathedral*, 500 of his *History of Imbanking and Draining* and virtually the entire run of the remaining parts of Sir Henry Spellman's *Glossary* and *Councils*. What was worse, only about thirty sheets of the third volume of Dugdale's *Monasticon Anglicanum* had been printed and the manuscript copy was burnt. His wholly understandable reaction was that 'The lamentable fire hath put an end to my determination', but Dugdale was too tenacious a scholar to be defeated by such a setback and the third volume of his *Monasticon* appeared in 1673.[56]

The clothiers were another group whose losses attracted comment. Much of the cloth produced in England was brought to London for finishing and export. It was sold through the factors, or agents, at Blackwell Hall, which was destroyed, together with cloth worth an estimated £25,000.[57] Some cloth was saved, by clothiers who were in London when the fire began and by those factors who were 'prudent and carefull', but news of the fire was received in the cloth-producing areas with the gloomy realisation that many clothiers with stock in London had probably lost it. The reaction from Coventry was that merchandise worth £2,000 belonging to the city's clothiers had been destroyed and some of them were ruined, 'their whole estate lying there in cloth', and the West Country clothiers were reported to have lost 'many thousand pounds worth of cloth'. The fire not only brought financial losses, but also struck confidence a considerable blow. Those clothiers in the West Country who had suffered heavily were said to have stopped operating, and both there and in Coventry concern was expressed about the impact of the fire on the local economy. This was especially so in the West Country, with its 'multitude of poore', and during the winter a petition was submitted to the House of Commons from the weavers, tuckers and spinners of the region complaining of their poverty.[58]

Dismay at the implications for trade with London was evident elsewhere. Thomas Waade wrote to Williamson that he had never seen so many sad faces as at Whitby, after the news of the fire had reached the town, which had 'a great trade' with London. The inhabitants of Norwich were 'at their wits' end' because of the uncertainty about the future of the city's trade with the metropolis, by far the principal outlet for its textiles.[59] Anxiety of this kind was tempered by the realisation that goods received from London would be in short supply, allowing prices to be increased. This, at least, was the allegation made at Bridgwater about the traders in Bristol who were raising their prices. Anthony Wood claimed that the cost of books and paper almost doubled after the fire, and subsequently remained at that level. In March 1667 Pepys was asked £2 10s for a book which before the fire was selling for only 8s, the scale of the increase apparently being explained by the fact that all but twenty-two copies had been burnt. He offered £1, but eventually paid £2 15s for the sixth and final copy of the superior edition, 'finely bound and truly coloured'.[60]

Pepys was also shocked at the price of coal, which continued to rise throughout the winter. The estimate of the losses in the fire that appeared in 1667 included a notional £20,000 for coal and wood burnt at the wharves, and it was difficult to restock them while the Dutch continued to harass the convoys of colliers.[61] Soon after the fire the corporation had petitioned the king, pointing out that the quantity of coal brought to London during the summer had been low and that much had been destroyed by the fire. They requested him to order that the colliers which were laid up, because their captains were waiting for seamen or a convoy, should be sailed to Newcastle. High prices led to allegations of profiteering.

Sir Edmund Berry Godfrey was in a fortunate position because his stocks of coal and wood had not been destroyed in the fire. In January 1667 he was accused of taking advantage of this by selling coal that had cost him no more than £2 7s per chaldron for £3 12s, which was 'a very great Extortion and Oppression, especially to poor People'.[62] (Ironically, Godfrey had been knighted for his conspicuous efforts during the fire.) The weather may have increased the resentment against those charging such prices; that month was the coldest January between 1659 and 1684 and there was another cold snap in early March, although the winter of 1666–7 was not especially cold overall, with seven colder ones during that period. Prices did not fall after the end of the winter, however, and indeed continued to rise during the coming months, reaching £5 10s per chaldron by June, more than twice their normal level.[63]

The most immediate price increase after the fire was in rents for surviving buildings in London. Within a few days house rents were said to be at 'an excessive rate' and Pepys heard of a house let for £150 which before the fire had cost only £40 per annum.[64] With pardonable exaggeration, Thomas Bromfield reported to his wife on 17 September that houses were ten times more expensive than they had ever been.[65] Those on the Earl of Southampton's new development at Bloomsbury Square and in Covent Garden were said to be much in demand, with houses in Covent Garden 'growing then dear'. A 'silkman' was prepared to pay a fine of £50 and a rent of £30 per annum for three rooms, including a garret, in a house in Covent Garden, with a further £40 yearly for board for himself and two apprentices. In these circumstances landlords were eager to take tenants at the higher rents that were now chargeable, which in some cases meant removing the existing occupants. Within a week of the fire Sir Nathaniel Hobart was given notice to quit, prompting him to describe his landlord as 'odious' and to make it clear that he would oppose eviction, in the courts if necessary.[66] The rise in rents levelled out as those who had been made homeless found accommodation, but they remained high and in 1668 the Venetian envoy complained that they were still 'severe and exorbitant'.[67]

Despite the increase in rents, some tradesmen were willing to meet landlords' demands in order to get space, or to adapt other buildings for their purposes. Pepys's mercer moved to 'a fine house' in Covent Garden within three weeks of the fire and in October an upholsterer took a shop in the same district.[68] By the beginning of November two traders had occupied outhouses adjoining the Charterhouse in southern Clerkenwell and were trying to contrive a new entrance to the property, while the parish of St Giles, Cripplegate, was able to let its fire-engine house for an annual rent of £7.[69] While many who had been burnt out moved west, beyond the City, the goldsmiths remained there, as close to Lombard Street as possible. Edward Backwell moved to Gresham Street, John Colvill took a house in Lime Street, the southern end of which had been destroyed in the fire, and Sir Robert Viner moved initially into the premises of the Royal Africa Company, off Broad Street, and later to Winchester Street, close by. Other tradesmen also preferred to stay close to their previous premises. John Sayer, a vintner, who had been the landlord of the Pope's Head tavern, a property of the Merchant Taylors' Company in Pope's Head Alley off Lombard Street, moved only a short distance, setting up in the nearby parish of St Helen, Bishopsgate. The bookseller James Allestry moved rather further, but his new premises in Duck Lane near Smithfield were among the closest undamaged buildings to his former base in St Paul's Churchyard.[70]

Deciding where to move was so important that it was not to be done lightly. So many physicians had moved to the West End that they were said to be short of patients, which caused William Denton to hesitate before making such a move and wait to see 'how practice will come in'.[71] Just how crucial such a decision could be was made particularly clear in the contrasting experiences of the brothers William and Anthony Joyce, both tallow chandlers. Before the fire William had moved to Russell Street in Covent Garden, where he prospered 'by the custom of the City coming to his end of the town'. Anthony and his wife, on the other hand, having had their own house burnt down and lost rents worth £140 a year from others destroyed, took an inn at St John's, Clerkenwell. They soon regretted it and hoped that Anthony would be able to obtain a government appointment. Disappointed in this, they moved to another inn, the Three Stags near Holborn Conduit. Despite his losses, Anthony claimed to have 'something left that he can live well upon' and by December 1667 he was planning to rebuild and trying to arrange a loan for the purpose. Yet in the following month he attempted to drown himself and died soon afterwards. Whatever the real reasons for his unhappy end, it was thought that 'the sense of his great loss by the fire, did bring him to it'.[72]

As well as the space available in existing buildings, additional accommodation was provided fairly quickly. The governors of St Bartholomew's, for example, met on 15 September and, aware of both the need to raise revenue and 'the great necessities of divers tradesmen which they are exposed unto for want of shops', authorised the erection of shops within the hospital precinct, obtaining a royal warrant for the purpose before the end of the month. Their first fifteen tenants, who took leases of twenty-one years, covered a range of trades and included a weaver, a merchant tailor, a cutler, three haberdashers, a goldsmith, a stationer, an ironmonger, a salter, a leatherseller and a fishmonger. The fines totalled £412 and the rents averaged £16 per annum.[73] The need for shops seems to have been met fairly quickly. Before the end of September Evelyn noted that the surviving part of the City and the suburbs were 'peopl'd with new shopps'. They were fitted up at Gresham College and occupied by those who had formerly traded at the Royal Exchange. Some shops were even set up at the Exchange itself, despite the ruins, on a pavement built of stones and bricks brought from Guildhall.[74]

The homeless who were unable to pay the rents demanded in the more substantial houses quickly made shift to provide themselves with some sort of accommodation. Canvas from the Navy yards was supplied for tents and many huts were erected. According to Clarendon, within four days virtually all of those who had initially moved out into the fields around the City had gone, finding room in the remaining buildings or nearby villages. Some returned to the burnt area, even though that could only be a temporary solution, where 'very many, with more expedition than can be conceived, set up little sheds of brick and timber upon the ruins of their own houses'. Michael Mitchell and his wife Betty sold spirits at a shop in Old Swan Lane, between Thames Street and the river, that was destroyed on the first day of the fire. They built a new shop, or 'booth', on the site before the end of October, which was taken down and replaced by a house early in 1668.[75] It was presumably in a similar structure that Arthur Winde, a fishmonger, was trading in Bridge Street in the spring of 1667, before rebuilding on the site had begun.[76] Although some of the temporary buildings may have been small and flimsy, costing no more than £20, others were more substantial. Indeed, houses erected on land leased from the corporation in Moorfields, outside the burnt area, were of two storeys 'and like to stand'.[77]

The speed with which the homeless found accommodation was impressive, although not entirely surprising, given that four-fifths of the houses in London remained intact. But it tends to conceal the difficulties and discomforts faced by some of the victims in the months after the disaster. Many hundreds of them appealed for assistance, such as Sarah Crofts, who in May 1667 claimed to be unable to support herself and stood out among the other supplicants as 'very sad an Object of Charity'.[78] The petition of Elizabeth Peacock, who described herself as a 'desolate & a disconsolate widdowe', explains how before the fire she, her husband and six children had lived 'in a very good and plentifull condition' in a 'faire and lardge Inne' called the Horseshoe in Snow Hill, on which they had spent £800 in the early 1660s in repairs and improvements. Her husband and eldest son had both died before the fire, however, and then the house had been 'utterly consumed' in the conflagration, 'together with her whole stocke of hay coales & beere layd in for her winter provision & alsoe all the furniture of her said house', leaving her with 'not soe much as a stoole to sitt uppon' and only £1 19s in money. She was granted just £1 10s from the charitable fund and allotted a plot of ground at Smithfield on which she began to build, but by March 1667 she had run out of funds, with the house unfinished. Her petition was supported by a testimony that she and her five children were 'in a very sad and deplorable case' and she was granted £10 more from the fund.[79]

The sum allowed to Elizabeth Peacock was modest in terms of building costs, but was a relatively large donation from the relief funds. Comparatively few beneficiaries received more, and by the early 1670s the typical sum allotted to claimants, the majority of whom were widows, was £2. Even Samuel Gellibrand, a stationer whose loss was put at a minimum of £1,700, was given only £10. The widow of George Kendall, a merchant, who had lost everything which her husband had bequeathed her, valued at £5,000, received £20. So did Charles Ubaldinole, but perhaps he was given special consideration, having come from a noble family in Italy, settled in London and converted to Protestantism, 'for which he hath left his nature Country freinds and enjoyments'.[80]

The many claimants and the scale of the losses necessarily restricted the amounts dispensed. Yet the relief effort after the Great Fire had one advantage, which was that the funds arrived fairly quickly after the fast day collections in October. By the end of December, £6,743 had been received and that rose to £10,568 by the end of February 1667 and to £11,296 a month later.[81] Because of this, the funds could be channelled to the victims, except for those excluded by the Bishop of London's restriction that 'none that have kept Alehouses or Tipplinghouses may have any Share in this Releif'.[82] Collections on briefs, in contrast, usually took so long that the income from them was not received until the immediate need had passed, and so it tended to be used towards the cost of replacing the public buildings that had been destroyed, rather than in donations to individuals. A feature of the Great Fire relief fund that did resemble some similar funds was the allegation of fraud. At London, it was no less than the lord mayor for 1666–7, Sir William Bolton, who was charged with 'Misimploying the great sume of Money hee received of the Collections for the releife of the poore distressed by the late dismall fire'. He was alleged to have siphoned off £1,800 and had to resign his place as an alderman. In 1675 he was convicted of misappropriation by the Commissioners for Charitable Uses and two years later he was so poor that the Common Council awarded him a pension.[83]

The distribution of relief employed the existing network of ward and parish, the administrations of which continued to operate, despite the buildings having been swept away in the fire. The officers of the wards were allocated funds to distribute among those in need, while the parishes were loaned money for placing as apprentices children who were receiving assistance, until such time as the sum could be recovered through a rate on the newly built houses.[84] Relief money was also used to supplement parish poor funds while they remained inadequate. The parish of St Olave, Old Jury, for example, paid for lodgings and care for Mary Whitehall, 'an impotent poor woman', with the relief fund contributing more than three-quarters of the cost.[85]

The rapid dispersal of suppliers and customers in the weeks following the fire made it difficult for them to find each other after contact had been lost. In order to remedy the 'interruption of trade' which this caused, a system was introduced whereby several people were designated to receive and disseminate new addresses. A house in Bloomsbury Square served as the clearing house for such information and as a kind of lost-property office, taking notices of goods lost and found. Some announcements of new addresses were included in *The London Gazette*, which also carried information about the arrangements made for the officials of the customs, excise, hearth tax, Post Office and the Admiralty and ecclesiastical courts, all of whom were quickly allotted new accommodation. The customs officials moved to Mark Lane, the petty customs to the west end of Fleet Street, the excise office to Southampton Fields and the hearth tax collectors to Leadenhall Street, with the Post Office established in Bishopsgate Street. Exeter House in the Strand was the new home for the Admiralty and ecclesiastical courts, the Vicar General's Office and the Faculty Office. The arrangements for the markets, too, were specified, and prisons were fitted up in Aldgate and Bishopsgate.

The government not only acted quickly on such practical matters, to enable business to resume as soon as possible, but was also concerned to deal with the rumours about the origins of the fire. The king ordered a Privy Council enquiry under Sir John Kelying, the lord chief justice, to hear the evidence. Towards the end of September the House of Commons set up its own committee, although not without opposition and only after a 'long and serious debate'.[86] The committee's report was not presented until 22 January and consisted only of statements, without any recommendations. Both hearings gave those who still clung to the conspiracy theory that the fire had been started deliberately and maliciously the opportunity to air their opinions. Indeed, the atmosphere in which they met was more conducive to the venting of suspicions verging on paranoia than a rational examination of the facts. War with France had produced a revival of xenophobic anti-Catholic passions reminiscent of the early 1640s, which the fire had reinforced. Tales of fire-balls, Farriner's testimony that the fires in his house and bakehouse were safely extinguished on the fateful night, the discovery of materials for making fireworks and a pile of daggers found in the ruins of a house where Frenchmen were alleged to have been lodging before the fire were enough to keep the pot simmering. Yet in the opinion of Sir Thomas Littleton, who sat on the committee, many stories that had been told with great confidence 'came to nothing upon a strict examination', and Sir Thomas Osborne, another of its members, thought that 'all the allegations are very frivolous, and people are generally satisfied that the fire was accidentall'. Clarendon even found it hard not to smile at the tales told to the Privy Council by some of the witnesses appearing at that enquiry.[87]

Others were not so sceptical and were reluctant to let the matter drop. Those who believed that the fire must have been started deliberately were able to point to the confession of Robert Hubert, a watchmaker and native of Rouen who had worked in London. Arrested at Romford when apparently trying to flee the country, on examination he described a journey that he had made with one Stephen Peidloe from France to Sweden and then on to London, where they arrived shortly before the fire. In his original story Hubert admitted to being guilty of throwing a fire-ball near to Whitehall Palace during the fire, but he later changed this and insisted that he and Peidloe had pushed fire-balls into a window of Farriner's house early in the morning of 2 September. Farriner and his two children said that no window had existed in the position described by Hubert, yet he could both find the ruins of the house without difficulty and describe its appearance before the fire. Convicted solely on his own unsatisfactory testimony, Hubert was hanged on 29 October.[88]

Neither Hubert's confession nor the evidence taken by the Commons' committee and its own enquiry altered the Privy Council's belief that, in Williamson's words, the fire was caused by 'the hand of God, a great wind, and a very dry season'.[89] Nevertheless, in March 1668 the City's Common Council prepared a petition requesting the House of Commons to reopen its investigation. Although that was not done, the emotions generated by the disaster and the suspicions, which had been there from the first, that it was the result of a conspiracy, gave the fire too much political potential for it to be allowed to fade. Those, such as Sir Thomas Crew and Andrew Marvell, who continued to believe that it was begun by Hubert and Peidloe as part of a plot, provided a body of opinion which could be reactivated when needed. Because of this, the suspicions surrounding the fire remained a potent political weapon for the next generation or so, regardless of its actual causes.[90]

While these investigations were going on the government took stock of the effects of the fire upon its own position. The most immediate danger was that it would be blamed for the disaster and the popular disturbances of 1641-2 might be repeated, but the resentment already directed against the French, Dutch and Catholics was not deflected on to the already unpopular court. The king nevertheless recalled George Monck, Duke of Albemarle, one of the principal architects of the Restoration, from the fleet to Whitehall to restore confidence. The old antagonisms between the House of Stuart and the Londoners were not forgotten. A Dutch account of the fire described how at first the king, his brother and the courtiers 'came to see King Charles I avenged', before being so shocked by the disaster that they began to help direct the fire-fighting. Whether this was literally true may be doubted, but it does reflect the court's ambivalent attitude to the fire, which had emasculated a potential political opponent, at least for the time being. Baptist May, Keeper of the Privy Purse, remarked at court that, apart from the Restoration itself, the fire was 'the greatest blessing that God had ever conferred' on the king, because the walls and gates had been wrecked, and he should not let the citizens replace them 'to be a bit in his mouth and a bridle upon his neck'. Instead, the City would be left open for his troops to enter, 'there being no other way to govern that rude multitude but by force'. While the king was said not to be amused at this comment, his courtiers 'highly approved' of it.[91]

If there was indeed a certain smug satisfaction that the City had been brought so low, it should have been tempered by a realisation that its important contribution to the government's revenues and the war effort would be impaired. Using the analogy of London as a fountain from which money flowed into the government's coffers, Clarendon commented that the reduced flow caused by the plague would be restored, but that 'this late conflagration had dried up or so stopped the very fountains, that there was no prospect when they would flow again'.[92]

The damage done to the revenues obtained from the hearth tax was obvious. The tax had been introduced in 1662 but had not achieved the revenue expected from it. Accordingly, in 1666 it was farmed to three City merchants, who were given responsibility for collecting the tax, paying a rent of £145,000 for the first five years, £150,000 for the next year and £170,000 in the final one. Their term began at Michaelmas, four weeks after the fire, and lasted for just three of the seven years of their contract, producing an average return of £103,000 per annum. The farmers claimed allowances and defalcations of £75,000, of which £20,000 related to the effects of the fire. This was a problem that they could not overcome; the revenue from the destroyed property was lost for seven years, not just until it was rebuilt, because the government exempted it from the tax for that period, to remove a possible disincentive to rebuilding. In fact, the exemption lasted for only five years, the City agreeing to the reduction in return for concessions on parliamentary taxation for 1665–8, but this came too late to help the farmers, although they were allowed £7,000 per annum for the loss of revenue due to the fire.[93]

Other branches of the revenue suffered from the impact of the fire. Approximately £52,000, or more than 4 per cent, of the shortfall in the expected yield from the assessment known as the Additional Aid was attributed to it, for example. London's inability to pay its full share of the eleven months' assessment granted by parliament in February 1667 was recognised by the government, which drastically reduced its share by £6,689 per month, from almost 7½ per cent of the total to under 2 per cent. The sum allowed to London was allocated elsewhere, but the fire was not the only problem affecting tax collection, for the effects of the plague and the war also made substantial inroads into receipts. The government's net income in the financial year 1664–5 was less than £893,000, falling in the two succeeding years to only £686,000 per annum, with its debt rising accordingly, to approximately £2,500,000.[94]

The financial blow which the fire represented to the government could not be concealed, and although it was by no means the chief reason for its fiscal problems – the decline in the customs receipts accounted for 70 per cent of the fall in its revenue – it came at a particularly bad time. No immediate solution could be found, although a mischievous suggestion emanating from Paris was that the valuables lodged in Whitehall Palace could be employed 'for the service of the country, for the fleet and for building the new city'. Whatever the temptation, the confiscation of the merchants' wealth was a political impossibility, as was the idea that some of the receipts from the charitable collections taken in October might be diverted to pay for the war.[95] More realistically, the court was aware that fresh revenue would have to be negotiated in the coming session of parliament if the war effort was to be sustained.

News of the fire had been welcomed in both Holland and France because it was thought that it must weaken British military endeavours. Johan de Witt, the Grand Pensionary, considered that it presented an opportunity which should be exploited and tried to persuade the Dutch naval commanders to mount an attack up the Thames estuary. In an attempt to counter such reactions, the government played down the military effects of the disaster. In its first issue after the fire *The London Gazette* stressed that no naval stores had been destroyed.[96] The Earl of Sandwich, now established as ambassador in Spain, took the same line, pointing out that the flames had not even come near the armouries and naval supplies, and going further by claiming that 'the most ignoble and useless was all buried together beneath the ashes, but what was precious and important had been preserved and was safe'. Sir William Temple, in Brussels, also put on a brave face, despite being so shocked when he received the news of the fire that 'I could at first hardly persuade myself that what I read was more than a dream'. He emphasised the positive aspect, that the City would be rebuilt in a more handsome manner, as well as stressing that trade had already recommenced and that the people's loyalty would not be shaken by the catastrophe.[97]

Diplomatic denials of this kind were all very well abroad, but the government had to face the practical problems which had been caused. Indeed, the encouragement which the fire had given to the enemy provided the king with a strong card in his dealings with parliament, which he played when the session began on 21 September. Parliament did not dispute that more money was needed and granted £1,800,000. This was conditional on the inspection of accounts by a subcommittee of the House of Commons, which reported favourably, although the issue resurfaced after acrimonious debates over the question of prohibiting imports of livestock from Ireland. Government hopes, raised when parliament agreed so swiftly to the new revenue, slowly deflated as time was taken by deciding how the money would be levied and preparing the necessary bills, with other issues being allowed to interrupt the process. The outcome of parliament's deliberations was that the two chief contributions to the new revenue would be a monthly assessment and a poll tax.[98] They did not provide the revenue immediately required; the assessment did not begin until 1668 and the poll tax, although collected in 1667, yielded less than had been anticipated, despite revisions in the format aimed at overcoming the defects of the previous such tax, levied in 1660.[99]

With the money voted but not received, the income from earlier grants slow to come in and its credit in the City exhausted, the government was hard pressed indeed. The Navy Board found itself quite unable to fit out the fleet for a campaign in 1667. Instead, the first- and second-rate ships were laid up and smaller ones only were fitted out, to serve as patrol vessels.[100] This strategy involved a considerable risk. The military initiative had swung against the Dutch following the St James's Day Battle and Holmes's bonfire, but the position was reversed after the Great Fire and by the end of 1666 they held the advantage, despite the severe plague epidemic in the United Provinces.

Negotiations with both the Dutch and the French for an end to the war got under way during the winter and an agreement with France was reached in April. Despite calls from Londoners for peace, talks with the Dutch were more protracted and continued throughout the spring, although the government was confident that a settlement of the differences was not far off. Before this was reached the folly of the naval policy that had been adopted was brutally exposed when, in June, the Dutch carried out a brilliant raid on the Medway. After capturing Sheerness, they burnt three of the biggest warships laid up in the river and towed away the flagship, *The Royal Charles*. What was worse, from the Londoners' point of view, was that the Dutch then proceeded to blockade the mouth of the Thames for over a month, amid fears that they would burn shipping as far up the river as London itself and could even mount an invasion.[101] Relief came with the signing of the Treaty of Breda in July, but it brought the war to an end in humiliating circumstances, with de Ruyter's fleet hovering off the Thames and English seaborne trade virtually at a standstill. While the Great Fire was only one of several factors that weakened the English efforts during the last year of the war, it has to be included in the contributory causes.

The appearance of the ruined part of the City and the shanty communities that had sprung up on and around it can have done little to raise spirits. Some householders had begun to rebuild almost at once, but the process was quickly halted until it was decided what form the new City should take. While the homeless had been accommodated and the principal streets at least were well enough cleared to take coaches, there were few other signs of a recovery from the disaster. To add to the gloom, the autumn of 1666 was punctuated by other fires, in Westminster and Southwark, and new fears of uprisings, perhaps even a general massacre. By the end of the year Pepys was so downcast at the prospects for the City that he concluded that it was 'less and less likely to be built again'.[102]

FOUR

PREPARATIONS FOR REBUILDING

I was yesterday in many meetings of the principal Cittizens, whose houses are laid in ashes, who in stead of complaining, discoursed almost of nothing, but of a survey of London, and a dessein for rebuilding.

Henry Oldenburg to Robert Boyle, 10 September 1666,
The Correspondence of Henry Oldenburg, ed. A.R. and M.B. Hall, vol. 3, p. 226

The delays which prevented the beginnings of reconstruction before the end of 1666 were an inevitable outcome of the immediate reactions to the fire. Almost as soon as the scale of the damage became clear, there was general agreement that the rebuilding should be subject to controls, involving at the very least the building materials to be used and the enforcement of the regulations introduced since 1580, and perhaps even a modification of the street plan. What was not acceptable was a hasty, piecemeal reconstruction, with individuals erecting new houses as soon as possible using whatever materials were available, in order to provide accommodation and resume business. Control of rebuilding entailed delaying property owners who were able and willing to go ahead, but because the fire had come close to the end of the building season this was less of a restraint than would have been the case after one that had occurred during the spring or early summer. In any case, as with all fires, practical matters of boundaries, ownership, liability, finance and supply of materials had to be resolved before large-scale rebuilding could get under way.

Among the common responses to a major fire were anxieties that rebuilding would be delayed so long that the community's prosperity would be diminished or even, as Pepys feared, that reconstruction would not take place at all. The general view of the House of Commons was that unless the controls governing the reconstruction were decided upon as soon as possible the City 'would be in danger never to be built'.[1] These should have been relatively minor worries after the Great Fire, despite the scale of the damage, for London's economic position was so dominant as to be virtually unassailable.

Yet some unease evidently did exist, especially regarding the City's position within the metropolis. A wholesale removal of tradesmen to the suburbs certainly was a danger, accelerating the existing trend, although the accommodation available could scarcely have provided space for all those leaving the City and new buildings could be erected there no more quickly than in the destroyed area. A building boom in the suburbs was undesirable, because it would bring competition for building materials and skilled labour when they were needed in the City. Such a boom was a possibility, although many members of the merchant and financial community had indicated their unwillingness to move out of the City, by choosing to remain close to their destroyed premises after the fire. Furthermore, the government could act to enforce or renew the earlier prohibitions of new buildings in the suburbs.[2]

Migration completely out of London was a further threat, apparently increased by the king's action. While the fire was still raging on 5 September, he had issued a proclamation directing that those who had been burnt out should be permitted to practise their trades elsewhere, regardless of restrictions limiting trading within a borough to its own freemen. This was one of the most jealously guarded privileges of the incorporated cities and towns, and most of them had taken steps to restore their regulations after the disruption of the Civil War. By overriding such controls, the proclamation may have been seen as increasing the likelihood that tradesmen would leave London and settle elsewhere. But this fear ignored the potential problems faced by newcomers establishing themselves in a community, where demand was already fully met, and at a time when trading conditions were difficult because of the war with the Dutch.

Similarly, although rebuilding was necessary if London was to maintain its primacy as a port, its privileges, the inertia of existing patterns and its strong locational advantages made it unlikely that other ports could challenge its position. During the Civil War the Royalists had tried to divert overseas trade away from London by promoting Exeter and Bristol, but with little success.[3] Positive replies could have been given to Sir William Petty's musings after the fire on such questions as whether London was the best place for a metropolis and what other

places competed with it 'for naturall advantages'.[4] Nevertheless, a rapid
recovery was desirable for both the City's mercantile community and
the king, whose prestige and revenues would both invariably suffer if
such a substantial part of his capital continued to lie in ruins.

The individual and collective need to rebuild was apparent in the
forward-looking comments which many made immediately after the
fire and the speed with which some owners began to rebuild. A new
house was being built at Blackfriars only a week after the end of the
fire, for example. But all such endeavours were brought to a swift and
premature end by the king's proclamation of 13 September prohibiting
any hasty rebuilding and empowering the City authorities to pull
down structures erected before regulations governing the process were
finalised.[5] While some controls, such as those stipulating the materials
to be used, were already in place, many other practical matters had to be
settled before rebuilding could begin, and the desire to rebuild quickly
had to be curbed until they were decided upon. A further element
in the deliberations arose from the proposals put forward for a radical
revision, not just of the fabric but also of the layout of the streets.

Almost inevitably, the fire was seen as providing an opportunity to
replan as well as rebuild the City, so that it could be 'finer than ever
it was'.[6] Evelyn naturally reacted to the opportunity for replanning
the City, having a few years earlier bemoaned its condition, with
its buildings 'compos'd of such a Congestion of mishapen and
extravagant Houses' and the streets 'so narrow and incommodious in
the very Center, and busiest places of Intercourse'. His comment that
the intention was to rebuild 'after the noblest model' reflected the
widespread optimism that London would emerge from the disaster
much improved, perhaps even as 'the most noble city that can be'.[7]
One of the objectives was to establish architectural 'uniformity', with
buildings of brick or stone, as laid down in the king's proclamation, all
erected in a similar style. It was anticipated that they would be 'at once
conspicuous and luxurious'. Sir William Temple's vision was for a city
that was healthier as well as better built, with open spaces, gardens and
wider streets than before. He also envisaged the construction of a quay
along the riverfront for the whole length of the burnt area, from the
Temple to the Tower.[8] This improvement would fulfil an obvious need
and had almost universal support, including that of the corporation.[9]
The necessity of broadening at least some of the principal streets was

also unquestioned. Graunt believed that the increased use of coaches, for which the narrow streets of the City were unsuited, was one reason for the drift of business westwards.[10]

These and the other ideas that were advanced had a wealth of theory and practice to draw upon. Much of the theory had been provided by Italian and German writers of the sixteenth and early seventeenth centuries, who were concerned with the creation of 'ideal' forms within the constraints imposed by the need to surround towns with the extensive artillery fortifications of the bastion trace. The most favoured designs were those based on polygons, with streets radiating from a central square or piazza, and rectangular grids. Only rarely were the theorists' geometrical solutions put into practice, although they were implemented at the circular fortress town of Palma Nova in northern Italy, begun in 1593, and in the septangular form adopted for the rebuilding of Coevorden in the Netherlands in 1597.[11]

Even though the theories were seldom given practical expression, the continent nevertheless provided numerous examples of town planning, ranging from the construction of new fortified towns, or rebuilding of those destroyed by warfare, to the addition of new developments to existing cores. Examples of the former were provided by the Dutch fortress towns, such as the late sixteenth-century Willemstad and Klundert. The opportunities for setting out wholly new towns of this kind in Europe were limited, however, compared with the development of colonial foundations in the Americas and Asia.

A far more common application of town planning in early modern Europe was the appending of districts to the existing built-up area. In 1607 and again in 1663 the burghers of Amsterdam embarked upon considerable expansions of their city and new districts were added to the burgeoning town of Leiden in 1644 and 1659.[12] An alternative approach was to construct a new town alongside an existing one. This was done at Nancy, where the *ville-neuve* begun in 1587 was actually larger than its medieval predecessor and comprised a gridiron street plan contained within a bastion trace that also enclosed the original town. Less systematic than this coherent plan, but on a far grander scale, was the development of Rome in the sixteenth century through a series of projects initiated by successive popes. These involved the setting out of grand avenues and piazzas to the east of the medieval city, that were ornamented by new churches, obelisks and statues.

This was a model of Renaissance town planning, incorporating not only grandiose features but also practical improvements, such as new aqueducts to improve the water supplies to the rapidly growing city. The achievements of the popes at Rome provided a paradigm for a city developed by its rulers who were anxious to provide a capital that would enhance their own dignity. This was indeed a common ambition in western Europe and led to the transformation of Turin, for example, although many rulers, including the French monarchs, were limited to piecemeal and restricted developments within the existing city. At Paris these consisted of residential squares lined with suitably grand houses and containing a statue of the monarch.[13]

The first London squares had been laid out in the reign of Charles I in the nascent 'west end', on sites beyond the existing built-up area. They were the developments of private landlords, not the Crown, but the building controls could be exercised in such a way as to achieve the desired uniformity. Nevertheless, such large-scale squares were inappropriate to the needs of the City, where more flexible planning was required. Nor could the bastides of the Middle Ages and their successors, the twenty-three towns established in Ulster during the early seventeenth century, be regarded as suitable precedents, even though the Ulster towns were laid out under the auspices of London's corporation and livery companies. The corporation itself added a modern fortified town to the existing medieval settlement at Derry City and the livery companies created new towns on their own estates, such as the mercers at Kilrea and the drapers at Moneymore. These typically had simple plans in which the axial streets met at a central square – the Diamond at Derry City – with a regular street pattern in each of the quarters. The straight streets ignored the topography, which was considered only in so far as defensive needs were concerned. As in many continental towns of the period, these were paramount, producing the fortifications of the fine bastion trace at Derry City. Yet the scale and functions of these Ulster towns made them of limited value for those planning the rebuilding of London.[14]

Indeed, despite the range of examples of new and expanded towns in western Europe in the sixteenth and seventeenth centuries, there was no comparable instance of such large-scale rebuilding after a fire. It was rare for the damage to be so extensive as to allow the kind of wholesale change as had occurred at Milan, where a conflagration in 1162 had been followed by the replacement of the Roman street plan, or Naarden on the Zuider Zee, which was moved to a new site following a fire in 1350.[15] Yet the changes imposed after a blaze at Stockholm in 1625 provided a more recent example of what could be achieved. The king, Gustavus Adolphus, had used the opportunity to construct a new straight street through and beyond the destroyed area, eliminating several alleys from what had been a tightly packed district. Furthermore, new regulations were introduced prohibiting timber buildings within the city. The result was that rebuilding was carried out in brick and the fire proved to be the stimulus for the replacement of low, often single-storey, cottages with tall brick houses. By the mid-seventeenth century, therefore, Stockholm provided an encouraging precedent for renewal after a fire, albeit in a city that was probably no larger than Norwich.[16]

Major fires in Britain in the recent past had wiped out large areas of towns, but they had not resulted in alterations to their plans. The rights of property owners were inimical to such changes, which could scarcely be effected unless the town was in the hands of one or two proprietors who were willing to impose a remodelling. As a result, boundaries remained unchanged, buildings were erected on the sites of their predecessors and street lines could be revised only with difficulty. Traditions of major changes after fires at Shifnal in 1591 and Southwold in 1659 are misleading in both cases. There is no evidence that Shifnal was rebuilt on a new site, and it seems unlikely that the greens at Southwold were laid out in the aftermath of the blaze there, to create fire-breaks.[17]

Nevertheless, London did seem to offer the possibility of radical change and the chance to build the finest capital in northern Europe, with the powerful corporation and the Crown acting in concert. Within a few days of the fire the corporation indicated its willingness to consider a new layout. Would-be town planners reacted with alacrity to the opportunity. Wren submitted a plan to the king on 11 September, Evelyn followed with his two days later and Robert Hooke's was shown to the Royal Society on 19 September, by which time it had already been examined by the corporation, together with that of the City's surveyor, Peter Mills. Other schemes were prepared by the cartographer Richard Newcourt, who produced two, and Captain Valentine Knight. The number of plans and their initial reception suggests that these were not regarded solely as exercises applying the ideas of town planning to a theoretical solution for the City. Evelyn for one felt that something might come of his proposals. Although aware that 'these things are as yet im'ature', he was encouraged by the amount of time that the king, queen and the Duke of York gave to his original submission, discussing it with him for nearly an hour.[18] Evelyn went on to make two revisions, admitting that he had not been fully aware of the facts, especially what had escaped the fire, until the appearance of Hollar's plan showing the destroyed area.[19]

Not all of the plans have survived, but those which are known show a completely new street layout in every case, not simply an adjustment of the old one. At least two of the designers even considered the possibility of extending the revision of the City's plan beyond the burnt area. Evelyn's first proposal included all the area within the walls, not just that affected by the fire, and Newcourt's plan extended even further, with his suggested layout set within a large rectangular box that covered an area well beyond the northern line of the city wall.

All of the designs involved plans based on a pattern of streets leading away from the river intersecting with those running across the City, although this arrangement was applied with varying degrees of rigidity. The more imaginative proposals were those submitted by Wren and Evelyn, both of which showed strong continental influences, with radial streets superimposed on the grid. An educated gentleman of Evelyn's interests could scarcely have failed to be aware of developments in planning and architecture, both in England and abroad. He had been able to widen his knowledge of contemporary urban design during his extensive tours in the 1640s, which had included spells in the Netherlands, Paris and Rome. Wren, born in 1632, was twelve years younger than Evelyn and had attracted attention at Oxford for a range of scientific work, before his appointment as Professor of Astronomy at Gresham College in 1657. He returned to Oxford as Savilian Professor of Astronomy in 1661 and at about that time he began to turn to architecture, producing his design for the Sheldonian theatre in 1663. Nevertheless, in the mid-1660s his practical experience was limited, although his awareness of urban forms had been increased during his stay in Paris, from the summer of 1665 until the spring of the following year.

Treating London Bridge and Ludgate as the points of entry into the City, Wren planned several long, straight principal thoroughfares.[20]

Inside Ludgate, his plan shows two such avenues diverging at an acute angle, one running to a new principal square and beyond it into Leadenhall Street, the second emerging at an open space around the Tower. St Paul's is prominently placed within the angle of the two avenues, in a part of the City where they are overlaid on a grid of streets. Similarly, he planned four streets radiating from a semi-circular piazza at the northern end of the bridge, one of them leading to the principal square, which is the focus of ten streets. The square was to contain the Royal Exchange and be ringed by buildings for those public offices displaced from the City by the fire; the Post Office, the Mint, the Excise Office and the goldsmiths' Insurance Office. In addition to that square, Wren included four other *rondpoints* as foci, surrounded by webs of streets, including a large one east of Temple Bar.

Evelyn's original plan is less densely filled than that of Wren, although his later modifications contain more detailed street layouts and incorporate a number of significant modifications. His initial design, like Wren's, treats the northern end of the bridge as a focal point for radiating streets. It also shows three streets diverging from a large oval space containing St Paul's, east of Ludgate, the central one of which runs through the principal square, which is aligned with the bridge, to the church of St Dunstan-in-the-East. The plan also includes a number of other squares and piazzas, where the diagonal streets meet those of the grid, which Evelyn visualised as embellished with fountains and which he consciously designed in a variety of shapes 'for their better grace and capacity'. A large octagonal *rondpoint* is placed between Temple Bar and the Fleet, with the eight avenues running from it linked by a concentric street. This feature remained in Evelyn's two later designs, but in a considerably scaled-down form. In the explanation of his proposals which he submitted with his first plan, Evelyn explains that the piazzas should be utilised as market places and that some of them could provide waiting places for coaches. His ideal was for a regulated city in which uniformity of building was of prime importance. This extended to the taverns and victualling houses, for 'even the very meanest, should exactly respect uniformity'.[21]

As the king acknowledged, the plans submitted by Wren and Evelyn contained a number of common features, although they had been drawn up quite independently. Both men were clearly indebted to sixteenth-century Rome and Henri IV's proposals for Paris for many of their ideas.

In particular, the fan shapes of the principal streets are reminiscent of the layout of the Piazza del Popolo at Rome and the plan by Claude Chastillon and Jacques Alleaume for the Place de France in Paris, drawn up in 1608–9.[22] Wren and Evelyn also adopted another feature characteristic of Renaissance town planning in their employment of rigidly straight streets, their vistas closed by a suitably imposing building, obelisk or fountain. The demands of such planning outweighed the effects of the topography of the site, which produced steep streets and even the use of steps where necessary, rather than the adaptation of the line of the streets to the gradient. Evelyn was aware of this, for he had described the Via Felix in Rome as 'a straite & noble streete, but exceeding precipicious', and suggested that in London some of the 'deepest valleys, holes, and more sudden declivities' could be at least partially filled up.[23] If his plan had been implemented, steep gradients would have been produced on the streets running northwards from the Thames quay and those which crossed the valley of the Fleet.

The other designs which are extant adhered more rigidly to the grid, although in some ways they were no less ambitious than those of Wren and Evelyn. Newcourt's has an unvarying, large-scale, chequerboard pattern on which the streets divide the ground into equal rectangular blocks, each 855 feet from west to east and 570 feet from north to south. Each block is, in turn, divided by cross streets, meeting at a square, which has a church at its centre. The design envisages a block as a parish. The pattern is broken only by five larger squares: a very large central one as the focus of the City and four others placed equidistant from it towards each corner of the plan. This arrangement of a large central square and a number of smaller subsidiary ones was a feature of the ideal city designs produced by both Pietro Cataneo and Vincenzo Scammozi. Newcourt's design makes no concessions at all to topography. This is equally true of Hooke's plan, which is also based on a regular grid, although with smaller blocks and squares than those proposed by Newcourt.[24]

Valentine Knight's solution described two principal streets crossing the City from west to east, with six equally wide streets and several narrower ones running northward from the quay. Within the irregular grid thus formed, the blocks were to be subdivided into long and narrow parcels by further east–west streets, creating divisions averaging 500 feet long and wide enough, at 70 feet, to accommodate two rows of houses. He also suggested the construction of a barge canal, 30 feet wide, running in an arc from the Thames at Billingsgate, through the burnt area, to the River Fleet near Holborn Bridge. An integral part of his scheme was the raising of revenue for the Crown, with a lump sum of £372,360 from fines and a recurrent annual income of over £200,000 in fees levied on the passage of the barges. His ingenious solution to the obvious problem of financing the new City received a distinctly cool reception at court. Knight was arrested and publicly rebuked for daring to suggest that the king 'would draw a benefit to himself, from so publick a Calamity of his people'.[25]

Knight's treatment may have been simply an exercise in public relations, for the question of finance had to be addressed. It was one of the subjects touched on by Petty, together with such matters as whether it was necessary to rebuild as many houses as had been destroyed and how the streets could be widened. Many of his reflections concerned a 'Modell for rebuildinge the Citty' and anticipated some of the measures subsequently adopted. He realised the need to assess the disadvantages of pre-fire London and determine what the objectives of the rebuilding should be. He also considered such practical matters as the quantities of materials and the numbers of workmen required, as well as the time-scale within which rebuilding could be achieved. Petty came to no definite conclusions on many of these matters, including finance, but he did consider that the whole nation could be taxed over a seven-year period and the sums levied later repaid 'with advantage'.[26]

A variation on the idea of a loan was put forward by Sir Edward Ford, who suggested that the existing system of credit could be extended, with bills of exchange issued on the security of parliamentary taxation.[27] Another proposal was for the compulsory purchase of the ground by the Crown and the corporation. It would then be conveyed to trustees while a new layout was put in place, when the revised sites would be sold, with preference given to their original owners. This scheme met Petty's requirement for a single owner of all the ground who was wealthy enough to afford the rebuilding. It received considerable support and was propounded in the House of Commons by John Birch, erstwhile Parliamentarian officer and now Member for Penryn. The proposal did not receive enough backing to proceed, but the fact that it had not been implemented was later bemoaned by such a powerful and well-informed figure as Sir Robert Viner.[28]

The Commons considered the fire and the rebuilding in the last week of September, both in general debate and committee, but were divided about what should be done. Some members favoured a new layout for the City and the implementation of Wren's plan, but they were outnumbered by those who spoke against such a radical solution. Others preferred more limited change, generally retaining the former sites, but with the construction of new streets from Temple Bar to Leadenhall and from Bishopsgate to the river, with the widening of the existing ones where necessary. There was also some support for the retention of the pre-fire plan, the only requirement being that the rebuilding should be in brick. The House came to no conclusion, although its mood seemed to be to reject both complete change and no change at all, and to favour the middle way of making some modifications.[29]

While the possibilities of a drastic remodelling were seriously considered by the court, the City and parliament, no solutions were found to the obvious problems. It was essential that the surveys of the sites within the ruined area should be completed if owners were to be bought out or compensated, or any redistribution of ground made, yet the response was so patchy that they probably remained unfinished. Furthermore, it is doubtful whether the administrative machinery available was adequate to the task of property conveyancing on the scale required. A bureaucracy of the size and experience needed did not exist and there was no possibility of recruiting and training one within an acceptable time, for the City was anxious that the rebuilding should begin as soon as possible, which meant in the spring of 1667. The time factor also applied to the question of finance, for the levying of a tax, as Petty suggested, was politically and practically impossible, especially in view of parliament's irresolution in September and the government's own very pressing needs. Reporting parliament's deliberations, Henry Oldenburg was well aware that 'The great stresse will be, how to raise mony for carrying on the warre and to rebuild the Citty, at the same time'.[30]

Without some form of extra revenue, neither the Crown nor the corporation could even contemplate setting aside money on the scale required for purchasing the sites. The government's finances were in a parlous condition by the autumn of 1666 and those of the corporation were scarcely in a better state. Indeed, the corporation's annual average deficit, already more than £11,000 during the early 1660s, could only be worsened by the diminution of its income because of the fire, for more than a quarter of its revenue came from property rents.[31] In any circumstances the problems would almost certainly have proved intractable, but as the fire coincided with a difficult and expensive war and followed so soon after a serious plague epidemic, they were indeed impossible to overcome.

Parliament's indecision and the gradual realisation that implementation of a new ground plan was impracticable did not bring progress on planning the rebuilding to an end, for the government and the City continued to take steps to determine how it should be regulated. Early in October the king set up a commission of six members, consisting of three of his own appointees and three nominated by the City, which reported on a weekly basis to the rebuilding committee of the Privy Council. The king appointed Wren, Roger Pratt and Hugh May, and the corporation Hooke, Mills and Edward Jerman. Their brief included the management of the survey of ruined property, consideration of the form and scale of the new buildings, and alterations to the streets.[32]

The proclamation of 13 September had set out some guidelines.[33] As well as halting progress on rebuilding until the necessary regulations were determined and repeating the requirement for brick building, it had laid down a number of other broad principles. With regard to the future prevention of fire it ruled that Fleet Street, Cheapside, Cornhill and 'all other eminent Streets' should be wide enough to prevent flames spreading from one side to another. Furthermore, no streets were to be rebuilt so narrow as to be inconvenient, especially close to the river, and alleys and lanes were to be eliminated as far as possible. The quay along the river was to be left clear of houses and an attempt at environmental control was made by prohibiting noxious trades from the riverside because 'their continual smoaks, contribute much to the unhealthiness of the adjacent places'. This may reflect a success for Evelyn, who had mounted a strong attack on the smoky riverside industries a few years before in his *Fumifugium*, in which he had taken particular exception to the premises of brewers, dyers, lime-burners and salt- and soap-boilers.[34] As far as new buildings were concerned, the king promised to replace the Custom House on the same site and commended the construction of the churches to 'well disposed persons'.

The commissioners developed the order concerning the width of streets, initially categorising them into 'high streets' of 70 feet width, other streets of 50 or 42 feet, and the 'least' streets of 30 or 25 feet. Such alleys as were permitted were to be at least 16 feet wide. By the end of October they had applied these general principles to a number of streets, ruling that Paternoster Row, Thames Street and Lombard Street, for example, should each be 40 feet wide. The question of the width of the streets was to be much debated, however, before being finally agreed.[35]

The concern for the easy flow of traffic reflected in these orders formed a major part of the commissioners' draft proposals, which were presented to Common Council on 30 November. As well as the width of the thoroughfares, they also dealt with the long-standing problem of large conduits in the middle of the principal streets, recommending that the City be given power to rebuild them in a smaller form than before, or remove them from the main streets altogether. Responsibility for paving, too, was to be transferred from the parishes and wards to the central authority of the City. This had been one of the defects of pre-fire London. A commission for 'reforming the buildings, wayes, streetes, & incumbrances' was set up in 1662 and had ordered the paving of some streets. Evelyn, one of its members, thought that in the aftermath of the fire bricks from the ruins could be used to pave the footways in front of the buildings, as in Holland.[36] The condition of the streets was to be further improved by an insistence that downpipes be fitted to carry away water from roofs, to prevent the cascade from gutters that spouted out above the street, which was 'troublesome and malicious'.[37] Bow windows and other projections were prohibited, although an exception was allowed for houses fronting the high streets, which could be fitted with balconies, as long as they were no more than 4 feet deep. The attempt to prevent projections reflected the concern in the pre-fire regulations to remove jettying because it was seen as a fire risk. Similarly, the earlier insistence on brick and stone was again repeated, and control of materials was now extended further, by banning wood from the outsides of all buildings. The only exceptions for external woodwork were window-frames and door-cases, and the bressummers and other features of shop-fronts, although the latter had to be of relatively fire-resistant, and expensive, oak.

The most far-reaching feature of the proposals, however, was the uniformity imposed on the rebuilding, by the categorisation of houses according to their site and detailed stipulations concerning such constructional matters as the height of storeys, depths of cellars and thicknesses of the walls. The desire for such uniformity of buildings in the City was not new. After the fire in the parish of St Magnus the Martyr in 1633, it had been pointed out that 'to rebuild with houses in one uniforme wilbe very gracefull to the place'.[38] What was novel in the regulations drawn up after the Great Fire was that this idea was given practical expression and the means of enforcement.

The regulations identified four categories of houses, according to their position. The smallest ones, of two storeys and garrets, were those in 'by-streets and lanes', those of the second sort were of three storeys and garrets on the 'streets and lanes of note' and facing the river, those in the next category were one storey higher and fronted the 'high and principal streets', while the biggest were 'mansion houses for citizens and other persons of extraordinary quality', not standing on the streets or lanes, but also limited to four storeys. All houses had to conform to these categories and the desired homogeneity of appearance was furthered by a ruling that the roof lines within the first three sorts of house should be uniform.

A further measure was that party walls should be set out equally on each owner's ground and that, if the adjoining houses were not to be built at the same time, the first owner was entitled to go ahead, leaving toothing for the second house to be built on to. The cost of the wall was to be shared equally by the owners, although the second owner was liable to pay interest at 6 per cent for the interval between the construction of the first house and his own. This was designed to remove a possible cause for delay. A further incentive for rebuilding was a clause permitting the corporation to compulsorily purchase ground that had not been built on within three years.

The commissioners' proposals were swiftly adopted and were incorporated into the bill to be submitted to parliament, which was finally approved by Common Council on 15 December. Another bill relating to the fire was already before parliament. This was for the establishment of a court 'to determine differences between landlords and tenants as to rebuilding' and replaced an earlier bill 'for present Prevention of Suits by Landlords against their Tenants, whose Houses were burnt in the late sad Fire'. The titles of the two bills reflect an obvious problem, which contained the potential for endless delays in rebuilding unless some procedure was devised to provide swift solutions to the many possible disputes likely to develop; 'a Legislative power to cut all Knots' in Petty's phrase.[39] Without a mechanism to handle the disagreements arising from rebuilding and related tenurial questions, the parties involved would probably have taken their case to the equity courts, Exchequer and Chancery. These were notoriously slow, with Chancery, in particular, having a bad reputation in that respect. In this period it attracted roughly eight times the number of suits that came before the Exchequer court and a quarter of its cases remained unresolved a year after submission.[40] The prospect of delays which this raised could only dismay the City.

The nature of the problems that could arise between landlords, tenants and subtenants was familiar from other fires and the destruction caused during the Civil War. Most fundamentally, there was the liability for rebuilding. Leases customarily contained a covenant that placed the onus for maintaining the property in good repair on the tenant. But repair was one thing, rebuilding in brick and tile to specified standards and dimensions quite another. This would almost certainly involve expense on a scale which many tenants would be unwilling to undergo, even if they could afford it, given that they would effectively be building a new and valuable property for their landlords. The tenants would have the benefit of the new building only until the end of their current lease. A loophole did exist, however, for if the destruction had been carried out by an enemy the tenants were judged to be not liable. This had been addressed against the background of the Civil War, when a tenant who was sued for arrears of rent had claimed that he had not had access to the property during the period for which the arrears were due because he had been expelled from it by an army commanded by Prince Rupert. The tenant's case that he was not liable for the arrears was based on the allegation that Rupert was 'an alien born' who had invaded the realm with a hostile army. Yet judgment had been given in favour of the landlord, on the basis that the tenant had failed to demonstrate that the entire army that had dispossessed him had consisted of foreigners.[41]

In the aftermath of the Great Fire the judges upheld existing opinion regarding leaseholders' liability to restore burned property, but also concluded that they were not responsible in this case because the burning had been caused by an enemy. That enemy was none other than the unfortunate Frenchman Robert Hubert, whose conviction was now used as a convenient legal scapegoat for the fire. Nevertheless, this 'excellent Salvo for the Tenants' was directly contrary to the government's consistently held view that the fire had been an accident.[42]

Despite this ruling, many disputes were bound to arise over such matters as liabilities, tenures, boundaries and rents, and the fire court was created to settle them. It was also expected to expedite rebuilding as far as possible, 'making new rules between owners and tenants for their material encouragement'. The court consisted of three or more judges of the courts of King's Bench and Common Pleas and Barons of the Exchequer. Cases were begun by petition and resolved by a decree; the only appeal permitted was to a larger meeting of the same court.[43]

The bill setting up the fire court passed the Lords in late January. The main bill, governing the rebuilding, had a more protracted passage through parliament and was subjected to a number of modifications. One of these dealt with the problem of building materials. If reconstruction did go ahead with the speed intended, there would be considerable and concentrated demand for bricks, tiles, lime and timber, as well as coal to fuel the kilns. Individual entrepreneurs had quickly realised that this would be the case. Within three weeks of the fire Pepys was toying with the idea of a partnership with Sir William Penn to bring timber from Scotland, which he foresaw would 'yield good money'. John Evelyn came to a similar conclusion regarding the need for timber, although he became engaged in a scheme to manufacture bricks.[44] The obvious danger was that, unless they were regulated, prices would rise to such a level that potential builders would be deterred. In November 1666 it was alleged that the prices of materials had already risen so much as to raise the cost of a small building between three and four times.[45]

Supplies of bricks, tiles and lime would be produced in or close to London and so could be regulated. Coal, lead and timber, on the other hand, had to be brought by sea, either coastwise or from abroad. So long as the war continued the coastal trade was liable to interruption by the Dutch, and the carrying trade in timber was chiefly in foreign hands, for English vessels were not suited to it. Earlier in the year the government had relaxed the Navigation Acts to facilitate imports, including timber, from Norway and the Baltic, and on 28 November extended this to cover London's direct trade with Norway and Sweden.[46] Britain's own regulations were only a part of the problem, however, for much of the trade from Scandinavia and the Baltic was in the hands of the Dutch.

But this was not necessarily an obstacle to supplies, for Dutch carriers recognised the opportunity presented by the fire and were soon offering their services, regardless of the war. On 24 September, the master of the *Blackamoor* of Rotterdam, which had brought over the body of Sir William Berkeley, killed during the Four Days Battle, asked the king for a licence to permit him to supply deal boards, and his petition was soon followed by one making a similar request for another vessel out of the same port. By October a group of merchants had contracted for building materials worth £5,000 or £6,000 from northern Europe.[47]

While the corporation clearly did not wish to discourage any suppliers of materials, its concerns about the prospect of profiteering were such that it promoted a separate bill regulating the manufacture of bricks and tiles. At the end of November the bill was introduced into the Commons, where an amendment was proposed that the City should appoint an inspector to check the quality of the brick and tile, who would be remunerated by a fee based on the number of items checked. Some Members viewed this with disapproval as representing a 'project'.[48] Presumably for this reason, the bill went no further, but a similar measure was incorporated into the main bill. This was designed to prevent profiteering by giving the Justices of the King's Bench power to fix the prices charged by brickmakers and other suppliers operating within five miles of the Thames, for both materials and transport. Those who did not comply with the justices' rulings were liable to imprisonment, although in fact the price control mechanism was never invoked.

The justices were also given the authority to determine wage rates in the building trades. The corporation faced a dilemma in this matter, for while a shortage of skilled labour would undoubtedly slow down rebuilding, it was anxious to maintain its regulations restricting trading within its jurisdiction to the citizens, which would prevent the influx required. The Common Council therefore referred the problem to the Commons, which duly inserted the relevant clause in the bill. This stated that those working in the building trades who were not freemen of the City should nevertheless be permitted to work there for seven years after the passage of the bill, or until the buildings were completed, with the right to trade thereafter as freemen.

The corporation had also addressed the problem of how the various improvements and the City's own buildings were to be paid for. Given the state of its finances, there was no doubt that some other source of funds would have to be found. The measure proposed by the aldermen and incorporated in the bill governing the rebuilding provided for the levying of a duty of one shilling on every ton of coal brought into the port of London. This was the obvious solution, for the trade was already well regulated and so the tax would be easy to collect, with little extra administration, and had the further recommendation that it was a local, not a national, imposition. But despite the City's intentions, the stipulations in the clause as included in the final bill failed to satisfy many of its needs, for they directed that the receipts should be applied to compensate the owners of land appropriated for street widening, the restoration of the wharves and the rebuilding of the prisons.[49]

With prompting from the king, during January and early February 1667 parliament turned its attention to the two bills relating to the rebuilding. Inevitably, a number of amendments and changes were made before they received the Royal Assent on 8 February. The act for rebuilding contained a mixture of measures, but failed to resolve all of the matters that needed to be determined before reconstruction could begin. While it detailed the specifications of the houses to be erected, the question of the layout of the new City was still less than fully dealt with. The act did include requirements for the widening of certain streets and the construction of a new one connecting Guildhall with Cheapside, but left the categorisation of the streets to the City, requiring that the task should be done by 5 April. Until that was completed and the lines of the streets staked out, building could not proceed, for an owner would not risk making a start on rebuilding only to find that a part of the plot was required for street widening.

The City did indeed act quickly in surveying the streets and presented its proposals to the king early in March. His response included recommendations modifying some of the suggested widths and a more far-reaching one that would remove market stalls from the streets at Cheapside, Leadenhall Street and Newgate to designated market places. The corporation balked at some of his suggestions, but by the end of the month it had prepared a full classification of the streets and their staking out, under the direction of the surveyors Peter Mills and Robert Hooke, had begun. An Act of Common Council issued on 29 April listed the streets and alleys that were to be widened. It also made provision for the widening of any other 'streight and narrow Passages', if the suggested improvements were thought to be desirable and the streets or alleys were set out before 20 May. Even when that task was completed, builders were not free to begin work immediately. The act had ruled that no builder could make a start until the site, the proposed foundations and party walls had been seen and approved by a surveyor, the builder paying 6s 8d per site towards the cost of the survey and the setting out of the streets. But in this respect, too, the corporation acted promptly, appointing the four surveyors before the end of March.[50]

While the act and the corporation's efforts cleared the path for house building to get under way in spring 1667, little had been settled regarding the reconstruction of the churches. Although it was clear that many of those destroyed did not need to be rebuilt and that the opportunity should be taken to amalgamate some parishes, no decisions had been taken by the time the rebuilding act was passed. Small and poor parishes were a problem inherited from the Middle Ages. Many of the livings in the City were held in plurality because the stipends were so low, and the curates' remuneration was particularly meagre.[51] The position had been worsened by the loss of income from tithes in the aftermath of the fire, with the parishes within the burnt area all but depopulated. Amalgamation offered an obvious solution, yet the number of interested parties prevented a quick agreement on the new arrangements being reached. A scheme to reduce the number of parishes to thirty-nine, overriding the rights of the patrons and impropriators and vesting the patronage of the churches in the corporation, failed because of the power of the various interests that it would have replaced. Nevertheless, the figure of thirty-nine new churches was included in the rebuilding act.[52]

The question of the churches was given greater attention in the Additional Building Act. This was set on foot by the corporation before the end of 1667 and the bill was discussed in the Commons in the following April and May, although it was not passed for a further two years. It raised the coal duty to 3s per ton and extended the original term of ten years by a further ten, until 1687 (the levy actually continued for over two centuries). The act also allocated three-quarters of the extra revenue towards the cost of reconstructing the churches, including St Paul's, and specified which were to be rebuilt. These now numbered fifty-one, to replace the eighty-seven destroyed in the fire, but the parishes were amalgamated for ecclesiastical purposes only and retained their own organisations, with the patrons presenting to the livings in rotation.[53]

The act also addressed other matters arising from the implementation of the acts of 1667. Among the most important of these was
the renewal of the jurisdiction of the fire court, which had lapsed at
the end of 1668. Because of the delay in the passing of the Additional
Building Act, there had been a hiatus in the court's activities. The
operations of the revived court regarding proof of ownership and
tenancy, complicated by the loss of so many of the relevant documents
in the fire, were facilitated by permitting proof of twenty-one years'
possession to be a valid basis for the granting of a new lease.[54]

Pending the passing of the legislation and the issuing of the
corporation's regulations early in 1667, individual owners and tenants,
if not actually chafing at the bit, were making their own plans for
rebuilding. Some may have been not a little anxious to see what changes
were to be imposed on the City and the effect they may have on their
own land. At the end of February, Thomas Hollier, a surgeon, told Pepys
that it was unsafe for him to begin rebuilding because 'he knows not
what restrictions there will be'.[55] By the end of March there was less
justification for such doubts, and as the uncertainties were resolved and
the procedures became known, plans could be consolidated.

For many owners and leaseholders the chief concern was how to
obtain the money to rebuild. Some could provide it from within their
own resources, although perhaps only if they could persuade their
creditors to settle outstanding debts. Inevitably, the Crown was a major
creditor, owing considerable sums to both its suppliers and employees.
The widow of William Procter, a wine merchant who had died in the
plague, had a substantial claim against the treasury, asking for payment of
£600 for wine supplied four years earlier. Sir William Wale, Purveyor of
Wines to the king, whose houses had been burnt down and his stock
of wine destroyed, requested payment of the outstanding balance on
his account of £1,697.[56] Losses in the fire also prompted the court
musicians to press for arrears of pay. John Gamble, one of the wind
players, petitioned the king for unpaid salary for the period since the
end of 1661, amounting to £221, pleading that he had lost everything
in the fire. His request was followed by a joint claim by twenty-two
members of the king's violin consort, who had also been unpaid during
that time and whose property and goods had been destroyed. The more
senior figures were owed even larger sums, with almost £600 being due
to Henry Cooke, Master of the Children of the Chapel Royal.[57]

Even without the payment of such debts, the apparently common practice among the citizens of hoarding a proportion of their wealth in money-bags and chests provided potential ready finance for building within the community. Tradesmen in late Stuart London left an average of £255 in cash at their death, with the figure for merchants being £671.[58] Those who did not need to use such reserves for their own rebuilding may have been ready to grant loans on the security of the new buildings. Pepys was most solicitous for the safety of his stock of coin, which at the time of the fire included gold worth £2,350 and at the end of 1666 totalled £6,200. Nevertheless, he was willing to lend some of it to finance the erection of a new house, which he evidently regarded as good security.[59] The release of such stocks of coin suggests that at least a part of the investment in building did not involve a diversion of funds from other outlets, such as trade. It certainly seems that considerable spare capital was available in London in the mid-1660s, for the concentrated adverse effects of plague, fire and war, including the panic demand for withdrawals from the bankers when the Dutch raided the Medway, did not lead to any bankruptcies.[60]

Within six months of the fire much had been resolved. The establishment of the fire court had provided the legal procedures to resolve disagreements and make rulings to expedite rebuilding, and the regulations governing that rebuilding had been decided upon. Any lingering regret over the failure to lay out a completely new street plan was unfounded, for although the idea may have been an appealing one its achievement was impracticable. The principal objective after the fire was to make possible the City's rapid recovery by ensuring that the conditions governing the rebuilding should be in place by the spring of 1667, and that was achieved. In any event, the straightening and widening of the streets, with the implementation of the plan to grade them and impose uniformity as well as minimum standards on the buildings, held out the promise of a much finer City than the one destroyed. Even a sceptic such as Pepys was cheered when he saw the lines of the streets staked out, remarking that if it were built in that form 'with so fair streets, it will be a noble sight'.[61]

FIVE

THE REBUILDING

... this great citty ... by reason of the Kings and Parlaments care
(then sitting), and the great wealth and opolency of the citty itselfe,
was rebuilded most stately with brick (the greatest part being before
nothing but lath and lime) in four or five years time.

Memoirs of Sir John Reresby, ed. A. Browning
(2nd edn, London, Royal Historical Society, 1991), p. 62

By the spring of 1667 all of the processes required for rebuilding
appeared to be in place. The fire court began sitting on 27 February,
hearing a case in which the landlord wished to redevelop a site which
had been held in multiple tenancies, with intermingled rooms. Only a
little later than the court in beginning their operations, the surveyors
were busy from late March, marking the lines of the streets and then
setting out house sites. With all of this work under way, it remained
only for individual property owners, including the livery companies
and the church, to arrange for the construction of the new buildings.

In those cases where the landlord had undisputed possession
of the site, unencumbered by previous leases or mortgages, and
could find a tenant who was willing and able to rebuild, this was a
relatively straightforward process. In April 1667 Thomas Brown leased
to Nathaniel Hill, a vintner, ground in Botolph Lane on which the
White Hart had stood before the fire, for fifty-one years at £12 per
annum. Hill undertook that within eighteen months of the start of
the term he would 'erect and build in workmanlike manner one good
firme and substantiall brick Messuage or Tenement. . . . According to
such scantlings of brickworke and Timber' as were laid down in the
rebuilding act. The form of the three-storey building had also been
agreed and the schedule accompanying the lease itemised the rooms
and some of the fittings.[1] This was a typical arrangement by which the

tenant was granted a lease without paying a fine for entry or renewal, to be held at a low rent, undertaking the rebuilding on the security of a long term. Many such building leases were granted in the next few years.

Not all landlords were so willing to commit themselves in the spring of 1667. Some may still have been uncertain about the financial implications. Before owners and tenants could set about raising the money required to rebuild, they needed some idea of the probable expense. A practical guide to estimating prices was provided by Sir Balthazar Gerbier's *Counsel and Advice to all Builders*, which had been published in 1663. But the anxieties of owners and tenants in the aftermath of the fire were more directly addressed by Stephen Primatt, a lawyer. He recognised that prospective builders were likely to be deterred by the fear that in the building boom they would be exploited by their workmen, who could charge high fees for their work. According to Thomas Manley, writing in 1669, wages in the building industry in and around London had been rising for 'some time' before the fire.[2] Nevertheless, Primatt alleged that the building workmen and surveyors were 'observed to make Harvest in the City Ruines and combine together for excessive Rates'. His response was *The City and Country Purchaser and Builder*, published in 1667, which was the first English work on the subject of property valuations and prices and was aimed at owners who were afraid of such exploitation. It gave practical information on the costs of erecting the various categories of house, providing owners with the knowledge they required when negotiating prices and settling disputes.[3]

Some owners were discouraged by the cost of construction, especially given the terms of the rebuilding act. In the aftermath of the fire the owner of an inn near Holborn Bridge had calculated the amounts of materials that would be required to rebuild and had made tentative arrangements for the delivery of timber, but was dismayed to discover that the specifications laid down in the act 'much altered the quantities required'.[4] The standards of building stipulated for the principal streets inevitably had an effect on costs. The estimated expenses of rebuilding a corner house in Lombard Street and a house on 'the best place in Cornhill' were £700 and £900 respectively, while a mansion house in Cornhill was expected to cost £3,000.[5]

Taking the whole range of houses, from mansions in the principal streets to tenements erected in such a 'very bad place' as the expressively named Dunghill Alley, the estimated costs of rebuilding given to the fire court in 1667 and 1668 averaged £516 per house.[6] The figure is inflated by the relatively high costs of taverns, which averaged £1,500 each, and mansions, which could require several thousand pounds. Yet modest houses on the rear of sites were also relatively costly and certainly more expensive to build than those of a similar size fronting the street. This was explained by the fact that the materials had to be carried by hand from the street to the site at the rear.[7] While some allowance has to be made for the exaggeration of projected costs in order to strengthen arguments put before the court, builders were also capable of making quite serious miscalculations. The eventual cost of building three houses in Love Lane, Aldermanbury, was roughly twice the original estimate of £1,500, for example.[8] The costs of houses built between 1667 and 1672 by Sir Robert Clayton and John Morris, two scriveners acting in partnership, on a range of sites, were £181 for a house in Finch Lane, £304 for three houses in Hand Alley, £441, £390 and £255 for houses in Cornhill and £1,268 for a coffee house, also in Cornhill. The outlay on Clayton's own mansion in Old Jewry was £1,669. This was a grand house, arranged around a courtyard, which Evelyn noted had been built 'at excessive cost', containing a dining room with cedar panelling and decorated by Robert Streater with paintings of 'the Historie of the Gyants War'.[9] The average for these nine buildings was £500 each, very close to the amount produced by the figures submitted to the hearings of the fire court.

The estimated expenses of building were only a part of owners' concerns, for it had also to be agreed who was to undertake the work. Despite the ruling that clauses requiring tenants to maintain the property in good repair could not be invoked to compel them to bear the cost of rebuilding, in practice landlords often did ask for a contribution from those who surrendered their old leases. Furthermore, such claims were upheld by the fire court. A tenant of the Drapers' Company in Sweeting Lane, having failed to persuade the under-tenants to rebuild, then attempted to get them not only to surrender their leases but also to contribute towards the cost of rebuilding. The court supported his appeal and directed his under-tenants to pay £30 in one case and £40 in two others, even though they were surrendering their leases and so would have no future interest in the properties. In a similar case, in St Nicholas Lane, the court ordered the tenant to contribute £380 in four instalments, paying £100 when each of the first, second and third storeys was reached and the balance when the house was roofed. Even so, it was clearly in a landlord's interest to retain an existing tenant and negotiate an agreement for rebuilding, rather than have to find a new tenant, or even bear the cost of the new building. In some instances, the ground landlord was prepared to make concessions to the head lessee in order to facilitate matters. The Saddlers' Company reduced its tenant's rent for a property in West Cheap and extended his term, enabling him to come to an agreement with the under-tenant whereby the costs of rebuilding were divided between them, the head lessee paying two-thirds of the costs and his under-tenant the remainder.[10]

The level of rent and liability for unpaid rents on a property were also matters to be agreed. Tenants were understandably unwilling to take a lease if the rent was higher than that charged during the previous term, and indeed attempts to raise ground rents in the new leases were frowned upon. The Bishop of Peterborough was called before the fire court and chided for trying to increase rents on his property in Fleet Street, being told by the court 'to consider the common calamity'.[11] Humphrey Henchman, Bishop of London, was even more intransigent. Demanding rents in full from his tenants near St Paul's for the period after the fire, when the buildings had stood in ruin, he refused to appear before the fire court, claiming parliamentary privilege as a peer. Many of the bishop's tenants were booksellers, who felt that he had treated them 'most basely, worse than any other landlords'.[12]

Even when the terms were agreeable, some existing tenants were unwilling to take on the cost of rebuilding, either because they could not afford to do so or they felt that they would not be making a good investment. If the property was in an unfavourable location, potential tenants feared that they would be unable to find under-tenants at a realistic rent once the building was completed. The clothworkers who held a lease of property in Paternoster Row in Cheapside, one of the best sites for retailers in the City, made a claim of this kind when negotiating their new terms. Their statement in November 1668 that 'the great trade which was formerly in Paternoster Row ... would never returne to that place in respect that the most part of the principall traders there have fixt themselves elsewhere and declared their intentions neither to build there nor returne thither' presented a particularly bleak forecast, although the court was apparently unmoved by it.[13]

A further point to be considered in negotiations was the condition of the property that had been burnt down. Tenants who had rebuilt or substantially renovated the property before the fire naturally asked for their previous investments to be taken into consideration. Since 1650 Roger Lewis had built four houses in White's Alley in the parish of St Stephen, Coleman Street, spending £600 in the process, which represented the 'cheife fruite of his forty yeares labour and paines in his trade', only to see them burnt down in the fire. Now in his late sixties, he was unwilling to rebuild unless he was granted some allowance by his landlord to compensate him for his previous investment. The court ruled that Lewis should be granted a lease of sixty-one years and that the rent should be halved.[14]

Existing tenants were reluctant to take a new lease of a property if it had been reduced in size by street widening and so became less valuable than before, or even no longer viable as a building plot. Compensation was payable out of the coal dues fund for land taken for street improvements, such as the £650 paid for the site of the Three Tuns tavern, which was 'totally taken away' for the enlargement of the passage through to Guildhall.[15] Similarly, at the time of the fire two houses had stood on a site at the junction of Ram Alley and Fleet Street, but the new street line and wider entrance to the alley made the site so narrow that a house could not be built upon it. On other sites street widening reduced the number of houses that could be erected. Because of the land lost from the ground formerly occupied by five houses in Ludgate Hill when the street was widened, there was space only for three or four of the 'faire fronting houses' appropriate on such a prominent site.[16]

Some of the remnants of sites reduced in size by street widening were incorporated into adjoining ones, but a number of owners were prepared to fight the changes, to the extent of trying to get the new street line altered. William Wheatly attempted to avoid losing a strip of ground 7 feet wide on his side of Water Lane by appealing to the City to widen the street by taking land solely from the opposite side. His petition seems to have been unsuccessful, but some changes to the initial plans were made elsewhere. The owners of property in Huggen Lane were afraid that if it were widened to 14 feet, as was proposed, it would become a thoroughfare for carts between Wood Street and Gutter Lane, making it less safe for the occupiers and more subject to repair through the damage to the surface that would be caused. They made a convincing case and were successful in getting the proposal withdrawn.[17]

The building regulations had also reduced the viability of sites through the ban on jetties and the stipulation of the number of storeys for each grade. A building near St Mary Aldermary churchyard was to be two storeys lower than its predecessor, built in 1661, and so too small for the tenant to continue his trade, and he refused to take a new lease. Similarly, the lessee of the Rose in Cheapside refused to rebuild, because the new building was to be a storey lower than the one on the site before the fire, and was to lose further floor area by not having jetties. The removal of the jetty over an alley at the side of the Weavers Arms in the parish of Allhallows, Honey Lane, had the effect of making the site too restricted to carry a house of the scale required by the rebuilding act for a house fronting a high street. That the prohibition of jetties and requirement to 'build upright' reduced the size of the new buildings was a point made by several tenants.[18]

Issues such as these had to be resolved before new tenurial and rebuilding arrangements could be agreed and many cases were taken before the fire court. It also dealt with other matters, including decisions as to who should rebuild what on those sites where the rooms of the destroyed buildings had been intermingled. Not all issues required the mediation of the court, for some had been resolved in advance of the hearing and the purpose of bringing them before the court was simply to get the decisions enrolled. In 1667 and 1668 the court handled just over 800 cases, before its authority lapsed and those with disputes took their suits to Chancery, despite its slowness. Indeed, the fire court itself had started to clog up with business in the spring of 1668, with some delays occurring to hearings. The defendant in a case heard in June failed to appear, her counsel claiming that he was unaware that it would come before the court on that day 'there being many causes at this time in arreare'.[19] After the court resumed business, following the 1670 rebuilding act, it dealt with another 800 cases. In many instances more than one site was involved, and it seems probable that as many as one in four pre-fire sites were included in suits that came before the fire court and Chancery.

In all cases, the fire court's aim was to expedite rebuilding. Yet its power in this respect was limited. It could indeed order tenants to build as soon as possible, but was unable to ensure that they did so. For whatever reasons, some tenants did not act promptly even after an order from the court. In the case of a house near Paternoster Row, for example, the court made an order in October 1667, but the request for the site to be staked out was not submitted for another year. Similarly, a decree made in November 1667 for rebuilding a house in St Mary Aldermanbury was not followed up by an application to the surveyors until January 1669. Perhaps unduly influenced by the address, the tenant of a site in Do Little Lane did not get the ground staked out until April 1673, five years after the decree. In roughly a third of cases, the request for the surveyors to set out the foundations came more than six months after the decree of the court and in one in seven of them the interval was more than a year.[20] The court attempted to impose a timetable on some tenants in order to avoid such long delays. At a hearing in June 1667 of the differences between the Pewterers' Company and Daniel Rawlinson, a vintner, respecting the Mitre in Fenchurch Street, it ruled that Rawlinson should rebuild and stipulated that the new building should be roofed by Christmas 1668. This date was specified for the completion of building in several agreements reached in the court during 1667.[21]

The number and variety of cases that required arbitration helps to explain the pace of the rebuilding process. It appeared to begin briskly. The first sites to be surveyed were set out in Budge Row and Fleet Street towards the end of March 1667 and some buildings were quickly raised. Kellway Guidott obtained a lease for the site of the St John's Head, in Chancery Lane, from the Society of Lincoln's Inn in April, and the carcass of the new tavern had been built by June.[22] The process of surveying seemed to be gaining momentum during the early summer, yet it came to a halt in the middle of June and scarcely any sites were set out during the second half of the month or in July. Only in August did the level of activity return to what it had been in the spring. Peter Mills was ill for a time in the summer and John Oliver – who was to become one of the surveyors in the following January – acted for him at a few sites, but that cannot account for the sudden fall off in activity, which must largely have been caused by the effects of the Dutch raid on the Medway and blockade of the Thames.

It could hardly have been otherwise, given the general alarm and blow to confidence which was caused. With the withdrawal of the Dutch fleet and the coming of peace the process revived. Nevertheless, there had been an almost total standstill in the setting out of new sites, and perhaps of building activity, during the peak period of the building season.[23]

Thus, despite the efforts to clear the path for rebuilding to get under way in 1667, the process had made a disappointingly slow beginning, reflected in the comment in the autumn that 'ground goes even a begging, & there is soe much to be sold that it becomes every day cheaper than the other'. This was a gloomy summary, but a more accurate one than the report that perhaps 700 or 800 houses had been rebuilt by March 1668, which was a considerable over-estimate.[24]

The number of buildings erected in 1667 was indeed a feeble response to the scale of the preparation of the legislative and legal framework. As we have seen, the war and the Dutch raid created severe difficulties and not all owners had resolved their problems and were ready to build, but there were other reasons for the sluggish start to rebuilding. While the opportunities for suppliers were obvious, it took time to attain the necessary momentum in making materials available in London on the scale required to sustain the building effort. Timber had to be selected, felled, shipped and seasoned before use, for example. Large quantities were needed, to provide roof trusses, joists, floorboards, doors, windows and wainscotting, as well as the frames of the buildings, for the brickwork and stonework required by the rebuilding act were cladding, not the load-bearing structure. Owners of woodlands realised the implications of the fire and did respond to the opportunity. The Fishmongers' Company immediately ordered a halt to sales of timber at its estate at Bray, on the Thames in Berkshire and so ideally placed to benefit, and ordered its surveyor to begin moving stocks to its wharf in the City. By February 1667 sixty-two barge-loads had arrived there. Even so, output at Bray or elsewhere could not be increased rapidly, and the softwoods, together with walnut, mahogany and some of the oak, had to be brought from abroad.[25]

Brick and tile making also took time to get started and did not yield the quick profits which some had anticipated. Within two years of the fire Evelyn had lost £500 on his venture into brick-making, although he had 'presumed to have got a great deal of money' from the enterprise.[26]

Clay had to be dug during the autumn and weathered during the winter months so that it was ready for firing in the following summer. Inevitably, there was an initial lag between demand and supply, until both labour and materials were available in sufficient quantities to produce the output required for rebuilding. It seems unlikely that the brick-making industry could have responded swiftly enough in the autumn of 1666 to dig sufficient clay to make bricks and tiles in considerable quantities in the summer of 1667. Although roughly three million bricks could be produced from each acre of suitable brick earth, it took time to raise output to that level. Henry Tindall produced only 6,400 bricks in the year to the end of September 1667, roughly 1.4 million in each of the next two years and 2.7 million in 1669–70. This represented over 5.5 million bricks in the four years 1666–70, three-quarters of them in the second half of that period.[27] Tindall's production was a significant contribution to the supply required, but not a major one, for 30,000 bricks were needed to build the average post-fire house and 200,000 were delivered for the construction of John Pollexfen's mansion in Walbrook.[28]

The same problems were faced by suppliers of stone and lead. Not only did the quarry owners have to increase the output of stone, but adequate shipping had to be made available to move it to London. Dealers in lead gradually geared their activities to the demand in the City, which kept the price high and allowed them 'to sell deare', but it took time to increase production to meet the new levels of demand.[29] The slowness in accumulating materials on the scale needed provides part of the explanation for the limited numbers of buildings completed in the first year after the fire. That sluggishness, together with existing obligations, may have contributed to an equally slow build up of the skilled workforce required before output could be increased significantly.

Yet with the coming of peace, the recovery of trade and revival of confidence, the process gradually picked up during the remainder of the 1660s. Only six British ships entered the Baltic in 1667, but during the following four years the annual average was 125, an increase on the numbers recorded in the early 1660s. Coal shipments from the Tyne also recovered after 1667, to the level they had stood at before the war with the Dutch.[30] The extent of the revival in both trades was partly attributable to the demand generated by rebuilding. Those merchants who already had links with their counterparts in northern Europe naturally were the best placed to benefit from the opportunity, with timber the principal commodity. Charles Marescoe, the London agent for many Scandinavian merchants and manufacturers, did not handle any timber in 1664 or 1665, but received four consignments late in 1666 and nine more, worth almost £5,600, in 1667. Encouraged by the fact that a cargo of good timber had found a ready market in London, in March 1668 one of Marescoe's contacts in Stockholm wrote to enquire whether deals and balks would sell quickly and at a good price, promising to respond. The smaller traders, too, took advantage of the market for timber, for example by adding quantities of planks and balks of wood to cargoes of pitch and tar. Other building materials were also in demand. A merchant in Norrköping was able to offer Marescoe as many as thirty or forty shiploads of sandstone 'for churches or mansions', while suppliers of lead also benefited, with lead costing £31,648 being used on the City churches. Sir Thomas Bludworth, the erstwhile lord mayor, was to the fore in the lead trade, selling £574 worth of lead to the Fishmongers' Company for its new hall.[31] The high level of seaborne trade caused by the rebuilding was such that in 1669 the government permitted the acquisition of sixty more Dutch flyboats, and the need for crews for the shipping that was being employed kept seamen's wages at the high level which they had reached during the Second Dutch War.[32]

The increasing commercial activity was reflected in the progress of rebuilding. The new house being erected for the goldsmith John Colvill was far enough advanced in March 1668 for him to show it to an admiring Samuel Pepys, who noted that Lombard Street 'will be a very fine street'. In the same month the diarist walked along Thames Street where 'many brave houses' were being built and he was impressed enough by that street, which had been widened and raised since the fire, to remark that it promised to be 'mighty fine'.[33]

It was 1668, when 1,450 houses were built, that really saw the beginning of large-scale rebuilding and the momentum was sustained during the next few years. By the end of 1670 almost 7,000 sites had been surveyed and 6,000 houses built. The numbers erected gradually declined thereafter and the bulk of the replacement housing was completed by 1672. Significantly, the fire court's jurisdiction, which was extended in 1671 for a further year, finally came to an end on 29 September 1672. The agreements with tenants for sites on the corporation's Bridgehouse estate reflected the general chronology of rebuilding, with seventy-four of them reached in 1667–9, ten more in 1670 and only seven in 1671–2. Indeed, the bulk of the house-building came in 1668–71, when 85 per cent of the houses erected in the aftermath of the fire were built.

The process of recovery was so far advanced by 1671 that the king attended the lord mayor's show in that year and inspected the City 'the handsomest part of which has been rebuilt with greater magnificence since the terrible fire'.[34] A comment in March 1672 that the City, had 'recovered its selfe in a great measure out of its asshes' was true, so far as the houses were concerned and by the end of that year 8,000 had been built. Nevertheless, fewer were rebuilt than had been destroyed and demand for sites slackened off during the early 1670s, so that 1,000 plots were still not built on in 1673.[35] Even by the 1690s, the numbers of houses were still below the pre-fire level. A sample of eight parishes shows a fall of 22 per cent between 1638 and 1695, with just one of them, St Michael Queenhithe, having an increase, and that a modest one of only 8 per cent.[36]

The reduction in numbers of houses was partly due to the amalgamation of sites and the opportunity taken by some owners to build larger houses. This applied to both small and large buildings. The six pre-fire houses in Swan Alley off Fleet Street were replaced by four and in George Alley, Lombard Street, just five houses were built where nine had formerly stood.[37] At the other end of the property scale, Sir Robert Viner took the opportunity to enlarge his site in Lombard Street by incorporating that of the adjoining tavern, using the bigger plot to construct 'a wandering expanse of buildings and courtyard covering a quarter of an acre'. Charles Marescoe had been a tenant of a house in Fenchurch Street before the fire, but he did not return to the area. In 1669 he began to acquire adjoining sites in Thames Street and Tower Street, eventually putting together a substantial plot, at a cost of £2,210. Part of it was used for houses, four of which he rented out, and on the remainder he built himself a mansion which was completed by 1672, when it was assessed for the hearth tax at twenty-three hearths.[38] Viner's fellow goldsmith Edward Backwell was even more ambitious. Further enlarging a site in Lombard Street and Cornhill that he had already been in the process of acquiring before the fire, his building plans were such that when Pepys saw them he thought that the area resembled 'a little town'. Backwell's own new house contained twenty-one hearths and was considerably larger than that destroyed in the fire, which had been assessed on only thirteen hearths. On a smaller scale, and in a less prestigious setting, the grocer Abraham Jaggard was responsible for the building of 'a great many' houses in Thames Street.[39]

Such extensive developments suggest a degree of confidence, at least among some of the wealthier property owners. Other landlords were less optimistic, having found it difficult to persuade tenants to take their properties. In 1671 new buildings belonging to St Bartholomew's Hospital in Knightrider Street and Peter Hill were still unlet, partly because of their location, which was 'not good for trading'. But even a tavern in Newgate Street was unoccupied, four tenants having failed in three years 'for lack of trading', and the rent of an inn in Warwick Street quickly fell into arrears because of 'a great damp in trading'. In these circumstances landlords found it hard to attract and retain tenants and the survey taken in 1673 showed that almost 3,500, or 45 per cent, of the houses built after the fire remained unlet.[40]

The number of empty sites and the sluggishness of the rental market suggest that the City's fears that the rebuilding would not be complete had been justified. The position was not helped by the government's financial and foreign policies, which, once again, impinged on the rebuilding process. In January 1672 its financial difficulties, especially the farming of the revenues, led to the decision to halt payments from the exchequer until the end of the year and to resume direct collection of taxes from the tax farmers. This was such a blow to those goldsmith-bankers who had lent heavily to the government that it was said to have 'almost blasted their very root'. They, in their turn, refused to pay merchants the money which they had deposited with them and only the king's intervention, his assurance that the money was secure and that the goldsmiths would be repaid, restored normal business.[41]

The stop of the exchequer was followed in March 1672 by the outbreak of another war with the Dutch, this time with Britain in alliance with France. It was not successful. Clashes between the two fleets in the North Sea in 1672 and 1673 left the Dutch undefeated, their Smyrna and East India convoys returned home in 1672 largely unscathed, and there was no realistic possibility of Charles II raising an army for an invasion of the Low Countries in order to make territorial gains, while the negative effects of hostilities on trade were broadly similar to those of the Second Dutch War. The number of British ships entering the Baltic fell from the average of 125 per year for the period 1668 to 1671, to thirteen in 1672 and just eight in 1673. Fuel supplies were again affected, as they had been in the mid-1660s, for the amount of coal entering the port of London in 1672 was only 70 per cent of the average for 1668–71, with a further decline in 1673 to 65 per cent of that average.[42] Furthermore, with the successful French invasion of the United Provinces, which led to a collapse of business confidence and sharp falls in prices on the Amsterdam Exchange, together with the threat posed by British and French privateers, the Estates General kept their merchant and fishing fleets in port for almost two years. Very few ships ventured out of Dutch waters and so the trades in which they were the chief carriers, such as that in Norwegian and Baltic timber, were badly affected. Moreover, the British privateers were thereby balked of their intended prey, while the Dutch commerce raiders were very successful, taking at least 700 British vessels in the war and, as the Venetian envoy in London reported, 'the Zeeland privateers infest these coasts with impunity'. Accounts of the losses among British shipping and reports that 'many Dutch merchants are turned privateers to intercept our ships' made gloomy reading. The impact on trade was such that the London merchant community became increasingly disgruntled, having little or no gains to show and plenty of losses to absorb, with trade 'daily perishing'.[43] Even so loyal a servant of the Crown as John Evelyn commented that there was no justification for the war, which was begun 'but because the Hollander exceeded us in Industrie, & all things else but envy'.[44]

Wartime conditions were no more conducive to investment in building than they had been in the immediate aftermath of the fire. In addition, although there may have been stocks of building materials, such as the timber that was in the process of being seasoned, the fall off in supplies did begin to affect the building trade. Indeed, higher building costs and longer intervals between the commencement of building and completion suggest that a timber shortage existed in London by the autumn of 1672. So, too, did a scarcity of labour, the consequence of the activities in London of the press gangs, which were busy trying to man the fleet.[45]

By the time that the stop of the exchequer and the deleterious effects on trade of the Third Dutch War put a damper on the rebuilding of houses, many of the livery companies were well on their way to building their new halls. This was not done without difficulty, for some companies were in a precarious financial position, partly a legacy of their financial contributions to the Parliamentarian cause during the Civil War. The loss of their rental income in the fire and the need to grant tenants new leases without levying a fine, as an incentive to taking a building lease, further deprived them of potential revenue. Many companies decided to sell some of their plate and to appeal to their members for subscriptions. These and other expedients were generally successful, although the members of the Grocers' Company responded to a collection for funds to rebuild the hall with only £700.[46]

Despite the financial problems, the rebuilding of their halls was a priority for the companies, for both practical and symbolic reasons. Several of them, including the fishmongers, weavers, drapers and mercers, engaged Edward Jerman, the City surveyor, to design their new buildings and some delays may have been caused by his death in November 1668. Others were encountered in those cases where it was thought necessary to enlarge the site, as the Coopers' Company did by repossessing from its tenants the ground adjoining the company's hall on which a 'great messuage' had stood.[47] Generally, however, the rebuilding of the halls was carried out between 1668 and 1673, albeit with internal decorative work continuing for a few more years. In spite of the economic circumstances, most companies did not stint in the quality or the workmanship of the new buildings, externally or internally. The halls of the fishmongers, drapers and mercers each cost in the region of £13,000, that of the Barber Surgeons – which was thought by Pepys to be 'very fine' – cost £4,292, and the weavers' hall £2,929. However bleak the financial outlook may have seemed in 1666, forty-one of the forty-four company halls burnt in the fire were replaced.[48]

The corporation's finances were in no better state than those of the livery companies. Nevertheless, its credit remained good and it was eventually able to pay much of the cost of reconstructing its buildings from the coal dues. This source of funds was not immediately available, however. The second rebuilding act of 1670 allocated the City for this purpose just a quarter of the 2s duty, a sum which totalled no more than £40,296 by 1677. This covered only a relatively small part of the City's needs for reconstruction, carrying out improvements and compensating those whose ground was appropriated for street widening. The solution, reached in 1672, was to assign its rebuilding costs to the revenues from the coal dues, disregarding the constraints imposed by parliament and effectively bringing in a windfall of £123,000.[49]

Work on restoring Guildhall began in 1667 and the building was so far completed by 1671 for the annual civic ceremonies to be held there. The complex of buildings at Guildhall was finally completed by the end of 1674, with all but £982 of the total cost of £37,422 paid for from the coal dues fund. Other revenue from the fund was allocated for rebuilding the prisons at Poultry and Wood Street, the gates and prisons at Newgate and Ludgate, the Sessions House, and the cloth markets at Blackwell Hall and Welch Hall. New market sites were created at Honey Lane and in a new square between Newgate Street and Paternoster Row, and the Stocks Market, acquired from the bridgemasters of London Bridge, was remodelled on the site of St Mary Woolchurch Haw. By 1674 only Bridewell of the principal public buildings remained incomplete. An additional structure erected by the City, to commemorate the fire, was the Monument. This was built between 1671 and 1677 where the church of St Margaret, New Fish Street, had stood, close to the site of Thomas Farriner's house in Pudding Lane. It is a fluted Doric column of Portland stone, 202 feet tall, that is surmounted successively by a drum, a dome and a flaming gilt urn. An internal staircase leads to a square balcony above the capital.[50]

The Monument had a symbolic significance, as did the swift replacement of the Royal Exchange and the Custom House, both 'for the general encouragement of all citizens' and the commercial need to have them operational again. The importance of the Exchange was signified by the king's ceremonial visit to the site on 23 October 1667 to lay the first stone of the new building.[51] Yet initial uncertainty about how to proceed with the design, Jerman's death in 1668, negotiations for the enlargement of the site and problems with the delivery of the stone produced such delays that the merchants were not able to occupy the new building before September 1669 and the shopkeepers did not move in until March 1671. The announcement of the shopkeepers' return proudly described the new Exchange as 'that most Stately and most Magnificent piece of Building'. This was by no means exaggerated praise for Jerman's ambitious design which was based, like Gresham's building, around an arcaded courtyard with an elaborate street front and a lofty tower at its centre. But the decision, influenced by the king, to erect a larger and grander structure than the one which had been destroyed pushed the cost up to £55,000, with a further £7,000 spent on enlarging the site. The responsibility for rebuilding was shared by the City and the Mercers' Company. It proved a considerable financial embarrassment for the company, which also had to rebuild its hall and chapel, St Paul's school and the Whittington almshouses. Tenants could not be found for all of the shops in the Exchange and the rents from those which were let did not even cover the interest on the loans raised to pay for the building.[52]

The Custom House was the Crown's responsibility and its reconstruction on its previous site was promised in the king's proclamation of 13 September 1666, despite a preference in government circles for it to be moved upstream to Whitehall. This would have been a more convenient location for the administration, but in political terms it was difficult to take it out of the City, and the king decided not to do so. Although the early replacement of the building was regarded as an important element in the City's economic recovery, in a microcosm of the difficulties that arose right across the burnt area prolonged negotiations were needed before the tenurial problems were sorted out and responsibility for the new building was established. The site and the adjoining quays were held by Sir Anthony Cope, and he, his tenants and the wardens of Queen Elizabeth's school and almshouses in Sevenoaks, who had received £139 annually as the freeholders of a quay forming part of the site, appeared before the fire court in order to determine the arrangements for rebuilding. All of this took time and it was not until the summer of 1668 that the court, in a typical ruling, placed the responsibility with Cope and allocated the term and rent due from his tenants, also satisfying the wardens' claims.

Even then the beginning of the work was delayed, partly because the Crown decided to acquire the site and erect the building itself, and partly because the question of financing had to be resolved, including the contribution from the farmers of the customs. The treasury's warrant authorising the commencement of the work was not issued until 23 June 1669 and only then could Wren's design be executed. Despite economies, the total cost of the building was £10,272, compared with the estimates, based on an earlier scheme, that £5,000 or £6,000 would be required. The customs officers may have been operating from their new building by September 1670, four years after the fire, although the king's undertaking in its immediate aftermath had been to 'use all the expedition We can' in the rebuilding.[53]

Both the Royal Exchange and the Custom House were replacements of existing buildings, albeit taking longer to erect and proving more expensive than anticipated. The City's improvement of the Fleet river, on the other hand, was a new scheme of public improvement, taking advantage of the opportunity provided by the fire. The need to improve the condition of the river itself and the insalubrious area around it, together with the potential commercial value offered by its banks, prompted the City to embark on a major project whereby the river below Holborn Bridge was straightened and canalised. Quays 40 feet wide were built alongside it on both banks, backed by large storehouses. The scheme was designed under Wren's direction and in consultation with Robert Hooke and John Oliver, acting for the City, and was completed by the end of 1674 at a cost of £51,307. This ambitious improvement can be counted a success in technical and constructional terms, but it failed as a commercial venture. Insufficient lighter traffic was attracted to the canal and the wharfage dues and rents of the storehouses were also lower than had been anticipated. By the 1720s it was 'very much neglected, and out of repair . . . the wharfs in many places are decayed and fallen in, which make it all look ruinous'. In 1733 the stretch of the canal between Holborn Bridge and Fleet Bridge was arched over and in 1766 this was also done over the remaining section below Fleet Bridge, a disappointing end for 'a work of great magnificence and expense'.[54]

The Thames Quay was a similar and more extensive improvement, provided for in the legislation and allowed for by the decrees of the fire court. Yet it was not constructed as planned, despite receiving almost universal support immediately after the fire. The scheme involved the clearing away of the host of narrow streets and passages down to the river and the construction of a quay, at least 40 feet wide, along the whole of the north bank of the Thames affected by the fire, from the Temple to the Tower. Its objectives were an open space separating the fire hazards of the vessels in the river from the buildings, ease of movement for traffic to and from the quays, and 'an open gracefull key' that was aesthetically preferable to a waterfront crowded with buildings running up to the water's edge. A more elaborate and ambitious version of the plan included the construction of an embankment, with the quay built out into the river, creating a uniform river front and removing the various indentations formed by the docks.

The rear line of the quay was duly set out and buildings between it and the river were prohibited, with the notable exception of Fishmongers' Hall just above the bridge. But further implementation of the plan was not feasible, chiefly because the City, aware of the enormous cost, did not attempt to acquire the land within the area of the quay, as was done along the Fleet, and to compel all of the owners to comply with the requirements would have been a difficult and expensive undertaking. Even the effective enforcement of the prohibition of all structures except cranes along the river front proved to be a problem, for the quay owners needed sheds and enclosures for storage, and their properties were divided by fences and walls. Yet the ban on permanent buildings was maintained and achieved many of the aims of the plan. Furthermore, although the scheme as a whole was not executed, piecemeal improvements were made by individual owners, by building out into the river and bringing the surface of adjoining wharves to a common level. The intention to construct a grand quay may have been frustrated, but the more limited objective of an open space along the river front, as envisaged by many in the aftermath of the Great Fire, was indeed realised.[55]

While the new houses and public buildings were beginning to appear in the devastated area, work had not started on the churches. There was little urgency, for although the parishes continued to operate as before so far as their administrative functions were concerned, until the population returned there was no need for places of worship. This situation had changed by 1670, when the decision on the number of new churches to be built was included in the second rebuilding act. By the end of the 1660s so many new houses had been built that the returning citizens required places in which to worship and so temporary buildings, commonly referred to as tabernacles, were constructed for the purpose. The first of these was set up in 1669 at All Hallows the Great, Thames Street. This was described as a shed and stood on the burial ground, but in some cases, as at St Michael, Wood Street, and St Mary Magdalen, Fish Street Hill, the ruins of the churches were extensive and safe enough for temporary accommodation to be provided by roofing over a section of the remains. Eventually, thirty such tabernacles were erected and, in addition, eight Nonconformist meeting houses were taken over.[56]

The design of the post-fire churches was entrusted to Christopher Wren, who began work on them in June 1670 and was responsible for all fifty-one required by the second rebuilding act. They were funded by the receipts from the coal dues, in some cases directly and in others by way of repayment of sums already advanced by the parishioners. Benefactors also contributed to the costs, in many instances by paying for the fittings, but in others providing funds for the actual fabric, such as the bequest of £5,000 by Henry Rogers for the erection of the nave of St Mary Aldermary. Considerable sums were raised from donations and revenue was also obtained by selling the bell metal, lead, iron, bricks and stone recovered from the ruins. By April 1671 such sales and contributions from parishioners had raised £1,500 at St Mary-at-Hill and £1,000 more was donated within the next two years, while loans totalling £500 were advanced towards the rebuilding of St Mary Aldermanbury, which were repaid in 1674. St Mildred, Poultry, benefited by the donation of a ton of iron by the ironmaster William Morgan. Where practicable, costs could be reduced by repairing surviving parts of the pre-fire buildings, such as the tower at St Mary Aldermary and the walls at St Vedast, Foster Lane, and St Christopher-le-Stocks, or by building on the old foundations, as at St Michael, Queenhithe. Despite the need for some parishes to economise, and the shortages of labour and materials, by 1678 the work done on thirty-two churches had cost £165,000 and ten years later the churches had received £265,467 from the coal dues.[57]

Wren was under considerable pressure in the early 1670s from impatient vestries that were anxious to press ahead with rebuilding. A start was made on sixteen churches before the end of 1670 and four more were begun in the following year. The vestry (or assembly of parishioners) of St Lawrence Jewry noted in February 1671 that 'Rebuilding does not go on as fast as was hoped' and in December of that year the churchwardens of St Magnus the Martyr were given a budget 'for the expediting and more vigorous carrying on the Building' which, the vestry felt, 'went but slowly forward all the last summer'. Wren was presented with gifts to reward his attentiveness and encourage him for the future. The churchwardens at St Mary Aldermanbury were instructed to pay him twenty guineas and Robert Hooke six guineas 'that they may be encouraged to assist in the perfecting' of the new church, and the vestry of St Mary Abchurch paid Wren twenty guineas for 'incouraging the forwarding of the building' of their church. The vestry at St Mary-le-Bow showed rather more subtlety in presenting twenty guineas to Wren's wife 'to incuridg and hast in the rebuilding the church' and entertaining both of them at a dinner at the Swan in Old Fish Street, although after the building was finished they were more direct and gave him a hogshead of claret.[58]

With such determination from the vestries and the finance provided by the coal dues, the work went ahead steadily during the 1670s. By 1678 Wren had prepared the designs of thirty-six churches. St Bride's, Fleet Street, was ready for worship in December 1675, having cost £11,430, excluding the steeple, making it the fourth most expensive of the new City churches, after St Mary-le-Bow, St Lawrence Jewry (the corporation's church) and Christ Church, Newgate Street.[59] By 1679 fifteen churches were finished and work was under way on nineteen more, while four years later twenty-five churches were built and another seventeen were nearing completion. Even so, work on three more had only begun in the early 1680s and six others were not started until 1684–6.[60] Such delays did not necessarily reflect tardiness on the part of those vestries. A committee was established by the newly united parishes of St Mary Abchurch and St Lawrence Pountney in June 1670 to deal with such questions as the raising of money and 'the form of building the Church'. The vestry did not let the matter rest, pressing in 1672 for Wren's attention regarding the demolition of the ruins of St Mary Abchurch and 'Rebuilding again the . . . Parish Church'. Nevertheless, it was not until 1681 that an order for the rebuilding was obtained and, despite several gratuities to Wren, his clerk and Henry Doogood the plasterer, the new, and relatively small, church was not ready until the spring of 1686, with payments to the joiner and wood-carver continuing until the end of the decade.[61]

Completion was generally taken to be when the interior fittings were installed and so the building was ready for use, but not necessarily when the tower or steeple was raised, which may have been some years later. Steeples were added to St Magnus the Martyr in 1705, St James Garlickhithe in 1714–17, St Michael Paternoster Royal in 1715–17 and to St Stephen Walbrook in 1717, for example.[62] Such delays reflected the need to assign the revenues from the coal dues to the construction of the churches themselves, and only when they had been built were funds released for towers and steeples. The parish officers of St Bride's made representations about the construction of the steeple to their church in 1682–3 and again in 1696, but it was not until 1701 that the first stone was laid and the work was not completed until 1703.[63] Excluding such additions, most of the fifty-one churches were finished before the end of the 1680s and the last six to be started were all in use by 1695. They cost an average of almost £5,400 each, a figure which conceals a range of costs that reflected their differing scale and the variety of their internal and external decoration, and also omits many of the steeples. Their total cost, including an estimate for the steeples, was roughly £326,000.[64]

Not all of the churches had to be completely rebuilt. St Dunstan-in-the-East and St Mary Woolnoth were not so badly damaged in the fire that they could not be restored. St Dunstan's largely survived the flames and was repaired by Wren, who added the tower and spire. He also repaired St Mary's, although it was demolished in 1716 and replaced by a new building designed by Nicholas Hawksmoor. Similarly, considerable sections of the pre-fire fabric of St Mary-at-Hill were incorporated by Wren into the new church, but subsequently had to be replaced. The tower was repaired after the fire and again in 1694–5, yet by the late eighteenth century it was in a bad condition and was substantially rebuilt in 1787–8, while the side walls were reconstructed as part of a programme of renovation undertaken in 1826–7.[65]

The adaptation of the surviving fabric was also considered at St Paul's Cathedral, with a proposal that the west end should be fitted up for worship, albeit on a temporary basis. Work began on the implementation of this plan, but had to be abandoned when a part of the masonry in that area collapsed.[66] In July 1668 a royal warrant authorised the demolition of the remains of the building and Wren was entrusted with the design of its replacement.

In destroying St Paul's the fire had resolved a major problem, for by the 1660s the great cathedral required a substantial amount of work. A lightning strike on the spire in 1561 had started a blaze which had spread rapidly and destroyed not only the spire, but also much of the roof. Although the roof was restored within five years, the spire was not replaced. Furthermore, falling timbers during the fire had cracked the vault and, as a result, in certain places the walls and pillars were no longer perpendicular. A campaign of repairs and restoration was begun in 1628 by William Laud during his time as Bishop of London and continued by his successor, William Juxon. This was designed to enhance the dignity of the cathedral and included the removal of the buildings that had clustered around it in the early seventeenth century. The clearance even included the demolition of the parish church of St Gregory, in 1638. By the time of the Great Fire St Paul's stood isolated in its churchyard 'on every side remote from houses', although this had not saved it from the conflagration. Improvements to the cathedral itself that were carried out during the 1630s, to the designs of Inigo Jones, included the addition of a Corinthian-style portico at the west end and the recasing of the nave, with classical pilasters replacing the buttresses.[67] In fact, this work had a number of structural defects that became evident after the Great Fire. In particular, his new casing was not satisfactorily tied in to the existing structure.[68]

Because of neglect and damage during the Civil War and Commonwealth, by the Restoration the fabric required further substantial renovation. The king set up a commission in 1663 to consider what should be done. Some commissioners thought that a repair of the existing structure would be sufficient, but others, including Evelyn and Wren, favoured a more drastic programme. Wren's proposals, submitted in May 1666, included the rearrangement of the interior and the construction of a lofty dome over the crossing to replace the existing tower. Towards the end of August the commissioners surveyed the building, accompanied by 'severall expert Workmen', and adopted Wren's scheme, but the fire made it redundant before it could be started.[69]

Wren's plans for the new cathedral had to satisfy both the aesthetic tastes of those with influence at court and the liturgical requirements of the clergy. Cost was also an important factor and his first scheme was for a relatively small building, which was opposed not only by Sir Roger Pratt on architectural grounds, but also because it was not grand enough. His next design, based on a Greek cross, with an extension to the westward arm, met with criticism because it did not have the traditional layout. In particular, it lacked a distinct choir, having the choir stalls placed on the segments of a circle, and Wren's low screen and gates were thought insufficient to separate it effectively from the remainder of the building. Moreover, the high altar could not have been seen from several parts of the church. It must also have been obvious that it was not going to be a cheap building. A solution to the problem of funding was to build the new cathedral in sections, completing the choir first and adding the remainder of the building as money became available. Allowing for that approach and providing a building that fulfilled the clergy's needs, by 1675 Wren had produced a design that consisted of a Latin cross with a choir of three bays, with an additional half-bay and apse at the east end, a nave of five bays with aisles, and transepts each of which was of three bays. Externally, the elevation of the nave broadly resembled that created by Jones in the 1630s, as did the portico. It was this essentially conservative design that was approved by the king's warrant authorising construction, which was issued in May 1675. The foundation stone was laid on 21 June.[70]

Once it was accepted that no part of the existing fabric could be kept in use, work on demolishing the remains went ahead. Gunpowder was used on two occasions to help break down the remains of the old fabric and a battering ram was eventually employed for the purpose. Although Pepys was impressed to see how quickly and easily the work was proceeding in the summer of 1668, the task proved an enormous one. By 1671 it was reported that no further demolition could be carried out because the site was full of the old materials and it was agreed that some of them should be sold, the timber and usable stone for the parish churches and the rag stone – 'which most encumbreth the ground' – to paviers. Clearance of the site was not completed until 1676. In all, 47,000 loads of rubbish were carted away for sorting and the retrieval of material that could be re-used.[71]

While the delay before building could begin had been considerable, it had the advantage that labour and materials were more readily available than they had been during the years when much of the rebuilding of the City had been taking place. By 1675 most of the secular buildings and some of the churches were completed, and the war with the Dutch had come to an end. Pressure on the funds from the coal dues had not entirely eased, however, and the commissioners entrusted by the king with overseeing the rebuilding of St Paul's harassed the City authorities, claiming that part of the allocation for the cathedral and the remaining churches was being withheld. By 1687, when parliament renewed the coal duty, the majority of the churches had been completed and so the bulk of the funds could be devoted to the cathedral. Before 1687 St Paul's received an average of £6,000 each year from that source, thereafter the comparable figure was £18,500.[72]

Although the increasing inflow of money from the coal dues helped to speed up progress, the scale of the work and the quantities of materials required made it inevitable that the building would take many years to complete. Unforeseen problems with the subsoil at the north-east corner added to the delays and expense. Nevertheless, work proceeded on several portions of the building simultaneously, and contracts were placed for the other sections several years before the choir was finished. Wren's preference was for Portland stone, and 50,322 tons were brought to the site at a cost of £81,357, over half of which was accounted for by the expense of carriage, together with 25,573 tons of stone from other quarries, which added a further £53,594. The total cost of the building was £738,845.[73]

By 1694 the new St Paul's was so far advanced that Evelyn was able to pass judgement, criticising indeed 'the placing Columns upon Pilasters, at the East Tribunal', but otherwise finding it 'certainly a piece of Architecture without reproch'. The choir was first used at the service held on 2 December 1697 to celebrate the Treaty of Ryswick, which ended the war with France, and the remainder of the building was brought into use in the next few years.[74]

Neither the idea of erecting the building by stages nor the design approved in the warrant of 1675 had come to pass. The king had permitted Wren 'liberty in the prosecution of this work to make some variations, ornamental rather than essential, as from time to time he should see proper' without requiring permission for each one, and this he took advantage of.[75] Almost from the outset, he set about adapting the design, although not limiting himself to 'ornamental' modifications, with the result that both the external appearance and the internal layout were considerably modified in the course of the work. The transepts were shortened by one bay, for example, considerable changes were made to the arrangement of the nave, the outer walls were continued above the roofs of the aisles to the full height of the nave and choir as 'false walls', side chapels were built at the west end that projected beyond the aisles, the two west towers were added and the two-storey portico of paired columns was substituted in place of the lower one of single columns that had been proposed. Perhaps most importantly, the design for a shallow dome with a tall drum above it that was topped with a lofty steeple of six stages (which has been described as 'a most grotesque design') was not executed.[76] Instead Wren reverted to the central dome that he had conceived for the pre-fire improvement of the cathedral and had also used for his design based on a Greek cross, although further developing that idea. Work on the dome was under way by 1706 and the building was completed in 1710, thirty-five years after it was begun and forty-four years after the Great Fire.

Any estimate of the total cost of the rebuilding of the City can be only a rough one. Allowing for a figure of £500 for building a house, rather than the £300 suggested in a contemporary calculation, produces a sum in the region of £4 million for housing.[77] St Paul's, the churches and chapels cost £1 million, or slightly more. The City's most expensive projects were the River Fleet improvement, the restoration of Guildhall, its share of the expense of rebuilding the Royal Exchange, and the construction of the Monument, which together cost roughly £132,000. By 1688 it had received £342,500 from the coal dues for rebuilding, improvements and compensation for owners who lost ground taken for street widening. Other expenditure was incurred by the livery companies for rebuilding their halls and the schools and almshouses for which they were responsible. The Crown bore the cost of the Custom House, and such buildings as Doctors' Commons and the College of Arms also had to be rebuilt. If £500,000 is allowed for the outlay by the companies and on the various other buildings, then the total cost of buildings and other post-fire improvements may tentatively be put at a figure approaching £6 million.

The completion of St Paul's and the addition of the steeples to some of the churches in the early eighteenth century mark the end of the post-fire rebuilding, but the bulk of the work had been finished much earlier, in the early 1670s. Indeed, much of the construction work on both the houses and the public buildings took place between the Second and Third Dutch Wars, that is in 1668–71. Despite some gaps in the frontages, empty church sites and the remaining ruins of St Paul's, by 1672 the City had largely recovered from the fire and a claim that it was 'well nigh rebuilded' within four or five years of the Great Fire was only a mild exaggeration.[78]

SIX

THE AFTERMATH

Divers Churches, the stately Guildhall, many Halls of Companies, and other Publick Edifices; all infinitely more Uniform, more Solid, and more Magnificent than before: So that no City in Europe (nay, scarcely in the World) can stand in Competition with it.

A Survey of the Cities of London and Westminster . . . By John Stow,
ed. John Strype (1720), book 1, chapter xxviii

From a horrified realisation that the Great Fire had been 'as tirrible a fire as ever was heard of' contemporaries gradually turned their attention to the rebuilding and then to its effects.[1] Yet while the transformation that the fire had wrought could be admired, the conflagration itself was an experience that those who had lived through it would never forget and one which they feared could be repeated. Pepys suffered sleeplessness and nightmares for many months afterwards 'with dreams of fire and falling down of houses'.[2] Presumably many others were troubled in the same way.

The old complacency regarding fire was replaced by a more urgent response to the many scares that followed the disaster. In June 1668, for example, Pepys was again called in the night and told of a blaze a few streets away. This time there was no question of taking a look and then going back to bed. His immediate reaction was to secure his gold and papers, but first he went to see where the outbreak was and realised that many others had reacted in the same way, for 'the whole town was presently in the streets'. Despite assuring himself that the fire was in a new brick house standing alone, he went to Allhallows church and watched from the roof until he was sure that the flames were dying down. When Pepys wrote up his account of this alarm he noted with satisfaction that 'the benefit of brick was well seen, for it burnt all inward and fell down within itself – so no fear of doing more hurt'.[3]

In addition to the important decision to enforce rebuilding in brick and tile, the practical measures taken after the fire included the replacement of the fire-fighting equipment that had been lost and destroyed. As early as February 1667 the parish vestry of St Martin Outwich bought two dozen new buckets and later in that year the Common Council made an order aimed at the comprehensive provision of new apparatus. It divided the City into four districts, each of which was required to maintain 800 buckets and 50 ladders, together with shovels, pickaxe-sledges and two hand-held squirts in every parish. Each of the twelve principal livery companies was instructed to provide an engine, thirty buckets, six pickaxe-sledges, three ladders and two squirts, while the lesser ones were to equip themselves with small engines and buckets at the lord mayor's direction. In addition, the aldermen were to keep equipment on their own premises. In response to this order the Drapers' Company bought two dozen buckets and in 1670–1 added a dozen more, together with a new fire-engine, and in January 1671 the court of the Ironmongers' Company ordered that an engine should be acquired. The wards, too, set about restoring their equipment. In 1670 the Cornhill ward-mote ordered the purchase of an engine, leather buckets, ladders and smaller implements.[4] Deployment of the engines seems to have been efficient enough; eight were taken to a fire in Creed Lane near St Paul's in 1679 and another blaze on the same day, in Fetter Lane, was quickly dealt with, 'all things being in a readiness it was almost as soon out as in'.[5]

In the 1720s Daniel Defoe echoed Howel's comment made almost seventy years earlier, writing that 'no city in the world is so well furnished for the extinguishing fires'. He supported this by describing the water supply, 'the great number of admirable engines' and the speed of response to an alarm, especially by the crews employed by the fire insurance companies. Almost every parish and a number of the livery companies had engines, as indeed did some of the citizens, so that soon after a fire had broken out, the house was 'surrounded with engines'. This reaction, he explained, was all the more necessary because of Londoners' incorrigible carelessness with fire.[6]

Earlier schemes for fire insurance had not matured, but in the aftermath of the Great Fire Nicholas Barbon, who was to become one of the greatest speculative builders in late seventeenth-century London, saw the opportunity and set up his 'Insurance Office'. The fire had demonstrated the inherent risks in such a venture, while on the other hand the rebuilding had lessened the hazards by enforcing stricter building regulations than before. Barbon quickly attracted business. Evidently he was not too selective in the premises which he insured, being prepared to grant a policy for a property in Redcross Street, outside the rebuilt area, occupied by a soapboiler, although that was a distinctly high-risk trade. Nevertheless, the success of his new business attracted imitators; the Phoenix and Hand-in-Hand were established before the end of the century and by the time that Defoe was writing six companies were operating in London.[7] It was obviously in the companies' interest to reduce the incidence of fire as far as possible and natural for them to set up teams of fire-fighters, supplementing the precautions taken by the City, livery companies and parish authorities.

Other cities and towns had reacted to the news of the Great Fire by renewing their own precautions. In an obvious and immediate response, on 15 September 1666 the Common Council at Bristol stipulated that bakers should store fuel only in their houses and not make piles of wood elsewhere. The authorities at a number of towns were prompted to check their fire-fighting equipment. On 10 September it was ordered that Reading's fire-engines should be tested and kept ready for use, and fifteen days later Exeter's Common Council specified the number of buckets that the parishes in the city should provide, which would have made 270 available from that source alone.[8] In November Beverley corporation ordered that two dozen buckets and two fire-hooks should be bought. A comprehensive scheme, similar to that in London, was introduced at Bristol in November 1668, which required the parishes, gild companies, aldermen, common councillors and individual citizens to provide a total of twenty-eight ladders, six fire-hooks and 1,523 buckets, while the corporation was to buy a second fire-engine.[9] The Great Fire clearly did much to heighten awareness throughout the country of the need to make proper provision in case of fire.

Despite the precautions and provision of equipment, fires continued to occur in the City. While the rebuilding after 1666 considerably reduced the likelihood of multiple house-fires, it did not remove it entirely. A blaze which began in Thames Street in 1715, when a boy making fireworks accidentally set off some gunpowder and blew up the house, spread and destroyed more than 100 houses in the vicinity.

The less-well-regulated and more shoddily built areas downstream were even more prone to such accidents. A fire at Shadwell in 1673 destroyed almost 100 houses, many of which were 'very old'; a few weeks later there was another, but less destructive, outbreak in an alley near East Cheap and a blaze at Wapping in 1682 caused losses valued at £56,394.[10] Attempts to impose controls were never tight enough to curb the problem entirely and in 1794 a conflagration at Ratcliff swept away 455 houses and 36 warehouses in one of the biggest urban fires of the eighteenth century. Nor was the south bank of the Thames secure. A blaze in Southwark in 1667 made forty families homeless and the area suffered from a devastating fire in 1676 which destroyed 624 houses.[11]

The reaction to the fire at Southwark in 1676 was to obtain an Act of Parliament to control the reconstruction, modelled on London's rebuilding acts. This had already been done in the aftermath of the fire at Northampton in the previous year and was to be copied on five further occasions, following the fires at Warwick in 1694, Blandford Forum and Tiverton in 1731, Wareham in 1765 and Chudleigh in 1807. As at London, commissioners were appointed and fire courts were set up to settle differences arising from the fires in order to promote rebuilding, to ensure that fireproof materials were used in the reconstruction and to make specific topographical improvements. Although the acts were based on those for London – that for Warwick included some passages taken directly from that legislation – they varied from them in some significant respects. For example, the town council at Northampton was excluded from the rebuilding process, while at London the corporation had been given a major role, and, although the legislation for London had contained detailed constructional specifications, the act for Northampton directed only that lead, slate or tile should be used to roof all buildings in future, and other constructional requirements were left to the fire court to determine. The act for Blandford was similar to that for Northampton in that respect, although it seems to have been the property disputes that had arisen after the fire which prompted the decision to obtain an act, rather than the need for parliamentary sanction to enforce the use of non-flammable materials.[12]

Not all of the features of London's rebuilding were universally applicable. This was certainly the case with the height specified for the second, third and fourth categories of buildings, for such tall three- and four-storey houses would have been inappropriate in the smaller provincial towns. Some adaptation was necessary and at Warwick it was decided that even the principal streets were to be lined with houses of two storeys and garrets, a modification of London's first category, with three-storey ones specified only for the intersection of the streets at the centre of the town, on its most prestigious sites. As in London, the topographical improvements imposed by the commissioners in these towns were limited and in none of them was there a wholesale revision of the street layout, although the uniformity of building materials brought a major visual change. The social effects of the legislation and rebuilding were also similar. As the London rebuilding acts produced social zoning by categorising the streets and specifying the type and size of houses in each category, so the commissioners at Warwick and Northampton created town centres that attracted members of the gentry and the professions.[13]

The practical effect of such reconstruction in reducing the incidence of large-scale fires was unquestionable, and the aesthetic benefits of rebuilding after a fire were also widely appreciated. Celia Fiennes was very impressed with Warwick, noting that 'the streetes are very handsome and the buildings regular and fine', and she also admired Northampton, as did Defoe, who described it as 'finely rebuilt with brick and stone'.[14] Such favourable reactions were not confined to those towns where rebuilding had been regulated by a fire court. A blaze in the small Lincolnshire town of Caistor in 1681 destroyed 'poor mean' buildings that were replaced by 'good modern' ones, prompting the remark that 'it is observed that every town is bettered exceedingly by being purified by fire'.[15] A social transformation was noted at Hingham in Norfolk, where a fire in 1688 was followed by rebuilding 'in a finer form, and the inhabitants, suitable to the place, are taken notice of as a gentile sort of people, so fashionable in their dress that the town is called by the neighbours "Little London".'[16] The changes to the fabric took longer where a major fire did not intervene to enforce reconstruction within a few years, but piecemeal rebuilding and refronting with brick gradually achieved the desired effects.

The move towards the adoption of brick and tile had begun in London well before the Great Fire, partly enforced by the building regulations. Their resistance to fire and the clear evidence that the prohibition of thatch was not enough to prevent the spread of a major blaze ensured that they would be adopted not only there, but also in most other cities and towns. By the early eighteenth century building in brick and tile, in the classical style, was being widely adopted. The example of London was of great importance in the process. In architecture, as with so many things – fashions in dress, decoration and modes of behaviour – the capital provided a model for the rest of the country.

Yet the adoption of the classical style marked a relatively recent change in taste. Classical ideas in planning and architecture had become increasingly widely known in England during the seventeenth century, partly through the powerful advocacy of Inigo Jones. But during Jones's lifetime it had remained largely a courtly style. Opposition within the City was reflected in the disagreement between Jones and the parishioners of St Michael-le-Querne over the style of their new parish church, a dispute that was probably won by the parishioners.[17]

Such resistance faced a major challenge with the erection of Wren's churches, which were seen as an opportunity to rectify English Protestantism's neglect in providing places of worship. Much effort had been put into building almshouses and hospitals, but not 'Works of pure Piety for advancing the Worship, the Praise, and the Glory of our Creator, which ought to be regarded in the first place'.[18] The new churches were indeed designed for Protestant worship, with their interiors arranged to suit services in which preaching played a major part, with all members of the congregation seated within comfortable hearing distance of the pulpit. This meant that the long nave at Christ Church, Newgate Street, for example, was not appropriate and Wren replaced it with a much shorter building occupying only the site of the former chancel. Indeed, many of his smaller churches, such as St Martin, Ludgate, and St Anne & St Agnes, were almost square. The use of galleries increased the seating capacity available close to the pulpit. The exteriors, too, were in marked contrast to those of their predecessors, especially where the towers and steeples were given lavish classical detail. But the new churches were not universally admired. Even St Paul's came in for criticism, with one of the humorist Ned Ward's characters describing it as 'more like half a goose pie' than a church.[19] Defoe was not entirely impressed by the churches and commented that some of them were 'rather deformed than beautified' by their spires. He did admire those at St Bride, Fleet Street, St Antholin and St Margaret Pattens, but he also favoured the towers at St Michael, Cornhill, St Mary Aldermary and St Christopher as 'not the worst in all the city'.[20] Perhaps the earlier wariness of the classical style had not been completely overcome, although the designs of the new City churches were imitated in provincial towns in the early eighteenth century.[21] The architect of St George's at Great Yarmouth, built in 1714–16, was John Price of Wandsworth, who clearly drew his ideas from Wren's churches, and the tower of All Saints, Bristol, of 1711–16 was inspired by that of St Magnus the Martyr.[22]

The skyline formed by the churches and the great dome of St Paul's was in marked contrast to that of the pre-fire City. So, too, was the appearance of the streets, which had undergone a dramatic change. Yet although the new City was much admired and the buildings were described as 'infinitely more beautiful, more commodious, and more solid' than their predecessors, the longed-for uniformity along their frontages had not been achieved. Neither Hawksmoor nor Evelyn would have agreed with the Reverend Kirk's judgement that 'Since the burning, all London is built uniformly, the streets broader, the houses all of one form and height'. Indeed, both expressed their disappointment with the result of the rebuilding, complaining about the quality of workmanship and the failure to produce a handsome and soundly built city.[23] Hawksmoor was particularly severe, contrasting the 'convenient regular well built Citty' that might have been expected to rise from the ashes of the fire, with the reality, which consisted of 'a Chaos of Dirty Rotten Sheds, allways Tumbling or takeing fire, with winding Crooked passages (Scarse practicable) Lakes of Mud and Rills of Stinking Mire Running through them'.[24]

Evelyn blamed the lack of 'more solid Directions' for the variety in appearance. In fact, small units of ownership, differences in decoration, balconies and doorways, and the stepped effect caused in streets built on an incline, had all prevented the creation of uniform fronts. According to Nicholas Barbon, the appearance of a house owed much to the trade of the master-builder responsible for it. He claimed to be able to recognise whether the master-builder was a bricklayer, stone mason, glazier or carpenter.[25] A greater variety in the appearance of the façades was possible because of the differing finishes of the bricks that were produced following the development of the London stock brick in the immediate aftermath of the fire. The London stock was produced by the addition of a mixture of ash and other materials, known as Spanish, to the clay. This practice of 'soiling' was later said to have originated in the production of bricks for the new Royal Exchange, when 'clear Sea-coal Ashes' were used. By the early eighteenth century it was arousing concern, partly because brickmakers had taken to including not just ash but almost any rubbish, even 'the Slop and Drift of the Streets', in the mixture, and partly because if they used too much Spanish, defective and weakened bricks were produced.[26] Builders also succumbed to the temptation of adulterating mortar, by the inclusion of earth with the lime. When an unfinished house in Lombard Street collapsed in 1668 the accident, and several similar ones, was attributed to the use of 'bad mortar and bricks'.[27]

The regulations contained in the rebuilding acts had not been specific enough to prevent such effects. Perhaps uniformity of appearance could only have come with large-scale changes of ownership and a rearrangement of sites, indeed with the implementation of the kind of ideas that were considered immediately after the fire but dismissed as impracticable. In fact, property boundaries were scarcely altered in the aftermath of the disaster and the post-fire surveys can form the basis for the reconstruction of the earlier pattern.[28]

Nor was the street plan greatly altered, apart from the changes decided on at the outset. The widening and paving of the streets was an undoubted benefit, as was the rebuilding of the Fleet Bridge and the construction of the new approach to Guildhall. Other work that was carried out as part of the post-fire street improvements was the easing of the gradient of the streets running down to the quays west of the Tower as far as St Andrew's Hill, which made the descent 'very easy and pleasant'.[29] But the changes did not go so far as eliminating the alleys of the earlier City, most of which were rebuilt. This had been a feature which the king's proclamation of 13 September 1666 had sought to remove, as had Richard Newcourt's plan for the new City, for he deplored the 'multitude of bye-lanes, rooks and alleys, huddled up one on the neck of another'. The courtyard houses of the wealthy merchants, characteristic of the medieval City, were also rebuilt. They were described as 'magnificent with courts, offices and all other necessary apartments enclosed to themselves' and admired for the richness of the decorations.[30] Yet despite the money and pride lavished upon them, such complexes were not necessarily up to date in stylistic terms. That of John Pollexfen cost £3,351 and included a warehouse and counting house, although the house was somewhat old-fashioned, both in terms of such features as its windows and its internal arrangements.[31]

Those with regrets for the survival of the pre-fire layout and what came to be seen as a lost opportunity have particularly censured the failure to implement Wren's plan. This train of criticism can be traced back to the 1730s and was furthered by the architect John Gwynn, who produced a version of the plan in 1749, claiming that it had been approved by parliament and then 'unhappily defeated by faction'. It was given added credibility by passages in *Parentalia*, an account of Christopher Wren's work written by his son, edited by his grandson and published in 1750. The editor, Stephen Wren, went much further than expressing regret that the plan had not been implemented and in uncompromising terms laid the blame on the self-interest of the citizens, with their 'obstinate Averseness . . . to alter their old Properties'. He also alleged that the practicability of the scheme had been assessed at the time and that it had been shown that it could have been carried through 'without Loss to any Man, or Infringement of any Property'.[32] The image conjured up was a powerful one of scheming opponents and unimaginative and obstructive citizens, and this was often repeated, despite its divergence from the truth. Wren's plan certainly had an appeal for later generations and the portrayal of the visionary architect whose proposals were frustrated by narrow-minded and selfish dullards helped to fuel the disappointment. Yet although his and the other schemes drawn up in the aftermath of the fire were not adopted for a new layout of the City, they did have an influence on future town planning, both in theoretical and practical terms. Newcourt's rigidly geometrical design, for example, may have been inappropriate for London, but it formed the basis for the setting out of two cities in North America: Philadelphia in 1683 and Savannah in 1733.[33]

The City as actually rebuilt is delineated on Ogilby and Morgan's map of 1676. Ogilby himself had soon set about repairing his fortunes after his losses in the fire and obtained the backing and financial support of the Court of Aldermen for a new plan of the City. The destruction of stocks of previous maps in the disaster and the need for the careful surveying of the streets and building plots in its aftermath provided an unprecedented stimulus for surveyors and map makers. This had been foreseen by William Leybourn, who had been one of the surveyors of the ruined area after the Great Fire. In 1667 he published a practical guide containing advice for surveyors in their use of Edmund Gunter's logarithmic line. Leybourn was engaged by Ogilby as the surveyor for the new plan of the City and although Ogilby died in September 1676 the project was taken over and completed by his widow's grandson, William Morgan. The result was the first large-scale printed plan of the City and nothing on so generous a scale covering the whole of the City was to be produced until the Ordnance Survey's plans of the mid-nineteenth century. The Ogilby and Morgan map was a true plan in two dimensions, whereas Hollar's uncompleted project of the 1650s, which had been equally ambitious, was for a plan-view, with the street layout shown in plan and the buildings in perspective.[34]

Comparable with the Ogilby and Morgan plan as a major initiative in its own field was Samuel Lee's *A Collection of the Names of the Merchants Living in and about the City of London* of 1677. This, the first London directory, lists 1,953 merchants and tradesmen within the walls, the majority of them based in the eastern part of the City, to the east of a line drawn along Dowgate Hill and Walbrook, then northwards to Moorgate. The number recorded shows that there had been a healthy flow of such people to the rebuilt area. Nor had the great merchants abandoned the City, for Ogilby and Morgan's plan identifies thirty-six of their mansions. Both that plan and Lee's directory suggest a steady economic recovery, with most of the street frontages rebuilt and numerous tradesmen in residence by 1677. Furthermore, rebuilding had not necessarily led to functional change. The goldsmiths had returned to Lombard Street, for example, with twenty-seven such firms there listed by Lee, and the wharves generally recovered their former specialisations in cargoes and areas of trade.[35] But, on the other hand, the drift of retailers, especially those in luxury goods, to the Strand and nascent West End had continued. Although this was a process that had been under way before the fire, and not one that was initiated by it, its effects were keenly felt in the areas formerly occupied by such traders. In 1676, ten of the twenty-two houses belonging to the corporation's

Bridgehouse estate in Paternoster Row were still unlet, with the mercers and haberdashers having moved away, and an early eighteenth-century assessment placed much of the blame for that migration on the fire.[36]

Problems of finding tenants, such as those faced by owners in Paternoster Row, appeared to confirm the City's anxiety that the fire would lead to the movement by tradesmen to the West End, the suburbs and the provinces. Something could be done about the first two areas by restricting building, and this the corporation successfully pressed for. Upon reports of 'divers buildings of late erected' that were not only undesirable as 'small and meane habitations', but could also be a 'great hindrance of perfecting the City buildings', the government decided to take action. In April 1671 the king issued a proclamation against such new buildings erected without licence. This evidently caught out many builders whose houses were 'some of them halfe erected, and some neer finished' and they petitioned to be able to complete their buildings. Others, disregarding the proclamation, during the following summer 'raysed severall new and meane buildings' in Westminster and the suburbs, and they were ordered to demolish them by November.[37] This was another phase in the struggle waged by governments for much of the seventeenth century to curb the growth of London. Apparently prompted by the effects of the Great Fire, it proved to be the last such attempt to prevent building in the suburbs.

Such controls on building may have discouraged those who were unable to re-establish themselves in the City from staying in the capital at all, but in any case some of those who found themselves in difficulties after the fire had moved away, perhaps to return to their original area. In September 1666 John Byrd of Caerleon wrote to his brother-in-law Thomas Pennant, a skinner, at London offering to 'furnish him with a house and what necessaryes I coulde, for which hee shoulde not paye any thinge'.[38] Others may have been encouraged by the king's proclamation allowing them to trade elsewhere and had overcome the problems of settling in a new community, benefited economically from their moves, and so were unlikely to return for that reason. At Chester, Samuel Heath claimed that he was the only confectioner in the city and Peter Bodvile reported that there was only one bookseller besides himself, while John Salmon, a haberdasher, had by the spring of 1668 set up 'a little manufactory'. All three men had come from London, as had Allan Smith, 'a great sugar baker' who settled in Liverpool.[39] Such dispersal need not have weakened London's position, however, for those who had left could well have continued to trade with their contacts in the capital. Indeed, the process may have provided more of a gain to the towns where such migrants settled, in terms of diversity of businesses and strengthening of economic links with London, than a loss to the City, where they could be replaced by others taking up their trades.

The corporation was not convinced that such movements were not going to have a deleterious effect and so took steps to compel the aldermen and freemen to live in the City, as they were bound to do. In addition, in 1672 action against non-freemen was halted and in the following year a major inducement was offered to such tradesmen in the form of admission to the freedom for the nominal sum of £2 6s 8d, so long as they lived in the rebuilt houses. Those who took advantage included a button-maker from Gloucester, a merchant tailor from York and an apothecary from Oxford. Craftsmen who had come to London to work on the rebuilding were entitled to become freemen and did so in increasing numbers, to safeguard their position in the future. The corporation's policy seems to have been successful, with 484 admissions to the freedom in the mayoral year 1673–4.[40] Action to compel members of the mercantile and financial élite to remain in the City was probably not needed, for they showed little inclination to move away from it. Of the forty-five aldermen elected between 1687 and 1701, thirty-one were living within the walls in 1695 and six more in the near suburbs.[41]

The admission of new members was a potential way for the livery companies to restore their fortunes. Some of them took many years to recover from the loss of rental income and costs of rebuilding their halls. The Haberdashers' Company was indebted to the tune of £10,000 in 1671, but it was noted in October 1673 that £1,200 had been raised from admissions to the Court of Assistants and other new members of that status brought in a further £1,000 early in 1675.[42] Sales of land and the raising of money from the membership by subscriptions were other methods adopted by the companies for increasing revenue. These sources had to offset the effect of the granting of building leases, which deprived them, and indeed other property owners, of the income from fines which in other circumstances were taken from tenants at the granting of a new lease. The long leases also created a lengthy delay before such fines could be received. A review of the finances of St Bartholomew's

Hospital in 1696 drew attention to this problem, concluding that no income could be generated from fines to settle the outstanding debts because 'the greatest part of the hospital's revenues was burnt by the late conflagration, and long leases granted in consideration of building'.[43] Only with the gradual expiry of such leases in the early eighteenth century could that income be generated. This not only deprived the landlords of that revenue, but by producing renewal dates within a relatively few years for buildings across the City, it created a distortion in the property market, with so many leases being due for renewal within a short time. Such distortion may have continued during the period of at least one more generation of leases, indeed for much of the eighteenth century. Yet despite such problems, many of the livery companies recovered, although the Mercers' Company's debts were such that by 1745 it was facing bankruptcy.[44]

The loss of rental revenue from buildings which formed the endowment of charities deprived them of their income from that source until the property was rebuilt and was again producing rents. Edmond Hammond had bequeathed the annual income of £80 from houses in Mincing Lane and Tower Street in trust to the Haberdashers' Company, to provide yearly payments of £1 each to twenty poor members of the company and £60 to maintain six pensioners in an almshouse, which was built in 1650. All of the houses were burnt in the fire and the company successfully argued that it could not be held responsible for the lost revenue. The solution was to forego the income from the tenants for two years after the fire and, as an incentive for rebuilding, to lower the rents from the properties to £60 per annum for forty years, thereby diminishing the charity's income by a quarter. Similarly, an almshouse for orphans in Westminster lost so much of its revenue because of the fire that 'there is not means left to maintain half the number of children formerly kept there'.[45]

Such loss of income applied not only to charities within London, but also to many others throughout the country which drew revenue from properties in the burnt area. Earlier in the century a member of the Merchant Taylors' Company had left a quarter of the rents from eight houses in the parish of St Gregory and two other properties nearby to the almshouse of St John the Baptist and St John the Evangelist in Sherborne, an early fifteenth-century foundation. In this case the fire court ruled that the rents must be maintained at the pre-fire level, but that the tenants should be granted an extension to their leases if they rebuilt the premises. The loss of revenue from the property forming the endowment of the Merchant Taylors' school at Crosby in Lancashire created a financial crisis which meant that the master and usher could not be paid their salaries until that income was restored.[46] These were already well-established charities, but the fire also had the effect of delaying the implementation of the wishes of Gilbert Keate, who had died in 1658. He had bequeathed £600 to the Grocers' Company that was designed to produce an income providing pensions of £4 annually to each of four elderly people in the village of Bishopstone in Wiltshire. The arrangements had not been completed before the fire and because of the company's losses and its desperate financial condition, payments did not begin until around 1680, more than twenty years after the benefactor's death.[47]

While those dependent on such charities suffered financially, at least in the short term, the dissenters later looked back on the period after the fire as one of religious toleration. Because so many churches were burnt down 'and the parish ministers gone', their meetings became 'very public' and they were able to preach openly in London for the next few years. This was an encouragement to dissenting congregations elsewhere, with one group in Bristol having 'liberty for about four years after, in some good measure'. Such freedom was curtailed rather sooner in London, however, with the Privy Council clamping down on Nonconformist conventicles in the capital in March 1669.[48]

The dissenters' brief experience notwithstanding, the Great Fire was far from being a force for religious and political toleration. Indeed, following the hostile reaction to Catholics and foreigners generally at the time, and while memories of the disaster were still relatively fresh, it retained great political potency during the 1670s and 1680s. This stemmed partly from the fact that it had been such an unforgettable event; it had left a legacy of fear that something similar might occur again, and not necessarily as the result of an accident. Memories were kept alive by an annual national fast day on 2 September and by a string of polemical publications. For example, the mayoralty of Sir William Turner, a bachelor, was celebrated by Robert Wild with verses entitled *Upon the rebuilding the City . . . the Lord Mayor, and the noble Company of Bachelors dining with him*, which praised the mayor and also attacked the Catholics for causing the fire.[49] Indeed, regardless of the findings of the enquiries into the causes of the Great Fire, that disaster quickly took its place with the Marian persecutions and the Gunpowder Plot as palpable evidence of a real and dangerous Catholic threat. As such, it had a political significance which resurfaced when, in the late 1670s, there was a resurgence of popular fears of a Catholic plot that created a panic akin to that which had gripped the capital in 1641–2 and had been feared in 1666. These apprehensions were largely based upon a dread of schemes by Catholics and Frenchmen to burn London as the prelude to the capture of the city and a massacre of the Protestant inhabitants. In the aftermath of the Great Fire this was more than an abstract threat, a crying of 'wolf', for had it not happened already in sixty-six? Of course it had, and it could happen again. Blazes in London in the aftermath of the Great Fire 'were thought to be by Popish treachery' and such fears resurfaced during later outbreaks, such as that in the Temple in 1679, which served to increase the fears of arson and treason.

In the feverish political atmosphere of the Popish Plot and Exclusion Crisis, there was much capital to be gained by the Whigs from all of this. Prints and pamphlets kept the idea alive, showing such scenes as the pope belching fire against a background of London in flames, and playing cards depicted Jesuits offering money as an inducement to people to set buildings alight.[50] Even such an apparently sober work as Thomas Delaune's history and description of the capital, *The Present State of London* of 1681, contained emotive references to the origin of the fire. Delaune was a Baptist scholar and schoolmaster who had converted from Catholicism, and he included a summary of William Bedloe's description of the methods employed by the papists to begin and promote fires, with the instructions alleged to be given them regarding such matters as the best places to commit arson and how to cut off water supplies once a fire had been started. The opening of the acrostic in the introduction carried the message, 'This is the City which the Papal Crew / Have by their Damn'd Devices overthrew / Erected on her old Foundations, New'.

The Duke of York was an obvious target, especially after his avowal of Catholicism in 1673, and the allegation that he had been involved in the plot which had led to the firing of the City in 1666 gained credibility. While it was undeniable that he had helped to direct the efforts of the fire-fighters, had he not gone around during those dreadful days with a smile on his face, watching London burn? This long-standing accusation became a familiar one, repeated by Titus Oates in his denunciations of the Catholics, told to the Court of Aldermen by Thomas Pilkington, and included in the Duke of Monmouth's declaration issued at the start of his ill-fated attempt to overthrow his uncle in 1685. But James's discomfiture was too limited an objective and the Whig propagandists sought to taint other political opponents with similar accusations. Even Sir Thomas Osborne, now the Earl of Danby and the king's chief minister, was accused of being implicated in the outbreak of the fire. Furthermore, not content with pointing the finger at Catholics and Jesuits, a petition of London apprentices presented to Sir Patience Ward, the Whig lord mayor, on the fifteenth anniversary of the outbreak of the fire extended the blame for the burning of 'that Famous Protestant City' to the Tories as well.[51]

The allegation that Catholics had been guilty of starting the Great Fire was not confined to popular opinion and lurid political propaganda, however. It was given parliamentary endorsement with the declaration of the House of Commons in January 1681 that 'it is the opinion of this House that the City of London was burnt in the year 1666 by the Papists; designing thereby to introduce arbitrary power and popery into this Kingdom'.[52] More publicly, an inscription was added to the Monument in June 1681, during Ward's mayoralty, which declared that 'This pillar was sett up in perpetuell remembrance of the most dreadful Burning of this Protestant City, begun and carried on by the treachery and malice of the Popish faction . . . in order to the effecting of their horrid plot for the extirpating the Protestant religion and English liberties, and to introduce Popery and slavery'. Erased after the Duke of York came to the throne as James II, this unequivocal statement was re-cut after the accession of William and Mary and not finally removed until 1830, following the passage of the act for Catholic emancipation in the previous year. To reinforce the message, also in 1681 a stone was set into the wall of the building erected on the site of Farriner's house that similarly declared that 'Here by ye Permission of Heaven Hell broke loose upon this Protestant City from the malicious hearts of barbarous Papists' and attributed the outbreak to Hubert, not mentioning the eighty Jesuits and priests that Oates had asserted to have had a hand in the fire.[53] But these gestures were becoming more defiant than triumphant, for by this time the Whigs were on the defensive and, following the dissolution of the Oxford parliament in March 1681, the king was regaining the initiative. The political pendulum also swung against the Whigs in London, with Ward succeeded as lord mayor by Sir John Moore, who had the support of the court, and he in turn by the Tory Sir William Pritchard. The Tories' victory was complete when two of their number were chosen sheriffs at the elections in 1682. Ward was forced to seek refuge in Holland in the following year, while Delaune was arrested for publishing his *Plea for the Nonconformists*, which was judged to be 'a false and seditious libel', and imprisoned in Newgate, where he died in 1685.[54]

The fears generated by the Great Fire were successfully exploited in the Whig propaganda of the 1670s and 1680s, yet the causes of the disaster were open to more than one interpretation and from the opposite perspective could be seen in a different light. London's support for parliament throughout the Civil War and acquiescence in the execution of the king were invoked by the Tories, for perhaps the Great Fire was not unconnected with its culpability in this respect. To put it bluntly, was the disaster not a case of 'the rebellious city destroyed'?[55] A late seventeenth-century painting based on the work of Jan Breughel the Younger vividly develops this point of view. A picture within the picture shows the execution outside the Banqueting House, which is being studied by a variety of creatures, including a masked fox which may represent Cromwell, while a couple of men with a distinctly conspiratorial appearance look furtively on. The scales of justice lie on the ground, perhaps having been cut down by the sword that is entwined with them, as do the works of the religious reformers. The military are rampant, lawlessness ensues. The accoutrements of war are scattered around, a soldier drags away a woman who is in a dishevelled state, while her child clings to her garments. Within vast classical ruins are the mouths of Hell itself, spewing forth famine, ignorance and an array of vices. Demons and a variety of grotesque creatures that would not be out of place in a painting by Hieronymus Bosch roam freely around, the moon has waned and a comet flashes across the sky. But retribution has been visited on the city which helped to unleash this mayhem and, beyond the picture of Charles's execution, London is being burned in the Great Fire, with St Paul's starkly outlined against the flames.[56] As with the Whig interpretation of the fire, the moral of the Tory message was clear, what had happened once could happen again and a disloyal City must expect to have such vengeance inflicted upon it.

While the ideological struggles were being fought out in the propaganda wars and, from time to time, in the streets, the scholars were trying to absorb the importance of the physical remains revealed by the 'great digging' after the fire.[57] Excavations for buildings and street improvements all over the burnt area produced remains, many of them obviously Roman, others not so clearly identified. Reference in a newsletter of 1687 to 'medals of 1,000 years standing' was unhelpful for dating purposes, for example, and discoveries made beneath Fleet Street in 1670 were described only in general terms. Other finds were meticulously recorded, however. Wren's workmen uncovered 'Walls, and Windows also, and the Pavement of a Temple, or Church of Roman Workmanship' while rebuilding St Mary-le-Bow and carefully measured the remains. Many finds were made during the work at St Paul's, which exposed the foundations of its medieval predecessors, revealing the extent of the successive buildings. This was not without interest, although the antiquarians' concern with the history of the site was focused much more on the debate which sought to establish whether the cathedral stood on the site of the temple of Diana.[58]

The discoveries attracted considerable attention and many of the artefacts were preserved by such assiduous collectors as John Conyers, an apothecary in Fleet Street, and John Bagford, a shoemaker and bookseller, yet they did not generate a study of Roman London during the late seventeenth century. Wren's interest was clearly aroused, but he did little to interpret the finds, and Edward Stillingfleet, who was Dean of St Paul's from 1678 to 1689, while much of the work on the cathedral was being carried out, ignored the archaeological evidence and prepared a study of Londinium that analysed only the literary sources. It was two scholars in the early eighteenth century who attempted to use the evidence revealed in the wake of the fire in a systematic way. John Strype was responsible for a new edition of John Stow's *Survey of London*, which was published in 1720, and contains a clear account of the City produced by the rebuilding, together with an appendix 'Of divers Roman and other Antique Curiosities found in London before and after the great Fire' that attempted to summarise the findings. The other scholar who took a close interest was Dr John Woodward, physician, geologist, naturalist, archaeologist and antiquarian. He was a careful worker in many ways, meticulous in his recording and aware of the views of his contemporaries. He attempted to interpret the distribution of Roman finds to discover the boundaries of Londinium and the location of temples. Woodward's methods were apparent in the care which he took to identify a statue found near St Paul's as being a Diana, before over-reaching the evidence to assume both that it was Roman and showed that a temple to that goddess had indeed stood on the site of the cathedral.

The inadequate recording and description of the wealth of finds from the period of rebuilding rendered them less useful to posterity than they could have been. They were, in any case, a relatively minor benefit of the conflagration. On the presumption that such a great event must have great consequences and form a watershed in the life of the City, much more significant effects came to be attributed to it than mere archaeological discoveries. The conjunction of the fire with the ending of plague epidemics in Britain was assumed to be a clear case of cause and effect, for example, even though only one-fifth of just this one city had been destroyed in the blaze. While this was generally attributed to the fact that the new buildings proved to be a hostile habitat for the flea-bearing rats responsible for spreading the disease, another view, as expressed by Walter Besant, was that the Great Fire had been a purifying agent that had cleansed the 'poisonous filtrations' then saturating the ground on which the City stood, to a depth of 'many feet'.[59]

Changes within London were also attributed to the disaster, such as the divergence of the capital into separate business and courtly societies in the City and West End and the adoption of brick and tile. In fact, in these and other cases, the Great Fire gave a boost to trends that were already under way; it did not initiate them. Again, while the post-fire planning process was innovative, especially in the legislation that categorised the streets and specified the types of houses to be built in them, control of such matters as building materials, storey heights, wall thicknesses and other constructional details had been foreshadowed in the building agreements for the development of the Bedford estate in Covent Garden in the 1630s.[60] Far from proving an irksome restriction, the house-types laid down in the rebuilding act were taken up by builders and erected in the areas newly developed during the capital's expansion in the late seventeenth century. Moreover, landlords wishing to control the kind of building to be erected on their ground adopted the terminology of house-types, specifying the 'rate' of house to be built long before it was given formal expression in the building act of 1774.[61]

As well as its consequences, the fire itself held a fascination for posterity, because of its sheer enormity and the unique scale of the disaster within the cities of western Europe. Although major outbreaks continued to occur, none rivalled that of 1666 in terms of the numbers of buildings destroyed. Furthermore, although urban populations greatly expanded in the late eighteenth and nineteenth centuries, the number of large-scale fires actually declined. A conflagration on the scale of the Great Fire was unthinkable in the vastly larger metropolis of the nineteenth century and one of the more destructive blazes, in Tooley Street, Southwark, in 1861, was shocking because of the value of the losses and the death of James Braidwood, Superintendent of the London Fire Brigade, rather than for the number of buildings destroyed or the area swept by the fire. The enforced use of fire-resistant building materials, the lower density of housing, with many dwellings standing in their own gardens, and the improvements in both the technology and organisation of fire-fighting served to limit the scale of outbreaks.[62] The Great Fire was seen to have played a part in this process by indicating, through the terms of the rebuilding acts, the procedures to be followed in order to reduce, indeed virtually eliminate, such disasters.

Although the threat of large-scale destruction from accidental fires receded, inevitably the fabric of the late seventeenth-century City was eroded, as it began to age and economic and social changes required new types of buildings. Even some of Wren's churches, seen as a major part of the legacy of the fire, fell prey to the inexorable needs of London's growing traffic and consequent street widening, as well as the fall in the population of the City, while others were subjected to alterations. Between 1781 and 1820 four of the post-fire churches were demolished, a further twelve followed in 1860–97 and three more were knocked down before 1940.[63] Finally, bombing during the Second World War did much to wipe away the remains of the late-Stuart City, destroying or gutting many more churches, eight of which were not rebuilt, and other surviving buildings, such as Beckford Court off Great Tower Street.

It was ironic that much of the wartime destruction came during raids in 1940, the year in which Thomas Reddaway's magisterial account of the rebuilding process was published. The parallels between the recovery in the years after 1666 and the rebuilding made necessary by bombing were too obvious to be overlooked. The Improvements and Town Planning Committee of the corporation included in its report outlining draft proposals for post-war reconstruction, submitted in 1944, an introduction dealing with the rebuilding after the Great Fire. It contained extracts from Reddaway's book and reproductions of Hollar's plan of the burnt area and the Act of Common Council specifying street widths. The introduction ended with a hope that the rebuilding that followed the Second World War would be carried out with such success that it would be possible to echo Dr Woodward's judgement on the effects of the disaster of 1666. In 1707 he wrote to Wren that the Great Fire 'however disastrous it might be to the then Inhabitants, had prov'd infinitely beneficial to their Posterity; conducing vastly to the Improvement and Increase, as well of the Riches and Opulency, as of the Splendour of this City'.

LIST OF ABBREVIATIONS

BL   British Library

CLRO   Corporation of London Record Office

CSPD   *Calendar of State Papers Domestic*

CSPVen   *Calendar of State Papers Venetian*

GL   Guildhall Library

HMC   Historical Manuscripts Commission

PRO   Public Record Office

RO   Record Office

VCH   Victoria County History

NOTES

ONE: DANGERS AND PRECAUTIONS

1. J.P. Malcolm, *Londinium Redivivum* (4 vols, London, 1802–7), vol. 4, p. 74

2. J.A.I. Champion, *London's Dreaded Visitation. The Social Geography of the Great Plague in 1665* (London, Historical Geography Research Series, 31, 1995), pp. 23–41, 102–3

3. P. Slack, *The Impact of Plague in Tudor and Stuart England* (London, Routledge & Kegan Paul, 1985), pp. 144–69

4. J. Goudsblom, *Fire and Civilization* (Harmondsworth, Allen Lane, 1992), pp. 143–50, 155–7

5. E.L. Jones, S. Porter and M. Turner, *A Gazetteer of English Urban Fire Disasters, 1500–1900* (Norwich, Historical Geography Research Series, 13, 1984), pp. 16–17

6. James Howel, *Londinopolis* (1658), p. 22. Kent Archives Office, Dering MS 220

7. BL, Thomason Tract E.104(25) *Mercurius Civicus*, 25 May–1 June 1643, p. 29. *Lords' Journals*, vol. 8, 1645–6, p. 30

8. BL, Thomason Tract E.589(16) *Death's Master-Peece: or, A True Relation of that Great and Sudden Fire in Towerstreet, London* (1650)

9. P.S. Seaver, *Wallington's World. A Puritan Artisan in Seventeenth-century London* (London, Methuen, 1985), p. 56. Howel, *Londinopolis*, p. 74. *The Fire Court*, ed. P.E. Jones (2 vols, London, Corporation of London, 1966–70), vol. 2, p. 77

10. C. Walford, 'King's Briefs: Their Purposes and History', *Transactions of the Royal Historical Society*, 10 (1882), 1–74. W.A. Bewes, *Church Briefs* (1896). *The Diary of Samuel Pepys*, eds R.C. Latham and W. Matthews (11 vols, London, Bell & Hyman, 1970–83), vol. 2, p. 128

11. S. Porter, 'Newspapers and Fire Relief in Early Modern England', *Journal of Newspaper and Periodical History*, 8 (1992), 28–33

12. VCH *Oxon.*, vol. 10 (London, 1972), pp. 8, 24. Nehemiah Wallington, *Historical Notices . . . of the Reign of Charles I*, ed. R. Webb (2 vols, London, 1866–9), vol. 1, p. 51; vol. 2, p. 295

13. W.M. Barnes, 'The Diary of William Whiteway, of Dorchester, Co. Dorset', *Proceedings of the Dorset Natural History and Antiquarian Field Club*, 13 (1891), 78–80.

DNB, sub John White. D.
Underdown, *Fire from Heaven:
The Life of an English Town in the
Seventeenth Century* (London,
HarperCollins, 1992), *passim*

14. BL, Thomason Tract E.12(11)
Mercurius Civicus, 3–10 Oct. 1644,
p. 677. S. Porter, 'Town Fires:
The Case of Tiverton', *Devon
& Cornwall Notes & Queries*, 33
(1977), 345–8; 'The Oxford Fire
of 1644', *Oxoniensia*, 49 (1984),
289–300

15. Jeremiah 17:27

16. Seaver, *Wallington's World*, p. 154.
*The State of Northampton From
the beginning of the Fire, Sept. 20th
1675 to Nov. 5th.* (London, 1675,
repr. Northampton, 1974), p. 6

17. *Swedish Diplomats at Cromwell's
Court, 1655–1656*, ed. M. Roberts
(Camden Society, 4th series, 36,
1988), p. 215

18. V.T. Sternberg, 'Predictions of
the Fire and Plague of London',
Notes & Queries, 1st series, 7
(1853), 79–80, 173–4

19. R. Hutton, *The Restoration. A
Political and Religious History of
England and Wales 1658–1667*
(Oxford, Oxford University
Press, 1985), pp. 185–7. J. Miller,
Charles II (London, Weidenfeld &
Nicolson, 1991), pp. 95–7

20. *Diary of Pepys*, vol. 4, p. 196

21. *The Diary of John Evelyn*, ed. E.S. de
Beer (6 vols, Oxford, Clarendon
Press, 1955), vol. 3, pp. 465–6

22. J.R. Woodhead, *The Rulers of
London 1660–1689* (London,

London and Middlesex
Archaeological Society, 1965),
pp. 15, 20, 24, 39–40, 96, 124, 163

23. I.M. Green, *The Re-establishment of
the Church of England 1660–1663*
(Oxford, Oxford University Press,
1978), p. 157. W.G. Bell, *The Great
Fire of London in 1666* (London,
John Lane, The Bodley Head,
1920), p. 307

24. Seaver, *Wallington's World*, pp. 48–
9, 54, where the fire is misdated
to 1634

25. Seaver, *Wallington's World*, p. 48

26. D. Keene, *Cheapside before the Great
Fire* (London, ESRC, 1985), p. 17

27. C.C. Knowles and P.H. Pitt,
*The History of Building Regulation
in London 1189–1972* (London,
Architectural Press, 1972), pp. 12–
15, 18–22. M.D. George, *London
Life in the Eighteenth Century*
(Harmondsworth, Penguin Books,
1965), pp. 78–80, 334 n.18

28. The comment was made in
respect of fires in Stratford-
upon-Avon: Shakespeare
Birthplace Trust RO, corporation
records, misc. docs., vii, 114

29. M. Wood, *The English Mediaeval
House* (London, Dent, 1965), p. 292.
J. Schofield, *Medieval London Houses*
(London and New Haven, Yale
University Press, 1995), pp. 96–7

30. John Stow, *The Survey of London*,
ed. H.B. Wheatley (rev. edn,
London, Dent, 1956), p. 76

31. S. Porter, 'Thatching in Early-
modern Norwich', *Norfolk
Archaeology*, 39 (1986), 310–12

32. Knowles and Pitt, *Building Regulation*, pp. 20–1. Jones, *Fire Court*, vol. 1, pp. 134, 276

33. Stow, *Survey*, pp. 129, 174. *The Itinerary of John Leland in or about the Years 1535–42*, ed. L.T. Smith (5 vols, London, George Bell, 1906), vol. 1, p. 7

34. *CSPD*, 1651–2, pp. 197–8

35. Jones, *Fire Court*, vol. 1, pp. 50–1, 117–18

36. Howel, *Londinopolis*, p. 398. *CSPD*, 1651–2, pp. 197–8

37. R. Finlay and B. Shearer, 'Population growth and suburban expansion' in A.L. Beier and R. Finlay, eds, *London 1500–1700: The Making of the Metropolis* (London, Longman, 1986), pp. 42–6

38. *Diary of Pepys*, vol. 6, p. 129; vol. 7, pp. 3, 5–6. *Diary of Evelyn*, ed. de Beer, vol. 3, pp. 417, 430

39. *Calendar of Treasury Books*, 1667–8, p. 296. Champion, *London's Dreaded Visitation*, p. 27

40. GL, MS 4069/1, f. 238. Jones, *Fire Court*, vol. 2, pp. 187, 331

41. R. Finlay, *Population and Metropolis. The Demography of London 1580–1650* (Cambridge, Cambridge University Press, 1981), pp 170–1

42. C.H. Firth and R.S. Rait, *Acts and Ordinances of the Interregnum* (3 vols, London, HMSO, 1911), vol. 2, pp. 1229–30. M. Ashley, *Financial and Commercial Policy under the Cromwellian Protectorate* (2nd edn, London, Frank Cass, 1962), pp. 88–9

43. Jones, *Fire Court*, vol. 1, p. 171. T.C. Dale, *The Inhabitants of London in 1638* (London, Society of Genealogists, 1931), pp. 99, 145, 168. *CSPD*, 1637, p. 180

44. *The London Surveys of Ralph Treswell*, ed. J. Schofield (London, London Topographical Society, 135, 1987). M.J. Power, 'The Social Topography of Restoration London' in Beier and Finlay, *London 1500–1700*, pp. 209–12

45. *Surveys of Treswell*, p. 17

46. *The Harleian Miscellany*, vol. 6 (London, 1810), pp. 399–401

47. GL, MS 4069/1, ff. 210, 212, 214, 216, 233v; 4069/2, ff. 273v, 290

48. *Harleian Miscellany*, vol. 6, p. 400

49. CLRO, Common Council Journal, 40, f. 31. GL, 4069/1, f. 242v; 11,394/1, unpaged

50. R. Jenkins, 'Fire-extinguishing Engines in England, 1625–1725', *Transactions of the Newcomen Society*, 11 (1930–1), 15–16, 23–4. S. Holloway, *Courage High! A history of Firefighting in London* (London, HMSO, 1992), pp. 5–8

51. Jenkins, 'Fire-extinguishing Engines', 17–18

52. *Privy Council Registers*, vol. 3 (London, HMSO, 1967), p. 19. *Analytical Index to . . . the Remembrancia . . . of the City of London. AD 1579–1664* (London, 1878), pp. 142–3

53. CLRO, Common Council Journal, 40, f. 31

54. GL, MS 16,697/4, pp. 368, 388. *Memorials of the Goldsmiths'*

Company, ed. W.S. Prideaux
(London, Eyre and Spottiswoode,
1896), vol. 1, pp. 202, 208.
Drapers' Company Archives,
M.B.14, ff. 15v, 26v; W.A.9/10, f.
22. Holloway, Courage High!, p. 8

55. Worcester RO, Worcester
Corporation Records, Audit of
Annual Accounts, 3, 1640–9, sub
1641. Norfolk and Norwich RO,
Norwich City Records, case 18a,
Chamberlains' Accounts, 1626–48,
f. 367. B.H. Cunnington, Some
Annals of the Borough of Devizes
1555–1791 (Devizes, 1925), p. 98

56. Bristol RO, Corporation Records,
Common Council Proceedings,
1642–9, p. 163; Great Audit
Book, 1645–9, pp. 155, 156.
Gloucestershire RO, GBR B3/2,
Corporation Minute Book,
1632–56, p. 447. Wiltshire RO,
G22/1/205/2, Marlborough
General Account Book, 1572–
1771, ff. 95v, 96

57. J.B.P. Karslake, 'Early London
Fire-appliances', The Antiquaries
Journal, 9 (1929), 233. Goldsmiths'
Company, vol. 2, pp. 35, 71, 75

58. Thomas Fuller, The History of
the Worthies of England, ed. P.A.
Nuttall (3 vols, London, 1840),
vol. 2, pp. 334–5

59. Mercurius Politicus, 21–28 Oct.
1658, p. 597

60. Keene, Cheapside, pp. 14–15

61. Seaver, Wallington's World, pp. 54–5

62. Wallington, Historical Notices, vol.
1, pp. 17–18. BL, Thomason Tract
E.589(16), Death's Master-Peece, p. 6

63. Jones, Fire Court, vol. 1, pp.
59–60. GL, MS 16,967/4, p. 307.
Stow, Survey, pp. 12–19, 323.
DNB, sub Sir Edward Ford

64. Seaver, Wallington's World, pp. 53–4

65. John Fox, 'A False Fearful
Imagination of Fire at Oxford
University' in Tudor Tracts
1532–1588, ed. A.F. Pollard
(Westminster, 1903), pp. 410–11.
Andrew Yarranton, England's
Improvements by Sea and Land, The
Second Part (1681), p. 102

66. Harleian Miscellany, vol. 6,
p. 400. S. Porter, 'The Oxford
Fire Regulations of 1671',
Bulletin of the Institute of Historical
Research, 53 (1985), 251–5

TWO: THE GREAT FIRE

1. B. Capp, Astrology and the Popular
Press: English Almanacs 1500–
1800 (London, Faber & Faber,
1979), pp. 174–5

2. Capp, Astrology, pp. 36, 258.
M. McKeon, Politics and Poetry
in Restoration England. The Case
of Dryden's Annus Mirabilis
(Cambridge, Mass., and London,
Harvard University Press, 1975),
pp. 222–3

3. Diary of Pepys, vol. 7, pp. 46–7, 55

4. Bell, Great Fire, pp. 20, 316, 341.
Diary of Pepys, vol. 7, p. 333

5. B. Capp, The Fifth Monarchy Men. A
Study in Seventeenth-century English
Millenarianism (London, Faber &
Faber, 1972), p. 214

6.   *The London Gazette*, 26–30 April 1666. Hutton, *Restoration*, pp. 150–1, 205–6, 231, 249–50

7.   *Diary of Pepys*, vol. 7, pp. 41–2, 72–3, 95. Hutton, *Restoration*, p. 246

8.   Slack, *Impact of Plague*, pp. 106–8. *Diary of Evelyn*, ed. de Beer, vol. 3, p. 435

9.   J.U. Nef, *The Rise of the British Coal Industry* (2 vols, London, Cass, 1966), vol. 2, app. D, opp. p. 380

10. J.I. Israel, *Dutch Primacy in World Trade, 1585–1740* (Oxford, Oxford University Press, 1989), pp. 214, 275, 278

11. McKeon, *Politics and Poetry*, pp. 120–1

12. R. Ollard, *Man of War. Sir Robert Holmes and the Restoration Navy* (London, Hodder and Stoughton, 1969), pp. 148–58

13. G. Manley, 'Central England Temperatures: Monthly Means 1659 to 1973', *Quarterly Journal of the Royal Meteorological Society*, 100 (1974), 393–4. H.H. Lamb, *Climate: Present, Past and Future* (2 vols, London, Methuen, 1972–7), vol. 2, pp. 571–2

14. D.J. Schove, 'Fire and Drought, 1600–1700', *Weather*, 21 (1966), 313–14. *Diary of Evelyn*, ed. de Beer, vol. 3, p. 466

15. Bell, *Great Fire*, pp. 22–3. HMC, *Fourteenth Report, Portland MSS, III*, p. 301. *Diary of Pepys*, vol. 8, p. 82

16. Malcolm, *Londinium Redivivum*, vol. 4, p. 73. *Diary of Pepys*, vol. 7, pp. 267–8

17. Bell, *Great Fire*, pp. 313, 321–2. P.D.A. Harvey, 'A Foreign Visitor's Account of the Great Fire, 1666', *Transactions of the London and Middlesex Archaeological Society*, 20 (1959–61), 83

18. *The London Gazette*, 3–10 Sept. 1666. G. Milne, *The Great Fire of London* (New Barnet and London, Historical Publications, 1986), pp. 111–15. *The Conway Letters. The Correspondence of Anne, Viscountess Conway, Henry More, and their Friends 1642–1684*, ed. M.H. Nicolson, rev. edn ed. S. Hutton (Oxford, Clarendon Press, 1992), p. 276

19. Milne, *Great Fire*, p. 29. 'Rege Sincera', *Observations, both Historical and Moral, upon the Burning of London; September 1666* (1667), reprinted in *The Harleian Miscellany*, vol. 3 (London, 1809), p. 296

20. Howel, *Londinopolis*, p. 22

21. *Harleian Miscellany*, vol. 3, p. 306

22. Gilbert Burnet, *History of My Own Time. Part 1: The Reign of Charles the Second*, ed. O. Airy (2 vols, Oxford, Clarendon Press, 1897–1900), vol. 1, pp. 412–14

23. *Diary of Pepys*, vol. 7, p. 268. Bell, *Great Fire*, p. 319

24. 'Autobiography and Anecdotes by William Taswell, DD', ed. G.P. Elliott (*Camden Miscellany*, vol. 2, 1853), 10–11. Milne, *Great Fire*, p. 28

25. *Diary of Pepys*, vol. 7, p. 268

26. Harvey, 'A Foreign Visitor's Account', 83. *Diary of Pepys*, vol. 7, p. 270

27. Harvey, 'A Foreign Visitor's Account', 83

28. *Diary of Pepys*, vol. 7, p. 269

29. Malcolm, *Londinium Redivivum*, vol. 4, p. 40. G.J.A., 'Fire of London', *Notes & Queries*, 5th series, 5 (1876), 306

30. Malcolm, *Londinium Redivivum* vol. 4, p. 77. *Diary of Evelyn*, ed. de Beer, vol. 3, p. 496

31. *Diary of Pepys*, vol. 3, pp. 270–1. *Diary of Evelyn*, ed. de Beer, vol. 3, p. 495. P. Earle, *The Making of the English Middle Class. Business, Society and Family Life in London, 1660–1730* (London, Methuen, 1989), p. 296

32. *Conway Letters*, p. 277. Malcolm, *Londinium Redivivum*, vol. 4, p. 41. HMC, *Twelfth Report, app. VII, Le Fleming MSS*, p. 485; *Fourteenth Report, Portland MSS, III*, p. 299. F.P. and M.M.Verney, *Memoirs of the Verney Family during the Seventeenth Century* (2nd edn, 2 vols, London, Longmans, Green, 1907), vol. 2, pp. 255–6. *Diary of Pepys*, vol. 7, p. 293

33. *Diary of Pepys*, vol. 3, p. 272. Bell, *Great Fire*, p. 319

34. *Conway Letters*, pp. 277–8. *CSPD*, 1666–7, pp. 99, 103.Verney, *Memoirs of the Verney Family*, vol. 2, p. 257. 'Autobiography by William Taswell', 13–14

35. *Diary of Pepys*, vol. 7, pp. 269, 271

36. Malcolm, *Londinium Redivivum*, vol. 4, p. 80

37. *CSPD*, 1666–7, pp. 94–5, 103–4

38. Edward Hyde, Earl of Clarendon, *Selections from the History of the Rebellion and the Life by Himself*, ed. G. Huehns (Oxford, Oxford University Press, 1978), p. 415. *Conway Letters*, p. 278

39. 'Autobiography by William Taswell', p. 11. Clarendon, *Selections*, pp. 415–16. Bell, *Great Fire*, pp. 75, 320

40. Harvey, 'A Foreign Visitor's Account', 84

41. *Conway Letters*, p. 278. Malcolm, *Londinium Redivivum*, vol. 4, p. 36

42. 'Autobiography by William Taswell', 11. Bell, *Great Fire*, p. 317

43. Clarendon, *Selections*, pp. 414–15

44. *Conway Letters*, p. 278. *Diary of Pepys*, vol. 7, p. 269. Malcolm, *Londinium Redivivum*, vol. 4, p. 63

45. Stow, *Survey*, pp. 217–18

46. 'Autobiography by William Taswell', 12

47. *CSPD*, 1666–7, pp. 95–6

48. G.J.A., 'Fire of London', 306. *Diary of Pepys*, vol. 7, p. 282

49. Bell, *Great Fire*, pp. 213, 318, 328. *Conway Letters*, p. 277. D.K. Clark, 'A Restoration Goldsmith-Banking House: The Vine on Lombard Street' in *Essays in Modern English History in Honor of Wilbur Cortez Abbott* (Cambridge, Mass., Harvard University Press, 1941), p. 27

50. Malcolm, *Londinium Redivivum*, vol. 4, p. 40. Bell, *Great Fire*, p. 324. G.J.A., 'Fire of London', 306

51. G.J.A., 'Fire of London', 306

52. Malcolm, *Londinium Redivivum*, vol. 4, pp. 75–6. Bell, *Great Fire*, pp. 164, 316–17

53. Clarendon, *Selections*, p. 418. R. Ollard, *Clarendon and His Friends* (Oxford, Oxford University Press, 1988), pp. 274–5. Bell, *Great Fire*, p. 316. *CSPD*, 1666–7, p. 99. *Diary of Pepys*, vol. 7, p. 278

54. CLRO, Ex–GLMS 298/111. Bell, *Great Fire*, pp. 141–3

55. Bell, *Great Fire*, p. 112

56. M. Whinney, *Wren* (London, Thames & Hudson, 1971), pp. 33–7. *Diary of Evelyn*, ed. de Beer, vol. 3, pp. 448–9, 452

57. *Diary of Pepys*, vol. 7, p. 270. Bell, *Great Fire*, p. 319

58. 'Autobiography by William Taswell', 12

59. 'Autobiography by William Taswell', 12. Bell, *Great Fire*, p. 325

60. Bell, *Great Fire*, pp. 160–1. *The London Gazette*, 3–10 Sept. 1666

61. *Diary of Pepys*, vol. 7, p. 276

62. Malcolm, *Londinium Redivivum*, vol. 4, p. 43

63. Ibid., vol. 4, p. 44. Bell, *Great Fire*, p. 317. *Diary of Pepys*, vol. 7, p. 277

64. *Diary of Evelyn*, ed. de Beer, vol. 3, p. 458. Jones, *Fire Court*, vol. 1, p. 3

65. *The London Gazette*, 3–10 Sept. 1666

66. Bell, *Great Fire*, p. 320. Clarendon, *Selections*, p. 419. *Diary of Evelyn*, ed. de Beer, vol. 3, p. 453

67. *CSPD*, 1666–7, p. 104. Bell, *Great Fire*, pp. 172–3

68. *Conway Letters*, p. 277. 'Autobiography by William Taswell', 13. *Diary of Pepys*, vol. 8, p. 42

69. *The Diary of Bulstrode Whitelocke 1605–1675*, ed. R. Spalding (London, British Academy, Records of Social and Economic History, new series, 13, 1990) p. 709. C. Welch, *The History of the Monument* (London, Corporation of the City of London, 1893), p. 64

70. *Diary of Pepys*, vol. 7, pp. 277, 282

71. *Diary of Evelyn*, ed. de Beer, vol. 3, p. 453. 'Autobiography by William Taswell', 13

72. Harvey, 'A Foreign Visitor's Account', 85

73. Bell, *Great Fire*, p. 316. *Diary of Evelyn*, ed. de Beer, vol. 3, p. 453

74. *Harleian Miscellany*, vol. 3, p. 300. 'Autobiography by William Taswell', 13

75. *DNB, sub* James Shirley. *The Correspondence of John Locke*, ed. E.S. de Beer (8 vols, Oxford, Clarendon Press, 1976–89), vol. 1, p. 292

76. Jones, *Fire Court*, vol. 1, pp. 44–5, 179

77. Clarendon, *Selections*, p. 417

78. Bell, *Great Fire*, pp. 316–18

79. Ibid., p. 320

80. Ibid., p. 321

81. *The History of Parliament: The House of Commons, 1660–1690*, ed. B.D. Henning (3 vols, London, Secker and Warburg, 1983), vol. 1, pp. 670–1. Woodhead, *Rulers of London*, p. 33

82. *Diary of Pepys*, vol. 7, pp. 187, 190, 393
83. Malcolm, *Londinium Redivivum*, vol. 4, p. 80. HMC, *Fourteenth Report, Portland MSS, III*, p. 298. Bell, *Great Fire*, p. 346. *Diary of Pepys*, vol. 7, p. 280
84. *CSPD*, 1666–7, pp. 167–8
85. Clarendon, *Selections*, p. 423

THREE: TAKING STOCK

1. *Diary of Pepys*, vol. 7, p. 276. 'Autobiography by William Taswell', 13. *Diary of Evelyn*, ed. de Beer, vol. 3, pp. 458, 461
2. S. Weston, 'Copy of a Letter from Sir Robert Atkyns ... Written from London during the Great Fire 1666', *Archaeologia*, 19 (1821), 105. HMC, *Le Fleming MSS*, p. 42
3. *Diary of Evelyn*, ed. de Beer, vol. 3, pp. 459–61. *CSPVen*, 1666–8, p. 87
4. *Diary of Whitelocke*, pp. 709–10
5. *CSPD*, 1666–7, pp. 107–8, 110, 113–14, 116, 124–5, 127, 129. *The Life and Times of Anthony Wood, antiquary, of Oxford, 1632–1695, Described by Himself*, ed. A. Clark, (4 vols, Oxford Historical Society, 1891–5), vol. 2, pp. 86–7
6. Bell, *Great Fire*, pp. 350–1
7. *Conway Letters*, p. 277. Bell, *Great Fire*, p. 328. *Diary of Evelyn*, ed. de Beer, vol. 3, p. 454
8. *CSPD*, 1666–7, pp. 119, 121–2. *Diary of Evelyn*, ed. de Beer, vol. 3, p. 464
9. *Diary of Pepys*, vol. 7, p. 283. Weston, 'Letter to Sir Robert Atkyns', 108
10. J. Spurr, *The Restoration Church of England* (London and New Haven, Yale University Press, 1991), pp. 54–5, 244
11. *Two East Anglian Diaries 1641–1729*, ed. M. Storey (Suffolk Records Society, 36, 1994), p. 113
12. *Diary of Pepys*, vol. 7, pp. 316–17; vol. 8, p. 21
13. J.E. Smith, *Bygone Briefs: ... A Schedule of More than a Thousand Briefs Laid in ... St Margaret, Westminster ...* (London, Wightman, 1896). *CSPD*, 1666–7, pp. 197, 200
14. *CSPD*, 1666–7, pp. 115–16, 119, 129, 185, 188. HMC, *Hastings MSS, II*, pp. 373–4
15. CLRO, Ex–GLMS 296
16. C.J. Kitching, 'Fire Disasters and Fire Relief in Sixteenth-century England: the Nantwich Fire of 1583', *Bulletin of the Institute of Historical Research*, 54 (1981), 183. *CSPD*, 1658–9, p. 171. Bodleian Library, MS Top. Northants c 9, p. 120
17. Kitching, 'Fire Disasters and Fire Relief', 184
18. BL, Thomason Tract E.694(7), *The Moderate Intelligencer*, 2–9 May 1653, p. 2. GL, MS 4458/1, p. 144 and unpaged entry, 23 Feb. 1676. CLRO, Ex-GLMS 271
19. *CSPD*, 1666–7, p. 101. *The London Gazette*, 17–20 Sept. 1666. Hutton, *Restoration*, pp. 246, 266

20. Slack, *Impact of Plague*, p. 133

21. CLRO, Ex-GLMSS 270, 271

22. The comment was made after a report of a fire at Crediton in 1732, *Derby Mercury*, 21 Dec. 1732, p. 3

23. *CSPD*, 1666–7, p. 111

24. Malcolm, *Londinium Redivivum*, vol. 4, p. 46

25. Bell, *Great Fire*, pp. 174, 323, 326, 330

26. *The London Gazette*, 20–24 Sept. 1666

27. T.F. Reddaway, *The Rebuilding of London after the Great Fire* (London, Jonathan Cape, 1940), pp. 62–4

28. *Calendar of Treasury Books*, 1660–7, p. 728

29. *The Correspondence of Henry Oldenburg*, ed. A.R. and M.B. Hall (13 vols, Madison, University of Wisconsin Press, 1965–86), vol. 3, p. 245

30. Reddaway, *Rebuilding*, pp. 64–6, 103. I. Darlington and J. Howgego, *Printed Maps of London circa 1553–1850* (London, George Philip, 1964), pp. 62–3

31. *The Economic Writings of Sir William Petty*, ed. C.H. Hull (2 vols, Cambridge, Cambridge University Press, 1899), vol. 2, p. 507

32. *Diary of Pepys*, vol. 7, p. 286

33. Bell, *Great Fire*, pp. 223–4

34. The figure was £15 for the 'moderated rent', which was three-quarters of the true value. Seaver, *Wallington's World*, pp. 238-9

35. *Economic Writings of Sir William Petty*, vol. 1, p. 105

36. The fires were at Wem, 1676, Beaminster, 1684, Warwick, 1694, and Blandford Forum, 1731; Jones et al., *Gazetteer*, pp. 18–21

37. Clarendon, *Selections*, p. 421

38. Bell, *Great Fire*, pp. 223–4

39. Jones et al., *Gazetteer*, pp. 11, 18–19. *CSPD*, 1666–7, p. 151

40. Bell, *Great Fire*, p. 318. *CSPVen*, 1666–8, p. 81

41. *CSPD*, 1666–7, pp. 100, 140, 171. A. Plummer, *The London Weavers' Company 1600–1970* (London, Routledge & Kegan Paul, 1972), p. 194

42. G. Whitteridge, 'The Fire of London and St Bartholomew's Hospital', *London Topographical Record*, 20 (1952), 55, 60. A.H. Johnson, *The History of The Worshipful Company of the Drapers of London* (5 vols, Oxford, Oxford University Press, 1914–22), vol. 3, pp. 275, 279. I. Doolittle, *The Mercers' Company 1579–1959* (London, The Mercers' Company, 1994), p. 75

43. CLRO, Ex–GLMS 297/21. Verney, *Memoirs of the Verney Family*, vol. 2, p. 259

44. Jones, *Fire Court*, vol. 2, p. 44. *Survey of London*, vol. 16 (London, Country Life, 1935), p. 209

45. *Conway Letters*, p. 278. 'Autobiography by William Taswell', 14

46. Weston, 'Letter from Sir Robert Atkyns', 108. *Diary of Pepys*, vol.

7, pp. 393, 401, 406; vol. 8, pp. 17, 87, 114

47.   Johnson, *Drapers' Company*, vol. 3, p. 275. B. Heath, *Some Account of the Worshipful Company of Grocers of the City of London* (London, 1869), pp. 22–3, 127. HMC, *Hastings MSS, II*, p. 372. *CSPD*, 1666–7, p. 340

48.   *Diary of Pepys*, vol. 8, pp. 60, 62

49.   Clarendon, *Selections*, pp. 421–2

50.   *Diary of Whitelocke*, p. 710. *Conway Letters*, p. 279

51.   *Diary of Pepys*, vol 7, pp. 386–7, 391

52.   Bell, *Great Fire*, p. 315

53.   Jones, *Fire Court*, vol. 1, pp. 134, 191, 262. Woodhead, *Rulers of London*, p. 97

54.   *Diary of Pepys*, vol. 7, pp. 297, 309–10. Clarendon, *Selections*, pp. 422–3. Bell, *Great Fire*, p. 226.

55.   *Aubrey's Brief Lives*, ed. O.L. Dick (Harmondsworth, Penguin, 1972), p. 382. H.F. Waters, *Genealogical Gleanings* (2 vols, Boston, Mass., 1901), vol. 2, p. 1060

56.   HMC, *Le Fleming MSS*, p. 48. *The Life, Diary, and Correspondence of Sir William Dugdale*, ed. W. Hamper (1827), p. 364

57.   Bell, *Great Fire*, pp. 227, 318

58.   *CSPD*, 1666–7, pp. 110, 168. HMC, *Portland MSS, III*, p. 298. *Commons' Journals*, vol. 8, p. 633

59.   *CSPD*, 1666–7, pp. 114, 133. U. Priestley, 'The Norwich Textile Industry: The London Connection', *The London Journal*, 19 (1994), 108–10

60.   *CSPD*, 1666–7, p. 197. *Life and Times of Anthony Wood*, vol. 2, p. 87. *Diary of Pepys*, vol. 8, pp. 121, 156

61.   *Diary of Pepys*, vol. 7, p. 401. *The Harleian Miscellany*, vol. 3, p. 300

62.   *CSPD*, 1666–7, p. 171. *Commons' Journals*, vol. 8, p. 676

63.   Manley, 'Central England Temperatures', 393. Lamb, *Climate*, vol. 2, p. 572. *Diary of Pepys*, vol. 8, pp. 98, 102, 105, 187, 295–6

64.   Weston, 'Letter from Sir Robert Atkyns', 107. *Diary of Pepys*, vol. 7, p. 280

65.   HMC, *Portland MSS, III*, p. 299

66.   Weston, 'Letter from Sir Robert Atkyns', 107. PRO, C5/96/17. *Diary of Pepys*, vol. 7, p. 296. Verney, *Memoirs of the Verney Family*, vol. 2, p. 258

67.   *CSP Ven*, 1666–8, p. 240

68.   *Diary of Pepys*, vol. 7, p. 296. *Survey of London*, vol. 36, (London, Athlone Press, 1970), p. 253

69.   Charterhouse Muniments, Assembly Books, vol. C, f. 62v. J.J. Baddeley, *An Account of the Church and Parish of St Giles, Cripplegate* (London, 1888), p. 155

70.   *The London Gazette*, 3–10, 10–13 Sept. 1666. Whitehead, *Rulers of London*, p. 51. Jones, *Fire Court*, vol. 1, pp. 167–8; vol. 2, p. 80. Clark, 'A Restoration Goldsmith-Banking House', p. 27. *Diary of Pepys*, vol. 7, pp. 323, 329; vol. 8, p. 521, n.2

71.   Verney, *Memoirs of the Verney Family*, vol. 2, p. 258

72. *Diary of Pepys*, vol. 7, pp. 277, 286, 293, 396, 398; vol. 8, p. 586; vol. 9, pp. 9, 16, 32–3

73. Whitteridge, 'St Bartholomew's Hospital', 50–3, 76–8

74. *Diary of John Evelyn*, ed. H.B. Wheatley (4 vols, London, Bickers & Son, 1906), vol. 3, p. 344

75. Clarendon, *Selections*, pp. 419–20. *Diary of Pepys*, vol. 7, pp. 338–9; vol. 9, pp. 75, 114

76. Jones, *Fire Court*, vol. 1, p. 105

77. *Diary of Pepys*, vol. 8, pp. 152, 155

78. CLRO, Ex-GLMS 298/80

79. Ibid., 297/6

80. Ibid., 297/4, 5; 298/105

81. Ibid., 271, unfoliated

82. Ibid., 298/19

83. Ibid., 297/72, 151. Woodhead, *Rulers of London*, p. 34. *Diary of Pepys*, vol. 8, p. 562

84. CLRO, Ex–GLMS 298 *passim*

85. Ibid., 298/107

86. *Commons' Journals*, vol. 8, p. 627. *The Diary of John Milward, Esq.*, ed. C. Robbins (Cambridge, Cambridge University Press, 1938), p. 7

87. Burnet, *History of My Own Time*, vol. 1, p. 415. *Diary of Pepys*, vol. 7, p. 357 n.1. Clarendon, *Selections*, p. 420

88. Bell, *Great Fire*, pp. 191–5. Burnet, *History of My Own Time*, vol. 1, pp. 411–12

89. *CSPD*, 1666–7, p. 175

90. *Diary of Pepys*, vol. 7, pp. 356–7. Burnet, *History of My Own Time*, vol. 1, p. 415 n.2

91. Bell, *Great Fire*, p. 322. Clarendon, *Selections*, p. 424

92. Clarendon, *Selections*, p. 455

93. C.D. Chandaman, *The English Public Revenue 1660–1688* (Oxford, Clarendon Press, 1975), pp. 92–7

94. Chandaman, *Public Revenue*, pp. 162–3, 177–80, 212

95. *CSPVen*, 1666–8, pp. 81, 87

96. K.H.D. Haley, *An English Diplomat in the Low Countries. Sir William Temple and John de Witt, 1665–1673* (Oxford, Clarendon Press, 1986), p. 101. *The London Gazette*, 3–10 Sept. 1666

97. *CSPVen*, 1666–8, p. 92. Haley, *An English Diplomat*, p. 98

98. Miller, *Charles II*, pp. 124–7. Hutton, *Restoration*, pp. 253–7

99. Chandaman, *Public Revenue*, pp. 180–1. *Surveying the People*, eds. K. Schurer and T. Arkell (Oxford, Leopard's Head Press, 1992), pp. 150–3

100. Hutton, *Restoration*, pp. 258–60

101. P.G. Rogers, *The Dutch in the Medway* (London, Oxford University Press, 1970), pp. 79–126

102. *Diary of Pepys*, vol. 7, p. 426

FOUR: PREPARATIONS FOR REBUILDING

1. *Diary of Milward*, p. 9

2. *The Wren Society*, vol. 18 (Oxford, Oxford University Press, 1941), pp. 19, 26

3. I. Roy, 'England Turned Germany? The Aftermath of the Civil War in its European Context', *Transactions of the Royal Historical Society*, 5th series, 28 (1978), 138–9

4. *Petty Papers*, p. 29

5. HMC, *Fleming MSS*, p. 42. *The London Gazette*, 13–17 Sept. 1666

6. *Correspondence of John Locke*, vol. 1, p. 293

7. *Fumifugium* (1661) reprinted in *The Writings of John Evelyn*, ed. G. de la Bédoyère (Woodbridge, Boydell Press, 1995), p. 131. *Diary of Evelyn*, ed. Wheatley, vol. 3, p. 345. HMC, *Portland MSS, III*, p. 299

8. *CSPVen*, 1666–8, p. 92. Haley, *English Diplomat*, p. 98

9. HMC, *Fleming MSS*, p. 42

10. *Economic Writings of Sir William Petty*, vol. 2, p. 381

11. H. Rosenau, *The Ideal City: Its Architectural Evolution in Europe* (3rd edn, London, Methuen, 1983), pp. 55–65. A.E.J. Morris, *History of Urban Form Before the Industrial Revolutions* (4th edn, Harlow, Longman, 1994), pp. 168–73. G.L. Burke, *The Making of Dutch Towns* (London, Cleaver-Hume, 1956), pp. 121–3

12. Burke, *Dutch Towns*, pp. 75, 118–21, 147–53

13. Morris, *History of Urban Form*, pp. 178–87, 194–205. M.D. Pollak, *Turin 1564–1680: Urban Design, Military Culture, and the Creation of the Absolutist Capital* (Chicago, University of Chicago Press, 1991). H. Ballon, *The Paris of Henri IV: Architecture and Urbanism* (Cambridge, Mass., MIT Press, 1991), pp. 252–3

14. J.S. Curl, *The Londonderry Plantation 1609–1914* (Chichester, Phillimore, 1986)

15. J.M. Houston, *A Social Geography of Europe* (London, Duckworth, 1963 edn), p. 179. Burke, *Dutch Towns*, p. 59

16. M. Roberts, *Gustavus Adolphus, A History of Sweden, 1611–1632* (2 vols, London, Longmans, Green, 1953–8), vol. 1, pp. 487–8

17. P.A. Barker, 'Excavations of the Moated Site at Shifnal, Shropshire, 1962', *Transactions of the Shropshire Archaeological Society*, 57 (1961–4), 195. N. Scarfe, *The Suffolk Landscape* (London, Hodder and Stoughton, 1972), p. 230

18. *Diary of Evelyn*, ed. de Beer, vol. 3, p. 463; ed. Wheatley, vol. 3, p. 345

19. *Correspondence of Henry Oldenburg*, vol. 3, p. 300

20. This and the following two paragraphs are based upon: Whinney, *Wren*, pp. 38–9. S.E. Rasmussen, *London: The Unique City* (rev. edn, Cambridge, Mass., MIT Press, 1982), pp. 102–10. N. Pevsner, *The Buildings of England: London I, The Cities of London and Westminster*, ed. B. Cherry (3rd edn, Harmondsworth, Penguin, 1973), pp. 62–3. Morris, *History of Urban Form*, pp. 256–9. J. Hanson, 'Order and Structure in Urban Design: The Plans for the Rebuilding of London after the Great Fire of 1666', *Ekistics*, 56 (1989), 25–9

21. *London Redivivum*, reprinted in *Writings of Evelyn*, ed. de la Bédoyère, pp. 337–45

22. Morris, *History of Urban Form*, pp. 184–6. Ballon, *Paris*, pp. 199–207

23. *Diary of Evelyn*, ed. de Beer, vol. 2, p. 241. *Writings of Evelyn*, ed. de la Bédoyère, p. 338

24. Rosenau, *The Ideal City*, pp. 57–8. Morris, *History of Urban Form*, pp. 257, 339

25. Bell, *Great Fire*, pp. 240–2. Rasmussen, *London*, pp. 111–12. *The London Gazette*, 27 Sept.–1 Oct. 1666

26. *Petty Papers*, pp. 26–30

27. Reddaway, *Rebuilding*, p. 70

28. HMC, *Portland MSS, III*, p. 299. *Diary of Pepys*, vol. 8, p. 81. *Petty Papers*, p. 28

29. *Correspondence of Henry Oldenburg*, vol. 3, p. 238. *Diary of John Milward*, pp. 7–9

30. *Correspondence of Henry Oldenburg*, vol. 3, p. 238

31. Reddaway, *Rebuilding*, pp. 68, 74, 171–81

32. Ibid., pp. 52–9

33. *The London Gazette*, 13–17 Sept. 1666. *CSPD*, 1666–7, pp. 121–2

34. *Writings of Evelyn*, ed. de la Bédoyère, p. 138

35. *Wren Society*, vol. 18, pp. 198–9. Reddaway, *Rebuilding*, pp. 60–1

36. *Diary of Evelyn*, ed. de Beer, vol. 3, pp. 318–19, 327–8. *Writings of Evelyn*, ed. de la Bédoyère, p. 344

37. *Writings of Evelyn*, ed. de la Bédoyère, p. 132

38. PRO, SP16/257/113

39. *Commons' Journals*, 8, pp. 640, 643, 650, 656, 659, 661, 664–6. *Petty Papers*, p. 28

40. H. Horwitz, *Chancery Equity Records and Proceedings 1600–1800* (London, HMSO, 1995), pp. 25–6, 35

41. John Aleyn, *Select Cases* (1688), pp. 26–8

42. Reddaway, *Rebuilding*, p. 77. *Diary of Pepys*, vol. 7, p. 357

43. Jones, *Fire Court*, vol. 1, pp. vi–viii

44. *Diary of Pepys*, vol. 7, pp. 298, 300–1. *Writings of Evelyn*, ed. de la Bédoyère, p. 345

45. HMC, *Hastings MSS, II*, p. 372

46. R. Davis, *The Rise of the English Shipping Industry in the Seventeenth and Eighteenth Centuries* (2nd edn, Newton Abbot, David & Charles, 1972), pp. 14, 18, 53. Reddaway, *Rebuilding*, p. 73

47. *CSPD*, 1666–7, pp. 156, 170. Reddaway, *Rebuilding*, p. 127

48. *Diary of John Milward*, pp. 46, 53–5

49. Reddaway, *Rebuilding*, pp. 84–5, 89

50. Ibid., pp. 102–10, 154. Knowles and Pitt, *Building Regulation*, pp. 30–3. *The Survey of Building Sites in the City of London after the Great Fire of 1666*, ed. W.H. Godfrey (5 vols, London, London Topographical Society, 1946–65), vol. 1, pp. viii–ix

51. P.S. Seaver, *The Puritan Lectureships. The Politics of Religious Dissent 1560–1662* (Stanford, Stanford University Press, 1970), p. 147

52. VCH, *London*, vol. 1, p. 339

53. Ibid., p. 340

54. Reddaway, *Rebuilding*, p. 92n. Bell, *Great Fire*, p. 248

55. *Diary of Pepys*, vol. 8, p. 87

56. *CSPD*, 1666–7, pp. 172, 384.
     Woodhead, *Rulers of London*, pp.
     133–4, 169–70

57. *CSPD*, 1666–7, pp. 171, 245.
     R. King, *Henry Purcell* (London,
     Thames & Hudson, 1994),
     pp. 54–5

58. Earle, *Making of the English
     Middle Class*, p. 121

59. *Diary of Pepys*, vol. 7, pp. 275,
     426; vol. 8, p. 586; vol. 9, pp. 9, 16

60. Ibid., vol. 8, pp. 263, 450

61. Ibid., vol. 8, p. 136

FIVE: THE REBUILDING

1.   Cheshire RO, DMD/C/13/1

2.   Thomas Manley, *Usury at Six Per
     Cent* (1669)

3.   E. Harris, *British Architectural
     Books and Writers 1556–1785*
     (Cambridge, Cambridge University
     Press, 1990), pp. 43, 380–1

4.   Jones, *Fire Court*, vol. 1, p. 202

5.   Ibid., vol. 2, pp. 76, 125, 233

6.   From 178 cases included in Ibid.,
     vols 1, 2

7.   Ibid., vol. 1, p. 136

8.   E. McKellar, 'Architectural Practice
     for Speculative Building in Late
     Seventeenth Century London'
     (unpublished PhD thesis, Royal
     College of Art, 1992), p. 107

9.   F.T. Melton, 'Sir Robert
     Clayton's Building Projects in
     London, 1666–72', *Guildhall
     Studies in London History*, 3
     (1977), 39. *Diary of Evelyn*, ed.
     de Beer, vol. 3, pp. 625–6

10. Jones, *Fire Court*, vol. 1, pp. 87–9,
     119–20, 150

11. Ibid., vol. 2, pp. 108–9

12. *Diary of Pepys*, vol. 9, p. 23. Bell,
     Great Fire, pp. 246–7

13. Jones, *Fire Court*, vol. 2, p. 328

14. Ibid., vol. 1, pp. 266–7

15. Ibid., vol. 2, p. 164

16. Ibid., vol. 1, pp. 20, 52–3

17. Reddaway, *Rebuilding*, pp. 142–3

18. Jones, *Fire Court*, vol. 1, pp. 228–9,
     278–9; vol. 2, pp. 14, 29, 53

19. Ibid., vol. 2, p. 178

20. Ibid., vol. 1, pp. 89, 102 and
     passim; vol. 2, p. 31

21. Ibid., vol. 1, pp. 82–3, 90, 92, 95,
     101, 104, 107–8, 139–40, 240;
     vol. 2, p. 78

22. *The Records of the Honourable
     Society of Lincoln's Inn: The Black
     Books. Vol. III. From AD 1660 to
     AD 1775* (London, Lincoln's Inn,
     1899), pp. 53–4

23. *Survey of Building Sites*, ed.
     Godfrey, vol. 1, pp. ix, 1–107

24. Verney, *Memoirs of the Verney
     Family*, vol. 2, p. 260. Reddaway,
     Rebuilding, p. 279

25. P. Metcalf, *The Halls of the
     Fishmongers' Company* (London
     and Chichester, Phillimore, 1977),
     pp. 59, 61. D.Yeomans, '18th
     Century Timber Construction:
     Trade and Materials', *Architectural
     Journal*, 10 July 1991, 53–4

26. *Diary of Pepys*, vol. 9, p. 314

27. Reddaway, *Rebuilding*, p. 128

28. L. Clarke, *Building Capitalism*
     (London, Routledge, 1992),
     pp. 132, 135. B. Cherry, 'John

Pollexfen's House in Walbrook' in J. Bold and E. Chaney, eds, *English Architecture Public and Private* (London, Hambledon Press, 1993), p. 92

29.   *Markets and Merchants of the Late Seventeenth Century: The Marescoe–David Letters, 1668–1680*, ed. H. Roseveare (London, British Academy, Records of Social and Economic History, new series, 12, 1987), p. 260

30.   Israel, *Dutch Primacy*, p. 214. Nef, *Rise of the British Coal Industry*, vol. 2, app. D, opp. p. 380

31.   *Markets and Merchants*, ed. Roseveare, pp. 25, 30, 224–5, 258, 268. G. Cobb, *London City Churches* (2nd edn, London, Batsford, 1989), p. 34. Metcalf, *Halls of the Fishmongers' Company*, p. 71

32.   Davis, *Rise of the English Shipping Industry*, pp. 135, 212, 214 n.2

33.   *Diary of Pepys*, vol. 9, pp. 112, 124

34.   *CSPVen*, 1671–2, p. 120

35.   Milne, *Great Fire*, pp. 93–8. Reddaway, *Rebuilding*, pp. 279–82. *Memoirs of Sir John Reresby*, ed. A. Browning (2nd edn, London, Royal Historical Society, 1991), p. 62

36.   Finlay, *Population and Metropolis*, pp. 168–71. *London Inhabitants within the Walls 1695*, ed. D.V. Glass (London Record Society, vol. 2, 1966), p. xxvi

37.   Jones, *Fire Court*, vol. 1, p. 18–19, 49–50; vol. 2, p. 195

38.   Clark, 'A Restoration Goldsmith-Banking House', p.

31.   *Markets and Merchants*, ed. Roseveare, p. 3

39.   *Diary of Pepys*, vol. 9, pp. 124, 517

40.   Whitteridge, 'Fire of London and St Bartholomew's Hospital', 71–2. Reddaway, *Rebuilding*, p. 301

41.   J.R., *The Mystery of the New Fashioned Goldsmiths, etc.* (1676), in J. Thirsk and J.P. Cooper, *Seventeenth-Century Economic Documents* (Oxford, Clarendon Press, 1972), p. 686. Miller, *Charles II*, p. 187

42.   Miller, *Charles II*, pp. 192–7. Israel, *Dutch Primacy*, p. 301. Reddaway, *Rebuilding*, pp. 185–6

43.   Israel, *Dutch Primacy*, pp. 293–9. *CSPVen*, 1671–2, pp. 204, 274. HMC, *Hastings Manuscripts*, vol. 2, pp. 159–60

44.   *Diary of Evelyn*, ed. de Beer, vol. 3, p. 620

45.   Melton, 'Sir Robert Clayton's Building Projects', 39. Reddaway, *Rebuilding*, pp. 214–15

46.   Heath, *Some Account of the Grocers*, pp. 127–30

47.   Jones, *Fire Court*, vol. 2, pp. 300–1

48.   Reddaway, *Rebuilding*, pp. 250–6. Doolittle, *Mercers' Company*, pp. 74–5. Johnson, *Drapers' Company*, vol. 3, pp. 286–7. Metcalf, *Halls of the Fishmongers' Company*, pp. 66–81. *Diary of Pepys*, vol. 9, p. 292. Plummer, *Weavers' Company*, p. 206

49.   Reddaway, *Rebuilding*, pp. 181–9, 193

50.   Bell, *Great Fire*, pp. 269–70. Reddaway, *Rebuilding*, pp. 193, 249

51.   *Diary of Pepys*, vol. 8, pp. 496–7

52. Doolittle, *Mercers' Company*, pp. 78–82. Reddaway, *Rebuilding*, pp. 267–70. *The London Gazette*, 17–20 April 1671

53. T.F. Reddaway, 'The London Custom House, 1666–1740', *London Topographical Record*, vol. 21 (1958), 1–14. Jones, *Fire Court*, vol. 2, pp. 205–9

54. Reddaway, *Rebuilding*, pp. 201–21. Daniel Defoe, *A Tour Through the Whole Island of Great Britain*, ed. P. Rogers (Harmondsworth, Penguin, 1971), pp. 301–2

55. Reddaway, *Rebuilding*, pp. 221–43. *Wren Society*, vol. 18, pp. 21–3. Metcalf, *Halls of the Fishmongers' Company*, pp. 67, 73

56. Cobb, *City Churches*, p. 32

57. VCH, *London*, vol. 1, p. 341. *Wren Society*, vol. 19 (Oxford, Oxford University Press, 1941), pp. 2, 23, 30, 32, 36. Reddaway, *Rebuilding*, pp. 186–7. Bell, *Great Fire*, pp. 310–11. G. Milne and A. Reynolds, 'St Vedast Church rediscovered', *London Archaeologist*, 7 (1993), 67–72

58. *Wren Society*, vol. 19, pp. 23, 26, 36. E.E.F. Smith, *The Church of St Mary Abchurch: City of London* (London, The Ecclesiological Society, 1983), p. 4. Cobb, *City Churches*, pp. 35–6

59. W.H. Godfrey, *The Church of St Bride, Fleet Street* (Survey of London, monograph no. 15, 1944), pp. 30–2

60. VCH, *London*, vol. 1, p. 342

61. Smith, *St Mary Abchurch*, pp. 4–5. *Wren Society*, vol. 19, pp. 30–1

62. Cobb, *City Churches*, pp. 36, 156, 158, 164, 171

63. Godfrey, *St Bride, Fleet Street*, p. 32

64. *Wren Society*, vol. 10, pp. 46–53. Cobb, *City Churches*, p. 34

65. Cobb, *City Churches*, pp. 151, 162, 164. P. Jeffery, R. Lea and B. Watson, 'The Architectural History of the Church of St Mary-at-Hill in the City of London', *Transactions of the London and Middlesex Archaeological Society*, 43 (1992), 197–9

66. *Wren Society*, vol. 13, p. 46

67. 'Autobiography by William Taswell', 12. C. Carlton, *Charles I: The Personal Monarch* (2nd edn, London, Routledge, 1995), pp. 164–6. J.A. Gotch, *Inigo Jones* (London, Methuen, 1928), pp. 154–60, 168–76

68. *Wren Society*, vol. 13, p. 46

69. Whinney, *Wren*, pp. 33–7. *Diary of Evelyn*, ed. de Beer, vol. 3, pp. 448–9, 452

70. Whinney, *Wren*, pp. 81–97. J. Lang, *Rebuilding of St. Paul's after the Great Fire of London* (Oxford, Oxford University Press, 1956), pp. 68–9

71. Lang, *Rebuilding of St. Paul's*, pp. 41–3, 51–3. *Diary of Pepys*, vol. 9, p. 288. *Wren Society*, vol. 18, pp. 30–1

72. Reddaway, *Rebuilding*, p. 199. Lang, *Rebuilding of St. Paul's*, p. 123

73. Reddaway, *Rebuilding*, pp. 124–5. *Wren Society*, vol. 13, p. 10; vol. 15, p. xvi

74. *Diary of Evelyn*, ed. de Beer, vol. 5, pp. 192, 278

75. Lang, *Rebuilding of St. Paul's*, p. 111

76. R. Blomfield, *A Short History of Renaissance Architecture in England* (London, Bell, 1900), p. 124

77. See above, p. 118. Edward Chamberlayne, *The Present State of England* (4th edn, 1673), 2nd part p. 201

78. *A Survey of the Cities of London and Westminster . . . By John Stow*, ed. John Strype (1720), bk 1, p. 231

SIX: THE AFTERMATH

1. *The Correspondence of John Cosin, DD, Lord Bishop of Durham, part ii*, ed. G. Ornsby (Surtees Society, vol. 55, 1872), p. 155

2. *Diary of Pepys*, vol. 7, pp. 280, 287, 296, 299; vol. 8, pp. 87, 128

3. Ibid, vol. 9, p. 245

4. *A Survey . . . By John Stow*, ed. Strype, bk 1, pp. 237–9. GL, MSS 11,394/1, unfol.; 16,967/6, p. 55; 4069/2, f. 301. Drapers' Company Archives, M.B.15, f. 35; W.A.21/3, 1670–1

5. HMC, *Ormonde Manuscripts*, new series, vol. 4 (1906), p. 356

6. Defoe, *A Tour*, pp. 318–19

7. H.A.L. Cockerell and E. Green, *The British Insurance Business* (London, Heinemann, 1976), pp. 16, 19. Thirsk and Cooper, *Seventeenth-Century Economic Documents*, p. 692. Goudsblom, *Fire and Civilization*, p. 151

8. Bristol RO, Common Council Proceedings, 1659–75, p. 142. HMC, *Eleventh Report, part 8*, p. 196.

Devon RO, ECA bk 11, Chamber Act Book, 1663–84, p. 100

9. Bristol RO, Common Council Proceedings, 1659–75, pp. 185–8. *Beverley Borough Records, 1575–1821*, ed. J. Dennett (Yorkshire Archaeological Society Record Series, vol. 84, 1932), p. 141

10. Bodleian Library, MS Tanner 42, ff. 20, 31. Jones et al., *Gazetteer*, pp. 18, 46. E.W. Brayley, *London and Middlesex* (4 vols, London, 1810–16), vol. 1, pp. 557–8; vol. 4, p. 300

11. *Diary of Pepys*, vol. 8, p. 191. Jones et al., *Gazetteer*, p. 18

12. *Statutes of the Realm*, vol. 5, pp. 798–801. F.A. Sharman, 'The Northampton Fire Court' in J.A. Guy and H.G. Beale, eds, *Law and Social Change in British History* (London, Royal Historical Society, 1984), pp. 118–25. *The Great Fire of Warwick 1694*, ed. M. Farr, (Dugdale Society, vol. 36, 1994), p. xv

13. P. Borsay, *The English Urban Renaissance* (Oxford, Oxford University Press, 1989), pp. 90–5. M. Turner, 'New towns for Old? Reconstruction after fires in the South West: The Case of Blandford Forum, Dorset, 1731' in R. Heigham, ed., *Landscape and Townscape in the South West*, (Exeter, University of Exeter Press, 1989), pp. 78–84. Jones et al., *Gazetteer*, pp. 52–4

14. *The Illustrated Journeys of Celia Fiennes 1685–c.1712*, ed. C. Morris (Stroud, Alan Sutton, 1995), pp. 114–17. Defoe, *A Tour*, pp. 405–6

15. *The Diary of Abraham de la Pryme*, ed. C. Jackson (Surtees Society, vol. 54, 1870), pp. 61, 141

16. Francis Blomefield, *An Essay Towards A Topographical History of . . . Norfolk* (11 vols, 1805–11) vol. 2, p. 443

17. H. Colvin, 'Inigo Jones and the Church of St Michael le Querne', *The London Journal*, 12 (1986), 38–9

18. Chamberlayne, *Present State of England*, 2nd part, pp. 201–2

19. B. Ash, *The Golden City. London between the Fires, 1666–1941* (London, Phoenix House, 1964), p. 43

20. Defoe, *A Tour*, pp. 302–3

21. Borsay, *English Urban Renaissance*, pp. 110–11; 'The London Connection: Cultural Diffusion and the Eighteenth-century Provincial Town', *The London Journal*, 19 (1994), 21–35

22. N. Pevsner, *The Buildings of England: North-East Norfolk and Norwich* (Harmondsworth, Penguin, 1962), p. 146; *North Somerset and Bristol* (Harmondsworth, Penguin, 1958), pp. 386–7

23. Pevsner, *London and Westminster*, p. 64. McKellar, 'Architectural Practice', p. 32

24. K. Downes, *Hawksmoor* (London, Zwemmer, 1959), pp. 241–2

25. J. Summerson, *Georgian London* (rev. edn, London, Barrie & Jenkins, 1988), p. 40

26. A. Cox, 'Bricks to Build a Capital' in H. Hobhouse and A. Saunders, eds, *Good and Proper Materials, The*

fabric of London since the Great Fire (London Topographical Society, no. 140, 1989), pp. 3–5. *Commons' Journals*, vol. 21, p. 77

27. *Diary of Pepys*, vol. 9, p. 392

28. V. Harding, 'Reconstructing London before the Great Fire', *London Topographical Record*, 25 (1985), 1–12

29. Reddaway, *Rebuilding*, p. 291. *Diary of Pepys*, vol. 9, p. 285

30. Edward Hatton, *A New View of London* (1708), cited in A. Saint and G. Darley, *The Chronicles of London* (London, Weidenfeld & Nicolson, 1994), p. 127

31. Cherry, 'John Pollexfen's House', 92–103

32. Reddaway, *Rebuilding*, pp. 32–3, 311–12

33. Morris, *History of Urban Form*, pp. 339, 346–8

34. P. Glanville, *London in Maps* (London, The Connoisseur, 1972), pp. 26–8. R. Hyde, 'Ogilby and Morgan's City of London Map, 1676', introduction to *The A to Z of Restoration London* (London Topographical Society, No. 145, 1992)

35. C.W.F. Goss, *The London Directories 1677–1855* (London, Archer, 1932), pp. 17–22. J. Chartres, 'Trade and shipping in the Port of London', *Journal of Transport History* (3rd series, 1, 1980–1), 29–33

36. Reddaway, *Rebuilding*, pp. 302, 306 n.2

37. *Wren Society*, vol. 18, pp. 19–20, 26, 31–3

38. Glamorgan RO, CL/MS 4.266, p. 74; I owe this reference to the kindness of Stephen Roberts

39. Chester City RO, Assembly Files A/F/39e/24; Assembly Book A/B/2, ff162v, 164v–5. Reddaway, *Rebuilding*, p. 245 n.3

40. Reddaway, *Rebuilding*, pp. 302–5. J.R. Kellett, 'The Breakdown of Gild and Corporation Control over the Handicraft and Retail Trade in London', *Economic History Review*, 2nd series, 10 (1957–8), 383

41. L. Stone, 'The Residential Development of the West End of London in the Seventeenth Century' in B.C. Malament, ed., *After the Reformation: Essays in Honor of J.H. Hexter* (Manchester, Manchester University Press, 1980), pp. 186–9

42. Archer, *Haberdashers' Company*, p. 93

43. Whitteridge, 'St Bartholomew's Hospital', 75

44. Doolittle, *Mercers' Company*, pp. 82, 101–3

45. Jones, *Fire Court*, vol. 1, pp. 23–4. *Calendar of Treasury Books, 1669–71*, p. 720

46. Jones, *Fire Court*, vol. 1, pp. 56–8, 199–201. VCH, *Lancashire*, vol. 2 (1908), p. 612

47. VCH, *Wiltshire*, vol. 12, pp. 5, 11

48. *The Records of a Church of Christ, Meeting in Broadmead, Bristol, 1640–1687*, ed. E.B. Underhill (The Hanserd Knollys Society, 1847), p. 88. Matthew Sylvester, *Reliquiae Baxterianae: or, Mr.*

Richard Baxter's Narrative . . . (3 vols, London, 1696), vol. 3, p. 19

49. *Diary of Pepys*, vol. 9, p. 552

50. J. Miller, *Popery and Politics in England 1660–1688* (Cambridge, Cambridge University Press, 1973), p. 161. T. Harris, *London Crowds in the Reign of Charles II. Propaganda and Politics from the Restoration to the Exclusion Crisis* (Cambridge, Cambridge University Press, 1987), p. 111

51. Miller, *Popery and Politics*, p. 182. Harris, *London Crowds*, pp. 112, 175

52. *Commons' Journals*, vol. 9, p. 703

53. Welch, *History of the Monument*, pp. 37–8

54. Harris, *London Crowds*, pp. 183–6. *DNB*

55. The title of a sermon by William Wray, delivered at St Olave's, Hart Street, and published in 1682

56. 'An Allegory of the Martyrdom of Charles I', after Jan Breughel the younger, is at Petworth House, picture no. 312

57. This and the following paragraph are based upon J.M. Levine, *Dr Woodward's Shield: History, Science, and Satire in Augustan England* (Ithaca and London, Cornell University Press, 1991), pp. 133–50

58. Lang, *Rebuilding of St Paul's*, pp. 65–7

59. W. Besant, *London in the Time of the Stuarts* (London, Adams & Black, 1903), pp. 233, 244

60. *Survey of London*, vol. 36, pp. 29–31

61. McKellar, 'Architectural Practice', p. 190. Charterhouse Muniments,

Committee Orders 1677–1736,
pp. 124–5

62.   E.L. Jones and M.E. Falkus, 'Urban
Improvement and the English
Economy in the Seventeenth and
Eighteenth Centuries', *Research
in Economic History*, 4 (1979),
198–203. L.E. Frost and E.L. Jones,
'The Fire Gap and the Greater

Durability of Nineteenth Century
Cities', *Planning Perspectives*, 4
(1989), 333–47. Goudsblom, *Fire
and Civilization*, pp. 176–80

63.   P. Jeffery and B. Watson, 'The
Templeman Report on London's
Churches: Can Wren's Legacy
Survive?', *London Archaeologist*, 7
(1994), 184–8

BIBLIOGRAPHY

Aleyn, John, *Select Cases*, 1688

Ash, B., *The Golden City. London between the Fires, 1666–1941*, London, Phoenix House, 1964

Ashley, M., *Financial and Commercial Policy under the Cromwellian Protectorate*, 2nd edn London, Frank Cass, 1962

Aubrey: *Aubrey's Brief Lives*, ed. O.L. Dick, Harmondsworth, Penguin, 1972

Baddeley, J.J., *An Account of the Church and Parish of St Giles, Cripplegate*, London, 1888

Ballon, H., *The Paris of Henri IV: Architecture and Urbanism*, Cambridge, Mass., MIT Press, 1991

Barker, P.A., 'Excavations of the Moated Site at Shifnal, Shropshire, 1962', *Transactions of the Shropshire Archaeological Society*, 57 (1961–4), 194–205

Barnes, W.M., 'The Diary of William Whiteway, of Dorchester, Co. Dorset', *Proceedings of the Dorset Natural History and Antiquarian Field Club*, 13 (1891), 57–81

Baxter: Sylvester, Matthew, *Reliquiae Baxterianae: or, Mr. Richard Baxter's Narrative . . .*, 3 vols, London, 1696

Beier, A.L. and Finlay, R., eds, *London 1500–1700: The Making of the Metropolis*, London, Longman, 1986

Bell, W.G. *The Great Fire of London in 1666*, London, John Lane, The Bodley Head, 1920

Besant, W., *London in the Time of the Stuarts*, London, Adams & Black, 1903

Bewes, W.A., *Church Briefs*, 1896

Blomefield, Francis, *An Essay towards a Topographical History of . . . Norfolk*, 11 vols, 1805–11

Blomfield, R., *A Short History of Renaissance Architecture in England*, London, Bell, 1900

Borsay, P., *The English Urban Renaissance*, Oxford, Oxford University Press, 1989

——, 'The London Connection: Cultural Diffusion and the Eighteenth-century Provincial Town', *The London Journal*, 19 (1994), 21–35

Brayley, E.W., *London and Middlesex*, 4 vols, London, 1810–16

Burke, G.L., *The Making of Dutch Towns*, London, Cleaver-Hume, 1956

Burnet, Gilbert, *History of My Own Time. Part 1: The Reign of Charles the Second*, ed. O. Airy, 2 vols, Oxford, Clarendon Press, 1897–1900

Capp, B., *The Fifth Monarchy Men. A Study in Seventeenth-century English Millenarianism*, London, Faber & Faber, 1972

——, *Astrology and the Popular Press: English Almanacs 1500–1800*, London, Faber & Faber, 1979

Carlton, C., *Charles I: The Personal Monarch*, 2nd edn, London, Routledge, 1995

Chamberlayne, Edward, *The Present State of England*, 4th edn, 1673

Champion, J.A.I., *London's Dreaded Visitation. The Social Geography of the Great Plague in 1665*, London, Historical Geography Research Series, 31, 1995

Chandaman, C.D., *The English Public Revenue 1660–1688*, Oxford, Clarendon Press, 1975

Chartres, J., 'Trade and Shipping in the Port of London', *Journal of Transport History*, 3rd series, 1 (1980–1), 29–47

Cherry, B., 'John Pollexfen's House in Walbrook' in J. Bold and E. Chaney, eds, *English Architecture Public and Private*, London, Hambledon Press, 1993

Clarendon: Edward Hyde, Earl of Clarendon, *Selections from the History of the Rebellion and the Life by Himself*, ed. G. Huehns, Oxford, Oxford University Press, 1978

Clark, D.K., 'A Restoration Goldsmith-Banking House: The Vine on Lombard Street' in *Essays in Modern English History in Honor of Wilbur Cortez Abbott*, Cambridge, Mass., Harvard University Press, 1941

Clarke, L., *Building Capitalism*, London, Routledge, 1992

Cobb, G., *London City Churches*, 2nd edn, London, Batsford, 1989

Cockerell, H.A.L. and Green, E., *The British Insurance Business*, London, Heinemann, 1976

Colvin, H., 'Inigo Jones and the Church of St Michael le Querne', *The London Journal*, 12 (1986), 36–9

Conway: *The Conway Letters. The Correspondence of Anne, Viscountess Conway, Henry More, and their Friends 1642–1684*, ed. M.H. Nicolson, rev. edn ed. S. Hutton, Oxford, Clarendon Press, 1992

Cosin: *The Correspondence of John Cosin, DD, Lord Bishop of Durham, part ii*, ed. G. Ornsby, Surtees Society, vol. 55, 1872

Cox, A., 'Bricks to Build a Capital' in H. Hobhouse and A. Saunders, eds. *Good and Proper Materials, The Fabric of London since the Great Fire*, London Topographical Society, no. 140, 1989

Cunnington, B.H., *Some Annals of the Borough of Devizes 1555–1791*, Devizes, 1925

Curl, J.S., *The Londonderry Plantation 1609–1914*, Chichester, Phillimore, 1986

Dale, T.C., *The Inhabitants of London in 1638*, London, Society of Genealogists, 1931

Darlington, I. and Howgego, J., *Printed Maps of London circa 1553–1850*, London, George Philip, 1964

Davis, R., *The Rise of the English Shipping Industry in the Seventeenth and Eighteenth Centuries*, 2nd edn, Newton Abbot, David & Charles, 1972

Defoe, Daniel, *A Tour Through the Whole Island of Great Britain*, ed. P. Rogers, Harmondsworth, Penguin, 1971

Delaune, Thomas, *The Present State of London*, 1681

Dennett, J., ed., *Beverley Borough Records, 1575–1821*, Yorkshire Archaeological Society Record Series, vol. 84, 1932

Doolittle, I., *The Mercers' Company 1579–1959*, London, The Mercers' Company, 1994

Downes, K., *Hawksmoor*, London, Zwemmer, 1959

Dugdale: *The Life, Diary, and Correspondence of Sir William Dugdale*, ed. W. Hamper, 1827

Earle, P., *The Making of the English Middle Class. Business, Society and Family Life in London, 1660–1730*, London, Methuen, 1989

Evelyn: *Diary of John Evelyn*, ed. H.B. Wheatley, 4 vols, London, Bickers & Son, 1906

——, *The Diary of John Evelyn*, ed. E.S. de Beer, 6 vols, Oxford, Clarendon Press, 1955

——, *The Writings of John Evelyn*, ed. G. de la Bédoyère, Woodbridge, Boydell Press, 1995

Fiennes: *The Illustrated Journeys of Celia Fiennes 1685–c.1712*, ed. C. Morris, Stroud, Alan Sutton, 1995

Finlay, R., *Population and Metropolis. The Demography of London 1580–1650*, Cambridge, Cambridge University Press, 1981

——, and Shearer, B., 'Population growth and suburban expansion' in Beier and Finlay, eds, *London 1500–1700*

Firth, C.H. and Rait, R.S., *Acts and Ordinances of the Interregnum*, 3 vols, London, HMSO, 1911

Fox, John, 'A False Fearful Imagination of Fire at Oxford University' in *Tudor Tracts 1532–1588*, ed. A.F. Pollard Westminster, 1903

Frost, L.E. and Jones, E.L., 'The Fire Gap and the Greater Durability of Nineteenth Century Cities', *Planning Perspectives*, 4 (1989), 333–47

Fuller, Thomas, *The History of the Worthies of England*, ed. P.A. Nuttall, 3 vols, London, 1840

George, M.D., *London Life in the Eighteenth Century*, Harmondsworth, Penguin, 1965

G.J.A., 'Fire of London', *Notes & Queries*, 5th series, 5 (1876), 306

Glanville, P., *London in Maps*, London, The Connoisseur, 1972

Glass, D.V., ed., *London Inhabitants within the Walls 1695*, London Record Society, vol. 2, 1966

Godfrey, W.H., *The Church of St Bride, Fleet Street*, Survey of London, monograph no. 15, 1944

——, ed., *The Survey of Building Sites in the City of London after the Great Fire of 1666*, 5 vols, London, London Topographical Society, 1946–65

Goss, C.W.F., *The London Directories 1677–1855*, London, Archer, 1932

Gotch, J.A., *Inigo Jones*, London, Methuen, 1928

Goudsblom, J., *Fire and Civilization*, Harmondsworth, Allen Lane, 1992

Green, I.M., *The Re-establishment of the Church of England 1660–1663*, Oxford, Oxford University Press, 1978

Haley, K.H.D., *An English Diplomat in the Low Countries. Sir William Temple and John de Witt, 1665–1673*, Oxford, Clarendon Press, 1986

Hanson, J., 'Order and Structure in Urban Design: The Plans for the Rebuilding of London after the Great Fire of 1666', *Ekistics*, 56 (1989), 22–42

Harding, V., 'Reconstructing London before the Great Fire', *London Topographical Record*, 25 (1985), 1–12

Harris, E., *British Architectural Books and Writers 1556–1785*, Cambridge, Cambridge University Press, 1990

Harris, T., *London Crowds in the Reign of Charles II. Propaganda and Politics from the Restoration to the Exclusion Crisis*, Cambridge, Cambridge University Press, 1987

Harvey, P.D.A., 'A Foreign Visitor's Account of the Great Fire, 1666', *Transactions of the London and Middlesex Archaeological Society*, 20 (1959–61), 76–87

Hearsey, J.E.N., *London and the Great Fire*, London, John Murray, 1966

Heath, B., *Some Account of the Worshipful Company of Grocers of the City of London*, London, 1869

Henning, B.D., ed., *The History of Parliament: The House of Commons, 1660–1690*, 3 vols, London, Secker and Warburg, 1983

HMC, *Twelfth Report, app. VII, Le Fleming MSS*

——, *Fourteenth Report, Portland MSS, III*

——, *Hastings MSS, II*

——, *Ormonde Manuscripts*, new series, vol. 4

Holloway, S., *Courage High! A History of Firefighting in London*, London, HMSO, 1992

Horwitz, H., *Chancery Equity Records and Proceedings 1600–1800*, London, HMSO, 1995

Houston, J.M., *A Social Geography of Europe*, London, Duckworth, 1963

Howel, James, *Londinopolis*, 1658

Howgego, J.L., 'The Guildhall Fire Judges', *The Guildhall Miscellany*, 2 (1953), 22–30

Hutton, R., *The Restoration. A Political and Religious History of England and Wales 1658–1667*, Oxford, Oxford University Press, 1985

Hyde, R., 'Ogilby and Morgan's City of London Map, 1676', introduction to *The A to Z of Restoration London*, London Topographical Society, No. 145, 1992

Israel, J.I., *Dutch Primacy in World Trade, 1585–1740*, Oxford, Oxford University Press, 1989

Jeffery, P., Lea, R. and Watson, B., 'The Architectural History of the Church of St Mary-at-Hill in the City of London', *Transactions of the London and Middlesex Archaeological Society*, 43 (1992), 193–200

Jeffery, P., and Watson, B., 'The Templeman Report on London's Churches: Can Wren's Legacy Survive?', *London Archaeologist*, 7 (1994), 184–8

Jenkins, R., 'Fire-extinguishing Engines in England, 1625–1725', *Transactions of the Newcomen Society*, 11 (1930–1), 15–25

Johnson, A.H., *The History of The Worshipful Company of the Drapers of London*, 5 vols, Oxford, Oxford University Press, 1914–22

Jones, E.L. and Falkus, M.E., 'Urban Improvement and the English Economy in the Seventeenth and Eighteenth Centuries', *Research in Economic History*, 4 (1979), 193–233

Jones, E.L., Porter, S. and Turner, M., *A Gazetteer of English Urban Fire Disasters, 1500–1900*, Norwich, Historical Geography Research Series, 13, 1984

Jones, P.E., ed., *The Fire Court*, 2 vols, London, Corporation of London, 1966–70

Karslake, J.B.P., 'Early London Fire-Appliances', *The Antiquaries Journal*, 9 (1929), 229–38

Keene, D., *Cheapside before the Great Fire*, London, ESRC, 1985

Kellett, J.R., 'The Breakdown of Gild and Corporation Control over the Handicraft and Retail Trade in London', *Economic History Review*, 2nd series, 10 (1957–8), 381–94

King, R., *Henry Purcell*, London, Thames & Hudson, 1994

Kitching, C.J., 'Fire Disasters and Fire Relief in Sixteenth-century England: the Nantwich Fire of 1583', *Bulletin of the Institute of Historical Research*, 54 (1981), 171–87

Knowles, C.C., and Pitt, P.H., *The History of Building Regulation in London 1189–1972*, London, Architectural Press, 1972

Lamb, H.H., *Climate: Present, Past and Future*, 2 vols, London, Methuen, 1972–7

Lang, J., *Rebuilding of St Paul's after the Great Fire of London*, Oxford, Oxford University Press, 1956

Leland: *The itinerary of John Leland in or about the Years 1535–42*, ed. L.T. Smith, 5 vols, London, George Bell, 1906

Levine, J.M., *Dr Woodward's Shield: History, Science, and Satire in Augustan England*, Ithaca and London, Cornell University Press, 1991

Lincoln's Inn: *The Records of the Honourable Society of Lincoln's Inn: The Black Books. Vol. III. From AD 1660 to AD 1775*, London, Lincoln's Inn, 1899

Locke: *The Correspondence of John Locke*, ed. E.S. de Beer, 8 vols, Oxford, Clarendon Press, 1976–89

McKellar, E., 'Architectural Practice for Speculative Building in Late Seventeenth Century London', unpublished PhD thesis, Royal College of Art, 1992

McKeon, M., *Politics and Poetry in Restoration England. The Case of Dryden's Annus Mirabilis*, Cambridge, Mass., and London, Harvard University Press, 1975

Malcolm, J.P., *Londinium Redivivum*, 4 vols, London, 1802–7

Manley, G., 'Central England Temperatures: Monthly Means 1659 to 1973', *Quarterly Journal of the Royal Meteorological Society*, 100 (1974), 389–405

Manley, Thomas, *Usury at Six Per Cent*, 1669

Marescoe: *Markets and Merchants of the Late Seventeenth Century: The Marescoe–David Letters, 1668–1680*, ed. H. Roseveare, London, British Academy, Records of Social and Economic History, new series, 12, 1987

Melton, F.T., 'Sir Robert Clayton's Building Projects in London, 1666–72', *Guildhall Studies in London History*, 3 (1977), 37–41

Metcalf, P., *The Halls of the Fishmongers' Company*, London and Chichester, Phillimore, 1977

Miller, J., *Popery and Politics in England 1660–1688*, Cambridge, Cambridge University Press, 1973

——, *Charles II*, London, Weidenfeld & Nicolson, 1991

Milne, G., *The Great Fire of London*, New Barnet and London, Historical Publications, 1986

——, and Reynolds, A., 'St Vedast Church rediscovered', *London Archaeologist*, 7 (1993), 67–72

Milward, *The Diary of John Milward, Esq.*, ed. C. Robbins, Cambridge, Cambridge University Press, 1938

Morris, A.E.J., *History of Urban Form Before the Industrial Revolutions*, 4th edn, Harlow, Longman, 1994

Nef, J.U., *The Rise of the British Coal Industry*, 2 vols, London, Cass, 1966

Oldenburg: *The Correspondence of Henry Oldenburg*, ed. A.R. and M.B. Hall, 13 vols, Madison, University of Wisconsin Press, 1965–86

Ollard, R., *Man of War. Sir Robert Holmes and the Restoration Navy*, London, Hodder and Stoughton, 1969

——, *Clarendon and His Friends*, Oxford, Oxford University Press, 1988

Pepys: *The Diary of Samuel Pepys*, ed. R.C. Latham and W. Matthews, 11 vols, London, Bell & Hyman, 1970–83

Petty: *The Economic Writings of Sir William Petty*, ed. C.H. Hull, 2 vols, Cambridge, Cambridge University Press, 1899

Pevsner, N., *North Somerset and Bristol*, Harmondsworth, Penguin, 1958

——, *The Buildings of England: North-East Norfolk and Norwich*, Harmondsworth, Penguin, 1962

——, *The Buildings of England: London I, The Cities of London and Westminster*, ed. B. Cherry, 3rd edn, Harmondsworth, Penguin, 1973

Plummer, A., *The London Weavers' Company 1600–1970*, London, Routledge & Kegan Paul, 1972

Pollak, M.D., *Turin 1564–1680: Urban Design, Military Culture, and the Creation of the Absolutist Capital*, Chicago, University of Chicago Press, 1991

Porter, S., 'Town Fires: the case of Tiverton', *Devon & Cornwall Notes & Queries*, 33 (1977), 345–8

——, 'The Oxford Fire of 1644', *Oxoniensia*, 49 (1984), 289–300

——, 'The Oxford Fire Regulations of 1671', *Bulletin of the Institute of Historical Research*, 53 (1985), 251–5

——, 'Thatching in Early-modern Norwich', *Norfolk Archaeology*, 39 (1986), 310–12

——, 'Newspapers and Fire Relief in Early Modern England', *Journal of Newspaper and Periodical History*, 8 (1992), 28–33

Power, M.J., 'The Social Topography of Restoration London' in Beier and Finlay, eds, *London 1500–1700*

Prideaux, W.S., ed., *Memorials of the Goldsmiths' Company*, London, Eyre and Spottiswoode, 1896

Priestley, U., 'The Norwich Textile Industry: The London Connection', *The London Journal*, 19 (1994), 108–18

Pryme: *The Diary of Abraham de la Pryme*, ed. C. Jackson, Surtees Society, vol. 54, 1870

Rasmussen, S.E., *London: The Unique City*, rev. edn, Cambridge, Mass., MIT Press, 1982

Reddaway, T.F., *The Rebuilding of London after the Great Fire*, London, Jonathan Cape, 1940

——, 'The London Custom House, 1666–1740', *London Topographical Record*, vol. 21 (1958), 1–25

'Rege Sincera', *Observations, both Historical and Moral, upon the Burning of London; September 1666*, 1667, reprinted in *The Harleian Miscellany*, vol. 3, London, 1809

Reresby: *Memoirs of Sir John Reresby*, ed. A. Browning, 2nd edn, London, Royal Historical Society, 1991

Roberts, M., *Gustavus Adolphus, A History of Sweden, 1611–1632*, 2 vols, London, Longmans, Green, 1953–8

——, ed., *Swedish Diplomats at Cromwell's Court, 1655–1656*, Camden Society, 4th series, 36, 1988

Rogers, P.G., *The Dutch in the Medway*, London, Oxford University Press, 1970

Rosenau, H., *The Ideal City: Its Architectural Evolution in Europe*, 3rd edn, London, Methuen, 1983

Roy, I., 'England Turned Germany? The Aftermath of the Civil War in its European Context', *Transactions of the Royal Historical Society*, 5th series, 28 (1978), 127–44

Saint, A. and Darley, G., *The Chronicles of London*, London, Weidenfeld & Nicolson, 1994

Scarfe, N., *The Suffolk Landscape*, London, Hodder and Stoughton, 1972

Schofield, J., *Medieval London Houses*, London and New Haven, Yale University Press, 1995

Schove, D.J., 'Fire and Drought, 1600–1700', *Weather*, 21 (1966), 311–14

Schurer, K. and Arkell, T., eds, *Surveying the People*, Oxford, Leopard's Head Press, 1992

Seaver, P.S., *The Puritan Lectureships. The Politics of Religious Dissent 1560–1662*, Stanford, Stanford University Press, 1970

——, *Wallington's World. A Puritan Artisan in Seventeenth-century London*, London, Methuen, 1985

Sharman, F.A., 'The Northampton Fire Court' in J.A. Guy and H.G. Beale, eds, *Law and Social Change in British History*, London, Royal Historical Society, 1984

Slack, P., *The Impact of Plague in Tudor and Stuart England*, London, Routledge & Kegan Paul, 1985

Smith, E.E.F., *The Church of St Mary Abchurch: City of London*, London, The Ecclesiological Society, 1983

Smith, J.E., *Bygone Briefs: . . . A Schedule of More than a Thousand Briefs Laid in . . . St Margaret, Westminster. . . ,* London, Wightman, 1896

Spurr, J., *The Restoration Church of England*, London and New Haven, Yale University Press, 1991

Sternberg, V.T., 'Predictions of the Fire and Plague of London', *Notes & Queries*, 1st series, 7 (1853), 79–80, 173–4

Stone, L., 'The Residential Development of the West End of London in the Seventeenth Century' in B.C. Malament, ed., *After the Reformation: Essays in Honor of J.H. Hexter*, Manchester, Manchester University Press, 1980

Storey, M., ed., *Two East Anglian Diaries 1641–1729*, Suffolk Records Society, 36, 1994

Stow, John, *The Survey of London*, ed. H.B. Wheatley, revised edn, London, Dent, 1956

Strype, John, *A Survey of the Cities of London and Westminster . . . by John Stow*, 1720

Summerson, J., *Georgian London*, rev. edn, London, Barrie & Jenkins, 1988

Survey of London, vol. 16, London, Country Life, 1935

——, vol. 36, London, Athlone Press, 1970

Taswell, 'Autobiography and Anecdotes by William Taswell, D.D.', ed. G.P. Elliott, *Camden Miscellany*, vol. 2, 1853

Thirsk, J., and Cooper, J.P., *Seventeenth–Century Economic Documents*, Oxford, Clarendon Press, 1972

Treswell: *The London Surveys of Ralph Treswell*, ed. J. Schofield, London, London Topographical Society, 135, 1987

Turner, M., 'New Towns for Old? Reconstruction after Fires in the South West: The Case of Blandford Forum, Dorset, 1731' in R. Heigham, ed., *Landscape and Townscape in the South West*, Exeter, University of Exeter Press, 1989

Underdown, D., *Fire from Heaven: The Life of an English Town in the Seventeenth Century*, London, HarperCollins, 1992

Underhill, E.B., ed., *The Records of a Church of Christ, Meeting in Broadmead, Bristol, 1640–1687*, The Hanserd Knollys Society, 1847

VCH, *London*, vol. 1

——, *Wiltshire*, vol. 12

Verney, F.P. and Verney, M.M., *Memoirs of the Verney Family during the Seventeenth Century*, 2nd edn, 2 vols, London, Longmans, Green, 1907

Walford, C., 'King's Briefs: Their Purposes and History', *Transactions of the Royal Historical Society*, 10 (1882), 1–74

Wallington, Nehemiah, *Historical Notices . . . of the Reign of Charles I*, ed. R. Webb, 2 vols, London, 1866–9

Warwick: *The Great Fire of Warwick 1694*, ed. M. Farr, Dugdale Society, vol. 36, 1994

Waters, H.F., *Genealogical Gleanings*, 2 vols, Boston, Mass., 1901

Weiss, D.A., *The Great Fire of London*, New York, Cumberland Enterprises, 1968

Welch, C., *The History of the Monument*, London, Corporation of the City of London, 1893

Weston, S., 'Copy of a Letter from Sir Robert Atkyns . . . Written from London during the Great Fire 1666', *Archaeologia*, 19 (1821), 105–8

Whinney, M., *Wren*, London, Thames & Hudson, 1971

Whitelocke: *The Diary of Bulstrode Whitelocke 1605–1675*, ed. R. Spalding, London, British Academy, Records of Social and Economic History, new series, 13, 1990

Whitteridge, G., 'The Fire of London and St Bartholomew's Hospital', *London Topographical Record*, 20 (1952), 47–78

Wood: *The Life and Times of Anthony Wood, Antiquary, of Oxford, 1632–1695, described by Himself*, ed. A. Clark, 4 vols, Oxford Historical Society, 1891–5

Wood, M., *The English Mediaeval House*, London, Dent, 1965

Woodhead, J.R., *The Rulers of London 1660–1689*, London, London and Middlesex Archaeological Society, 1965

Wren: *The Wren Society*, 20 vols, Oxford, Oxford University Press, 1924–43

Yarranton, Andrew, *England's Improvements by Sea and Land, The Second Part*, 1681

Yeomans, D., '18th Century Timber Construction: Trade and Materials', *Architectural Journal*, 10 July 1991, 51–6

INDEX